Sustainable Design

Sustainable Design

ECOLOGY, ARCHITECTURE, AND PLANNING

Daniel E. Williams, FAIA

**Forewords by David W. Orr and
Donald Watson, FAIA**

John Wiley & Sons, Inc.

This book is printed on acid-free paper. ⊗

Copyright © 2007 by John Wiley & Sons. All rights reserved

Published by John Wiley & Sons, Inc., Hoboken, New Jersey

Published simultaneously in Canada

For general information about our other products and services, please contact our Customer Care Department within the United States at (800) 762–2974, outside the United States at (317) 572–3993 or fax (317) 572–4002.

Wiley also publishes its books in a variety of electronic formats. Some content that appears in print may not be available in electronic books. For more information about Wiley products, visit our web site at www.wiley.com.

Library of Congress Cataloging-in-Publication Data:

Williams, Daniel E.
  Sustainable design: ecology, architecture, and planning / Daniel E. Williams.
    p. cm.
  Includes bibliographical references and index.
  ISBN: 978-0-471-70953-4 (cloth)
   1. Sustainable architecture.   I. Title.
  NA2542.36.W548 2007
  720'.47—dc22   2006102173

Printed in the United States of America

10 9 8 7 6 5 4 3 2 1

WILEY BICENTENNIAL LOGO DESIGN: RICHARD J. PACIFICO

contents

Foreword by David W. Orr   ix
Foreword by Donald Watson, FAIA   xiii
Preface   xv
Acknowledgments   xxi
Introduction   xxiii

Part 1

CHAPTER ONE: The Ecological Model   **1**

Ecology   2
Ecology as a Model   3
Waste Debts   5
The Value of Land   7
Paradigm Shift   8
Thinking as a System: Connectivity, Not Fragmentation   9

CHAPTER TWO: Sustainable Design   **13**

Where Do We Want to Go?   13
Design Matters   13
Why Architects?   14
Green Design versus Sustainable Design   15
Why Now?   16
Approaching Sustainability   17
Place-Based Energy and Resources   18
Principles for Designing Sustainably   18
Where to Start?   20

CHAPTER THREE: Regional Design   **23**

Evolving from Nonrenewables   25
Another Weak Link: The Power Grid   25

The Regional Design 26
Water: A Common Denominator 27
Make No Small Plans 29
The Regional Design Process 30
Regional Case Studies 43
    Cache Valley, Utah 43
    Farmington, Minnesota: Building within the Community
        Watershed 50
    Smart Growth: Southeast Florida Coastal Communities 59

CHAPTER FOUR: Sustainable Urban and Community Design **69**
A Matter of Place 70
Principles for Sustainable Communities 72
Regional Ecology and Biourbanism 72
Sustainable Urban and Community Case Studies 81
    Lessons from Belle Glade: Can We Save the Everglades
        and Sustain Agriculture? 81
    Rio Nuevo Master Plan 84
    Growing the Great River Park 91

CHAPTER FIVE: Architectural Design **103**
The Site: Challenges and Opportunities 103
Site Design and Environmental Analysis 106
Sustainable Infrastructure 116
The Skin 116
Evolving a Sustainable Design Practice 120
Sustainable Design and Existing Buildings 121
Sustainable Interior Architecture 126

Part 2

CHAPTER SIX: The AIA/COTE Top Ten Green **129**
Projects Program
1997 AIA/COTE Top Ten Green Projects 130
1998 AIA/COTE Top Ten Green Projects 140
1999 AIA/COTE Top Ten Green Projects 147
2000 AIA/COTE Top Ten Green Projects 159
2001 AIA/COTE Top Ten Green Projects 170
2002 AIA/COTE Top Ten Green Projects 182

2003 AIA/COTE Top Ten Green Projects   200
2004 AIA/COTE Top Ten Green Projects   218
2005 AIA/COTE Top Ten Green Projects   230
2006 AIA/COTE Top Ten Green Projects   248

Afterword   255
Sustainability Terms   257
Bibliography   261
Index   265
Photo Credits   274

foreword by david w. orr

The practice of architecture occurs on a continuum between form making and place making. The former is driven by the desire to create novelty or great art or to accommodate the styles and fashion of the period and has been, by far, the dominant trend in the making of buildings and landscapes. But place making, which implies the careful attention to the effects of building on the ecological health of a site and site occupants' health, has an ancient pedigree that dates back, at least, to Vitruvius in the first century BCE. Ideally, buildings and landscapes would blend both, but these are often warring concepts.

The historically predominant concern for form, however, is giving way to a more balanced view of architecture and landscape design. The driving forces in the change include rising costs for energy and materials and the growing awareness of the ecological impact of buildings, which include 40 percent of all greenhouse gas emissions and substantial ecological damage that can be attributed to the extraction of materials. Not to put too fine a point on it, we are building our way to oblivion. The recent success of the U.S. Green Building Council represents a considerable shift along the continuum of art and place making. But this is only the merest of beginnings.

Harvard biologist Edward O. Wilson describes the twenty-first century as a "bottleneck" in which the forces of rapid climate change, species extinction, and population growth converge. Unless managed with unusual skill and wisdom and graced with considerable luck, the future of *Homo sapiens* could well be "nasty, brutish, and short," as Thomas Hobbes put it in the seventeenth century. Cambridge astronomer Martin Rees, for one, believes that our chances of making it to the year 2100 are no better than 50–50 (Rees 2003). Independent scientist James Lovelock is even more pessimistic (2006). Aside from the ongoing threat of nuclear weapons, two converging crises will make the years ahead particularly challenging. The first challenge is climate change, which will raise sea levels by as much as 20 feet, increase the severity of storms, raise the likelihood of severe droughts and heat waves, change ecosystems, increase the number of novel diseases, and disrupt political and economic systems everywhere. The other challenge is posed by the end of the era of cheap, portable fossil fuels. Unusually astute leadership will be required to avoid the possible catastrophe that scientists such as Wilson, Rees, and Lovelock see ahead.

Looking back on our time from a century or two hence, from the other side of the bottleneck, our descendants will see those small beginnings, perhaps unnoticed by us, that altered the human prospect for the better. One such change, I think, will be the changes design professionals made toward place making that began a sea change in the human presence on Earth. Collectively, this will represent a force rather like what we see in the Enlightenment of the eighteenth century; but it will be a global change and much more pervasive. It will alter how we provision ourselves with shelter, food, energy, materials, and water. It will revolutionize economies and foreign policies alike. And it will begin with a shift from energy inefficiency toward hyperefficiency now technically possible and economically feasible. It will culminate in a world powered by current sunlight captured as wind, solar energy, and biomass. The design revolution they will see and perhaps take for granted will grow from disciplines that we call biomimicry, industrial ecology, natural-systems agriculture, and ecological engineering. Will it be nirvana? No, but it will be a world considerably more decent and durable than what lay in prospect in the early years of the twenty-first century.

How might the design professions lead that revolution? The education of designers will have to change a great deal, and that is beginning to happen (AIA 2006). Design professions will need an equivalent to the Hippocratic oath. My suggestion is that it read: "We will cause no ugliness, human or ecological, somewhere else or at some later time." The first rule of making any place is that it should not impair some other place. But they will also need a compass by which to orient themselves to the larger issues of the time. Drawing on Thomas Jefferson, Aldo Leopold, and Bill McDonough, I suggest that that compass read: "No generation has any right whatsoever to alter the biogeochemical cycles of Earth or impair the stability, integrity, and beauty of natural systems, the consequences of which would be a form of intergenerational tyranny." They will learn the moral art of assessing costs and risks across generations in ways that do not deprive those to come of life, liberty, and property.

Daniel Williams's *Sustainable Design: Ecology, Architecture, and Planning* is a description of a transition from the exclusive concern for form making to the art and science of place making. But it is more than a primer. It is a thoroughly practical call for the design professions to take the next steps in a transformation of the human prospect toward a future that is sustainable and sustaining of the best in human life—one that is lived in partnership not domination.

Sources

American Institute of Architects (AIA). 2006. *Ecology and Design.* Washington, DC: AIA.

Lovelock, James. 2006. *The Revenge of GAIA*. New York: Penguin.

Rees, Martin. 2003. *Our Final Hour*. New York: Basic Books.

David W. Orr is the Paul Sears Distinguished Professor of Environmental Studies and Politics and Chair of the Environmental Studies Program at Oberlin College. He is best known for his pioneering work on environmental literacy in higher education and his recent work in ecological design.

Daniel Williams has given us an important book. *Sustainable Design: Ecology, Architecture, and Planning* is a passionate call to architects and planners to respond to the challenges of global climate change through sustainable design.

This call carries this important message: *Through ecological design, the professions of architecture, landscape architecture, and planning can make a positive contribution to environmental health, community benefit, and the experience of natural beauty in everyday life.*

Ecology as Model and Metaphor

The author uses the terms *ecological model* and *ecological design* to describe the approach to architecture and planning that is based on understanding of environmental, biological, and natural processes. In this model, a building and its site are made a beneficial part of the larger environmental context. Instead of depleting resources and creating negative impacts of pollution of air and water, a building and site can be designed to restore land value, increase vegetation, and purify air and water. In the author's words, ecological design is based on "the bioclimate of a region—solar energy, soil, water, humidity, wind, topography, altitude, and natural energies." It is specific to its particular place in the sun and on Earth, like all of nature.

This may appear opposite to conventional approaches to design and planning that follow the *economic model,* which uses and excuses standard practices that deplete limited and nonrenewable resources. But the author properly states that the best economic investment is in sustaining natural resources and biological diversity, now commonly referred to as *natural capital.*

The author describes how ecological design is implicit in indigenous building, Native American cultures, and in the writings of Thomas Jefferson, "in placing community first with individuals as part of a whole." He cites, as significant sources of his own life's work, Ian McHarg's *Design with Nature,* Victor and Aládar Olgyay's *Design with Climate,* and the work of ecologist Howard T. Odum, one of the author's former teachers, who developed the concept of embodied energy flow as a unifying principle of living systems.

Principles of Ecological Design

This book makes a unique contribution in outlining design principles by which to conceive of projects and plans in terms of watershed viability and creating or restoring a *green infrastructure* that is as powerful and important in community life as any utility grid. From this larger view, water is the common denominator.

Among the guiding principles of ecological design described in the book is *to design for connectivity, avoiding fragmentation.* In ecology, fragmentation of land, waterways, and forests decreases functional choices for species survival. In design, connectivity of natural systems such as watershed streams and open spaces creates logical places for pedestrian walkways, bikeways, and recreation, alongside protected corridors for wildlife and plant habitat.

Another guiding principle of ecological design put forth here is *to conceive of local rainfall as a precious and limited resource.* Depending on the rainfall conditions prevailing at a site, the water goals of a project can be established so that the building roofs and landscape can serve to *store* water (reducing and slowing stormwater flow impacts), to *clean* water (improving water quality by filtration as it returns to the local aquifer), and to *recycle and reuse* water (reducing the drawdown of precious fresh water resources). Sustainable design, the author asserts, achieves all three goals.

The Potential of Design

The book is founded on the positive contribution that designers can make to improve environmental quality through ecological design of architecture, community design, and regional planning.

This book provides a comprehensive summary of the principles of ecological design, with helpful "To Do" and "Where to Start" guidelines. Its case studies demonstrate a maturing body of work of designers who have succeeded, through building community and regional projects, in improving environmental health and civic benefit.

These ecological design principles and practices make the positive case that the future of a healthy world on a healthy planet rests in the inspiration, knowledge, and practice of environmental design.

With the call to "make no small plans," the author adapts a well-known quote from a past century, Architect Daniel Burnham's "Make no little plans. They have no magic to stir men's blood and probably will not themselves be realized." *Sustainable Design: Ecology, Architecture, and Planning* makes a convincing case that this ambitious claim is once again a timely and significant call to action.

Donald Watson, FAIA, is an architect and author/editor of books on architecture, urban design, and environment. He is a former dean and professor of architecture at Rensselaer Polytechnic Institute (1990–2000) and chair of the Environmental Design Program at the Yale School of Architecture (1970–1990).

preface

La aritmetica non e opinione
—arithmetic is not an opinion.

The media has saturated us with the measurements, the "arithmetic," on how badly we have been doing as stewards of our home: global warming, drought, sprawl, asthma, and obesity are direct results of the way we have chosen to live. Implicated in the equation of global climate change is the way we plan, design, and build on the land. We have consumed precious natural landscape and depleted vegetation, soils, and water, using up the resource base that has been our benefactor. To understand what it might take designers to change this arithmetic, we must first understand both the magnitude and complexity of what brought us to this point, and second, we must learn ways to change our direction.

We do know that we must aggressively commit to designing sustainably—that is, designing within the limits of our natural resources and natural laws. Some choices are obvious and readily available to us. For example, we can develop and employ renewable resources, find alternatives to scarce and diminishing resources, and use less more efficiently and wisely. This does not mean accepting a lower quality of life but, instead, designing ways to achieve a higher quality of life for the present and future by designing for an "unplugged" life that functions well without exploitation of nonrenewable resources and increases renewable capacities for present and future generations.

The scope of global issues that account for the arithmetic of climate and cultural change demands more of us. This book reviews the range of impacts that planning and design might undertake to redress global consequences. The collection of design principles and practices set forth in this book illustrates the meaning of *deep sustainability*, which is a commitment beyond the standard energy-efficiency responses—demonstrating the best of what sustainable design can accomplish. This book presents multiple scales and a comprehensive overview of sustainable-design principles and practices, which are defined to set high but realizable goals, and these principles and practices are illustrated by examples and case studies.

Sustainable design is an approach to design based on natural-systems functioning—what Ian McHarg aptly titled his book *Design with Nature*. The considerable energy in nature can provide enough to power a sustainable future if we listen and learn from it. Designs that use the available site energies are approaching sustainability—these designs connect everything and are the ecological model.

Architects and Climate Change

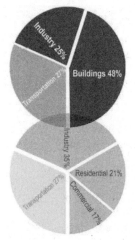

GRAPHIC 1: Combining the annual energy required to operate residential, commercial, and industrial buildings along with the embodied energy of industry-produced building materials like carpet, tile, glass, and concrete exposes buildings as the largest energy consuming and greenhouse gas emitting sector.

Key Points

➻ *The biggest source of emissions and energy consumption both in this country and around the globe: buildings.*

➻ *The Building Sector, as the major U.S. and global source of demand for energy and materials that produce by-product greenhouse gases, is poised to fuel the world's rush toward climate change.*

Buildings Account For Half Of All Greenhouse Gas Emissions

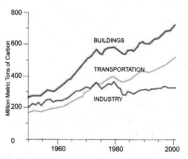

GRAPHIC 2: U.S. CO2 Emissions by Sector.

In our quest to dramatically cut greenhouse gas emissions and lessen our dependence on fossil fuels, we have overlooked the biggest source of emissions and energy consumption both in this country and around the globe: buildings and the energy they consume each year. Buildings and their construction account for nearly half of all the greenhouse gas emissions and energy consumed in this country each year. This includes energy used in the production and transportation of materials to building construction sites, as well as the energy used to operate buildings, Globally the percentage is even greater. The Building Sector is the key source of demand for energy and materials that produce by-product greenhouse gases.

U.S. annual energy consumption is projected to increase by 37% (34 quadrillion Btu) and greenhouse gas emissions by 36% over the next twenty years. Annual global energy consumption is projected to increase by 54% (230 quadrillion Btu) over this same period.

Building Sector Emissions Are Increasing Dramatically

Buildings have a lifespan that lasts for 50 to 100 years throughout which they consume energy and produce emissions. The Building Sector as the major U.S. and global greenhouse gas emitting sector, is poised to fuel the world's rush toward climate change. The U.S. alone is projected to need 1,300 to 1,900 new power plants over the next 20 years (about one power plant per week). Most of this new energy will be needed to operate buildings.

The United States will add 22 million buildings that will not only consume electricity produced at a central power plant, but also directly burn oil, natural gas and/or propane in boilers, furnaces and hot water heaters. In fact, 58% of end-use energy needed to operate a building is consumed by the burning of fuel onsite.

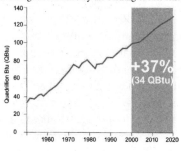

GRAPHIC 3: U.S. Energy Consumption Projections

1 quadrillion Btu is equal to annual energy output of 40 - 1,000MW power plants.

Climate change is everyone's challenge, and architects must play an important role commensurate with their impact.

Architects and Climate Change

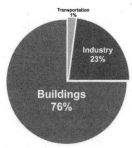

GRAPHIC 4: 76% of all power plant generated electricity is used just to operate buildings.

Key Points

↪ *Architects know that buildings can be designed to operate with less than half the energy of today's average U.S. building at little or no additional cost*

↪ *By the year 2035, three quarters of the built environment in the U.S. will be either new or renovated.*

This Background Sheet was prepared in collaboration with Edward Mazria AIA, founder of Architecture 2030. For further information see www.architecture2030.org or contact: info@architecture2030.org. The AIA, through its Sustainable Design Task Force and its Committee on the Environment, is working to develop a detailed action plan to meet the greenhouse gas reduction goals set out above.

A Perspective On How To Curb Emissions

Scientists tell us that in order to avoid dangerous climate change we must keep global warming under 2°C above pre-industrial levels (we are currently at 0.7°C above pre-industrial levels). To avoid exceeding this threshold a way forward would involve:

● Promoting sustainable design including resource conservation to achieve a minimum 50 percent reduction from the current level of consumption of fossil fuels used to construct and operate new and renovated buildings by the year 2010.

● Promoting further reductions of fossil fuel consumption by 10 percent or more in each of the following five year intervals so that the cumulative reduction from today's baseline is:

> 60% in 2015
> 70% in 2020
> 80% in 2025
> 90% in 2030
> carbon-neutral by 2035 (Meaning that the construction and operation of buildings will no longer require the consumption of fossil fuel energy or the emission of greenhouse gases.)

● Driving these reductions through: 1) creating building performance standards in building codes and standards to address private sector structures, and 2) creating governmental mandates that federal and state buildings meet energy efficiency targets.

● Supporting government action to use incentive-based regulatory means to reduce greenhouse gas emissions.

Architects know that buildings can be designed to operate with far less energy than today's average U.S. building at little or no additional cost. This is accomplished through proper siting, building form, glass properties and location, material selection and by incorporating natural heating, cooling and ventilation and day-lighting strategies.

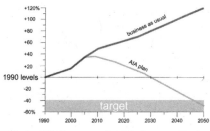

GRAPHIC 5: By enacting a Building Sector initiative like this we can meet a greenhouse gas reduction target of 40% to 60% below 1990 levels by 2050.

With about 5 billion square feet (sf) of new construction, 5 billion sf of renovation and 1.75 billion sf of demolition taking place in the U.S. each year, by the year 2035, three quarters of the built environment in the U.S. will be either new or renovated. This transformation over the next 30 years represents a historic opportunity for the U.S. architecture and building community, with the support of the federal government, to lead in addressing greenhouse gas emission reductions.

Form follows energy.

The five chapters that follow address the challenges of sustainable design on a range of physical scales. *The ecological model* is discussed in Chapter 1. In this chapter the case is made for learning from biological and ecological system functioning and using ecological principles as a working model for sustainable design.

Chapter 2, Sustainable Design, reviews the challenges before us and argues for a deeper look into and beyond green design, making the case that a critical element in the change to sustainable living is in how we practice design and how we must, in fact, design a sustainable future.

Chapters 3 through 5 are discussions and case-study examples on various scales of design from regional to urban to architecture, based, in part, on an ecological model.

The focus of Chapter 3, Regional Design, is on the *regional scale*. The importance of large-scale design and planning illustrates systems thinking and systems solutions at the larger scale, suggesting that the design of regions is the most critical to sustainability at other scales.

Urban design is discussed in Chapter 4, Sustainable Urban and Community Design, showing that sustainability at the urban scale requires the design of livable communities that are efficient, that possess a human scale, and that provide a high quality of life for people with diverse incomes and cultural interests. The functional foundation for these communities is rooted in ecological principles and the use and cycling of sustainable local energies and renewable resources.

Chapter 5 is on architectural design and the building scale. The primary focus is on buildings and structures, several of which function more like organisms than static objects. Sustainably designed buildings are connected to their site and natural place in order to capture, store, and distribute the natural site energies, the neighborhood scale, and local climate conditions.

Part II, Chapter 6 presents the winning entries from the AIA/COTE (Committee on the Environment) Top Ten Green Awards from its inception in 1997 through 2006. This section illustrates how quickly sustainable design has become part of acceptable and mainstream design practices and how the lessons-learned metric for performance has become increasingly better defined. These examples give credence to thinking that sustainable designs are achievable, affordable, and compelling.

The sustainable-design challenge is about designing places that increase natural and human capacity. These designs better fit the planet, the local climate, the site, and the specific places we build and live and work in. Sustainable design is achievable if we understand how ecological systems provide sustainable flows and storages of materials and energies from the place—to design and build an ecology—as an organism might build and live in an ecosystem.

The first challenge is to understand ecology, to become literate about our home, and to learn what sustainable forces and energies are available on the project site and, then, design to make use of this knowledge—to design the connections. A primary goal is to unplug our designs and power them with only on-site energy. Once the idea of using site energies is understood, the exciting process of sustainability begins, through designs that are connected to and reflect the natural place and that are loved and truly sustainable.

The comparative value of community and ecology is that they both revere connections, relationships. The rethinking of design—not as an object but as an organism with flows and storages of energy and materials—is basic to sustainability. Creating designs that facilitate connections—capturing, concentrating, and storing energy and materials—between the sustainable energies and materials of the site and region will create sustainability.

Architects and planners relish complex challenges, and designing sustainable buildings and communities is just such a challenge. *Sustainable Design: Ecology, and Architecture, and Planning* is intended to help architects, planners, landscape architects, engineers, and public officials—the professional agents of change—understand the deep issues of sustainability and gain the knowledge necessary to meet the sustainable-design challenge.

Because a magnifying glass uses available sustainable energy—sunlight—it serves as a metaphorical *sustainable match*. It captures and concentrates a sustainable energy.

acknowledgments

It takes a village to write a book, and I have had the unique experience of working with some of the best in the village. Many people and events helped provide the inspiration and shaped the need for this book. One of the many that stand out is Dr. H. T. Odum. Dr. Odum, a general systems ecologist and holistic thinker, constantly challenged his students to connect things and—for those of us in design—to design the connections. Our initial talks and walks through the swamps, uplands, and estuaries of Florida changed my thinking about architecture and planning and provided a rich and challenging introduction into ecological thinking.

My gratitude to professors Leland G. Shaw and Bernard Vocysonk. They skillfully set my early design education on a foundation of problem solving and complex design challenges. Their push to look deeper into design problems and to develop an even greater love of searching for and researching solutions through creative problem definition continues to feed my passion for design to this day.

In 2003, I had the honor of chairing The American Institute of Architects (AIA) Committee on the Environment, or COTE. Evolving from the AIA Committee on Energy, COTE has been for many years the gathering spot for architects passionate about connecting design, science, and the environment. Thanks to Gail Lindsey, Bob Berkebile, Randy Croxton, Bill McDonough, Muscoe Martin, Sandy Mendler, Joyce Lee, Mark Rylander, Vivian Loftness, James Binkley, and Kira Gould for their valuable input over several years of work and conversations that are woven into this book. The contributions of many of these people were critical to the development of the Department of Energy's High Performance Building Standards and energy conservation work; the Environmental Protection Agency's Smart Growth and the AIA's *Environmental Resource Guide;* the U.S. Green Building Council and the development of LEED (Leadership in Energy and Environmental Design); and the early work from the AIA Foundation addressing passive design and energy-efficient buildings.

The support of the AIA leadership is much appreciated: Norman Koonce, Susan Maxman, Thom Penny, Gene Hopkins, Doug Steidl, Kate Schwennsen, R. K. Stewart, and Chris McEntee have helped promote the integration of sustainability into the foundation of our profession. The AIA staff, including Richard Hayes, Helene Dreiling, Barbara Sido, and Jeff Levine, have helped to create an environment open to the critical issues facing the profession, and they have stewarded the environmental issues with intellect, interest, and care.

Additional input and editorial comments made by Richard Hayes, Kira Gould, Patricia Kahn, and Max Williams were important and instructive. If there is clarity to this book, it is due in large part to their assistance.

To my publisher John Wiley & Sons and editor John Czarnecki, editorial assistant Raheli Millman, production manager Leslie Anglin, and developmental editor Christine Gilmore, thank you for the opportunity and the assistance in completing and publishing this manuscript. The many discussions with John during the development of this manuscript were instructive and helpful. Major assistance in collecting the information on the AIA/COTE Top Ten Award projects for this book came, in large part, from Kate Rizzo from the AIA; thank you.

There is no way to credit the many others who have, at one time or another, associated with me or inspired me through their work other than to list them. Each has been an important inspiration to this effort as a friend, associate, or mentor of sustainable design. They are as follows: Kaid Benfield, Fernando Navarro Bidegain, Bill Bobenhausen, Lance Brown, Mark Brown, Bill Browning, Scott Bernstein, Lance Brown, Dan Burden, Dru Crawley, David Crockett, David Dixon, Christine Ervin, Robert France, Greg Franta, Diane Georgopulos, Robert Goo, Walter Grondzik, Christopher Gronbeck, Charles Harper, Denis Hayes, Paul Hyett, Ken Kay, Jamie Learner, Dr. Richard Jackson, Alan Jacobs, Huey Johnson, Douglas Kelbaugh, Charles Kibert, Walter Kulash, Rai Okamoto, Dennis Olie, Amory Lovins, Bill Morrish, Ed Mazria, John McRae, Nadav Malin, Larry Peterson, Bill Reed, Harrison Rue, Soren Simonsen, Tom Singleton, Roger Schluntz, Alex Wilson, and Robert Yaro.

Thanks also to the future generations of COTE chairs and advisory groups who remain the AIA's critical link to the multidisciplinary challenges fundamental to sustainable design.

A special thanks to Donald Watson, FAIA, an early advocate of bioclimatic and passive design, who has been a friend and colleague for many years and has helped me immensely to refine and focus the material for this book.

This book is dedicated to Max and Megan and all of the neighbors and residents of the planet—and to a future yet to be decided and clearly contingent on what we design and plan to do today.

introduction

We are nature—all changes to nature and to the habitat have an impact on us.

The radically degrading landscape requires radical changes to the design professional's process and practice. This book is not about small steps. It asks the designer to first strive to create solutions that do not use nonrenewables. Rather than using fewer nonrenewables, use *none:* Instead, create designs that use and reuse only the energy and resources that reside on site and within the bioregion. These are the same sustainable energies that power ecology. Designs can function *unplugged* from the nonrenewable grid and, instead, be powered by the energies that reside on the site. To do this, projects must be designed to collect, store, and distribute sustainable energy and resources.

The largest resource of energy on the planet is sustainable natural energy. Although this natural energy is taken for granted, it does virtually all of the work that makes the planet and the places within hospitable and livable. Natural energy powers all of the life-essential processes on the planet. Many of these processes are powered by energies not normally thought of as energy—examples include sunlight, wind, water, gravity, tides, and hydrological cycles. There are huge amounts of these free energies, and they are the only energies that are sustainable.

Most natural energy is geographically, spatially, and diurnally unique and site specific. Some is only seasonal, some constantly changing, and some fairly consistent. Sustainable energies vary with the seasons, change annually, and are changing significantly due to global warming. Sunlight is diurnal, huge, and yet diffuse.

Energy that is local to an area is *resident energy.* Because resident natural energies and resources vary with region, location, site, and site context, analyzing the climate-specific conditions of the site is central to the sustainable-design approach. In the pursuit of design for human habitation, most climates offer comfort during certain times of the day and year, but these climatically comfortable periods depend on geographic location and climate. Seattle, Washington, cannot count on solar energy to run its buildings, and New Mexico cannot count on tidal energy to power its buildings. Designing to collect, store, and concentrate the resident renewable energy is the sustainable-design challenge. To provide comfort by relying on the resident energies will create unique structures that are specific to the region while

"Pollution," Buckminster Fuller once said, "is the consequence of bad design."

reducing or eliminating reliance on nonrenewable materials and energies. In sustainable design, there is no one-size-fits-all.

Every site has useful and sustainable energies. The sustainable-design challenge is to collect, incorporate, and distribute those energies to meet specific needs. Much of the nonrenewable energy and resources consumed by architecture, communities, agriculture, and transportation can be supplied by renewable sources when the structures and communities are designed to integrate them.

Sustainable development was defined by the World Commission on Environment and Development in 1987 as "meeting the needs of today without compromising the ability of future generations to meet their own needs." To design for sustainability, it is helpful to look at the processes of nature and create designs that both fit and connect with that larger ecological-system framework. An *organism* designed for living would use, supply, store, and renew resources, as well as clean and distribute waste products. It would provide a basis for creating better communities and improve the economic engines so important to development. If architecture in the twentieth century was challenged with designing a "machine for living," then in the twenty-first century the challenge of architecture is designing "organisms for living."

Dr. Howard T. Odum posed an ecological problem in his University of Florida Systems Ecology class in 1973. The problem was about exponential growth. For years the greatest concern in the population-explosion and ecological-degradation discussion was not so much about the rapid rate of growth, but that it would happen the day after the concern was validated. Odum used for his example the water hyacinth, which is a lily pad–like plant that doubles its biomass, its size, each day. His point was that once a pond was 50 percent covered with hyacinth, it was too late to do anything—the next day it would be 100 percent covered. The dense mat of hyacinth blocked out sunlight to the lower levels of the pond and quickly changed the oxygen demand and balance of the whole system.

The 50 percent benchmark is an interesting and critical observation in ecology. It marks the day before—in exponential-growth terms—the "pond" was fully covered and indicates that significant change is imminent.

In 2005, the number of people living in U.S. cities equaled the population in rural areas. China's consumption of nonrenewable materials and energies by 2010, although small on a per-capita basis, will exceed that of the United States. This is fuel consumption on an exponential growth curve, while new discoveries and storages are on an exponential decay curve. Fossil fuel is so addicting that we use it despite knowledge that it is killing us. That benchmark was passed in 2003, when the Natural Resources Defense Council (NRDC) reported that more people died as a result of auto emission pollution than auto accidents.

Human settlements have been around for more than 6,000 years. Until the early 1800s, they functioned somewhat sustainably, powered by a multibillion-year sustainable energy source—the sun. Then came the use of fossil fuels, an amazing resource that supplied more energy than what was required to retrieve it. At the turn of the second millennium, the global community and economy was nearly 100 per-

"Sustainability is the [emerging] doctrine that economic growth and development must take place, and be maintained over time, within the limits set by ecology in the broadest sense—by the interrelations of human beings and their works, and the biosphere . . . It follows that environmental protection and economic development are complementary rather than antagonistic processes."

WILLIAM D. RUCKELSHAUS,
SCIENTIFIC AMERICAN
(SEPTEMBER 1989).

cent dependent on it for every part of its functioning. Food, water, jobs, transportation, comfort, medicine, and security were all dependent on a nonrenewable, corrosive, and limited polluting-energy supply.

This gift of cheap nonrenewable resources, which clearly seemed a blessing, is now increasingly seen as a curse. Instead of using this gift to improve quality of life, it has been used mostly to grow, to expand usage, leaving the current challenging condition of hyperextended growth patterns that rely on nonrenewables and that cannot function without them. The remarkable ability of nonrenewables to be converted to electricity, building products, fertilizer, gasoline, medicine, and literally thousands of essential products with many uses has nurtured a lazy attitude in the construction industry and in architectural and urban-design practice. Present-day developments—habitats for most people in developed countries and the billions of people in developing countries—are habitats that are uninhabitable without fossil fuels.

Since the 1950s, and the ubiquitous incorporation of air conditioning into buildings and the accompanying loss of operable windows and common-sense building orientation, the design and construction industry has built trillions of dollars' worth of buildings and urban structures. Powered only by nonrenewables, these structures cannot function without them. During the Northeast blackout of 2003, the buildings and infrastructure in the impacted communities were without power and were consequently nonfunctional. The design of these structures—homes, businesses, factories, schools, libraries, courthouses, hospitals, and industrial buildings—relied on an energy supply that was not sustainable or even available. The nonrenewable-powered mechanical systems were down, so air did not flow, unhealthy interior temperature and air quality made the spaces uninhabitable, and even toilets could not be used. Potable water became immediately undrinkable as treatment plants, also powered by electricity, shut down. The only available drinking water was bottled and selling at more than $4 per gallon, and there was not enough. Some estimated that 50 million people were affected.

It is not just blackouts that require the rethinking of reliance on and use of nonrenewable power. The hurricanes of 1992 to 2005 left many people without power for weeks. Millions of people paid mortgages and rents on residential and commercial property that they could not use, and without the use of the structure, where is the value? Designing buildings that can only function with electricity is a terrible legacy for homes and businesses alike.

But what if these communities and their buildings were sustainably designed? The windows would be oriented to collect usable daylight, and operable windows would provide controllable ventilation. The roof would collect and store rainwater so that a gravity-reliant distribution system would supply the toilets during power outages. Potable water would also be harvested on the roof, and it would be filtered and distributed by gravity. These buildings would be functional even during a blackout, because they would be running off available site energy—sunlight, wind, or gravity. The form and structure of the building would have been designed to capture what it needed to provide the occupants comfort when the electrical, natural gas, or

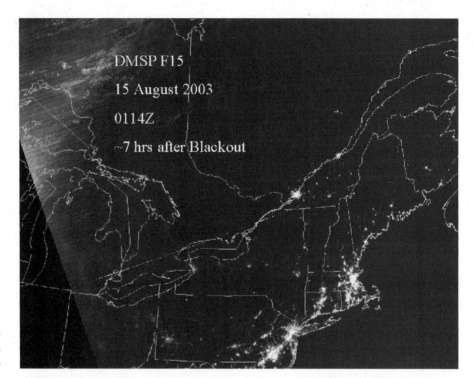

50,000,000 without electricity; where is the commodity?

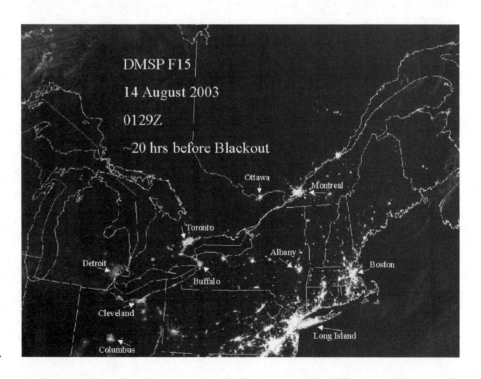

50,000,000 with electricity.

other power was not available. The architect who creates such responsive buildings is designing to meet the challenge of sustainability. As a result, the buildings function, and the users are productive and safe when other buildings and structures unsustainably designed are vacant and degrading.

Sustainable structures collect, store, and concentrate the local energy for the buildings' users, owners, and neighbors. The buildings are designed and built as organisms that draw upon Vitruvius' principles of firmness, commodity, and delight.

Sustainable designs are *system designs*. They help solve the economic, social, and environmental issues *simultaneously* and as a single system. By solving these challenges simultaneously—as a systems problem—real economic development and investment can be attained. An exceptional environmentally sensitive solution that does not survive economically is no better than one that is socially irresponsible or one that has high returns based only on first costs and in time becomes a financial and environmental drain on the community and future occupants.

PART ONE

CHAPTER ONE

the ecological model

The first law of ecology is that everything is related to everything.
—Barry Commoner

M any books and articles suggest that nature will inspire design to provide for a sustainable future. These sources provide lessons that tend to lead to patterns or forms that copy nature's solutions in form only. The deeper lesson of ecology is that nature's form is a direct response to capturing the flow of energies and materials that reside within that bioregion. The huge diversity in natural forms teaches us that there are many ways, many forms, to capture and use available energy. The form itself, made up of biological processes, maximizes the use and storage of energy and materials for its needs and functions within its ecological and energy location.

Ecology is the study of the *relationship* of plants and animals to their environment. The flow of material and energy between things within their environment is their spatial context—their community. It is the study of that spatial connectivity between organism and environment that makes ecology an excellent model for sustainable design. Conceptually, sustainable design expands the role of the design program, moving the design goal from object to community, and then designs the connections, illustrating the relationship between available energy and the natural place. The flow of renewable energy, which powers all the essential processes needed for life, dwarfs the power and use of nonrenewable energy sources. These energies power functions at no cost and without pollution-loading the environment. The removal of natural systems not only increases costs, but it reduces the functioning of natural systems—as nature is reduced, the cost of life and to life increases.

The physical environment includes the sun, water, wind, oxygen, carbon dioxide, soil, atmosphere, and many other elements and processes. The diversity and complexity of all the components in an ecological study require studying organisms within their environments. Ecological study connects many fields and areas of expertise, and in so doing illustrates holistic aspects of components and their relationships to one another within their spatial community.

Planning and architecture must work together to be sustainable. Sustainable design challenges the designer to design connections to the site and to the site's resident energy—to design holistically and connectedly and address the needs of the building and the environment and community of which it is a part. Sustainable design and planning make use of the regional climate and local resources. To design *sustainably* is to integrate the design into the ecology of the place—the flows of materials and energy residing in the community.

Ecology

German biologist Ernst Heinrich Haeckel introduced the term *ecology* in 1866. The term, derived from the Greek *oikos*, means "household," which is the root word for economy as well. Charles Darwin developed his theory of evolution by making the connection between organisms and their environments. Earth contains huge numbers of complex ecosystems that collectively contain all of the living organisms that exist. An organism's household includes the complex flow of materials within and outside of the system, and it is all powered by sustainable energies. Systems powered by sustainable energy tend to grow to a mature state called a *climax state* and then slow their growth and develop hardy species and environmental connections (e.g., redwood forests). Systems powered by nonrenewables grow rapidly to a point where growth and their structure can no longer be sustained, and then—at the point of growing past the resource base and structural abilities—die back (e.g., weed-filled lots). Nonrenewables, such as fossil fuel, due to their high net energy (usable energy), accelerate growth beyond what renewable energy can do, but then when nonrenewables become scarce or are used up, the growth decelerates to disorder and the system toward failure.

The biosphere is composed of the Earth plus the sliver of thin air extending out six miles from the Earth's surface. All life in this zone relies on the sun's energy. The biosphere has specific bioclimatic zones called *biomes*, which are tailored to their climate, soil, physical features, and plant and animal life. These components uniquely support their ecosystems, and they provide a working balance for the *basics*, as ecologist Ben Breedlove called them—feeding, breeding, resting, and nesting.

Ecology makes use of what is there. Since ecology is the study of organisms and their environment, it includes the study of the relationships and interactions between living organisms—including humans and their natural and built habitats.

Ecology as a Model

Architects are well aware of the value of a *model,* a scalar but accurate representation of a designed solution to a specific program. The ecological model is somewhat different. It still illustrates an accurate representation, but it does so by showing pathways between energy and material flows. An ecological model shows the processes that drive the ecological system under study, as well as the cycles associated with the flow of energy and materials essential to its existence.

We are a part of nature; all changes in nature and to our habitat affect us. It is important to understand what is being affected and how. This knowledge is basic to defining the sustainable design problem. *Odum's model,* devised by systems ecologist and holistic thinker Dr. Howard T. Odum, illustrates the relationship between flows of energy and materials, between system components, and between producers and consumers. All of life functions this way. We can change the relationship between the components by changing the connections and flows between the components: for example, increasing agriculture's gross output with the use of fertilizers and pesticides and converting natural landscape into agricultural or urban *land use.* This land-use change results in the gain of a community but also the loss of the valuable contributions from nature—clean air and water. The sun powers photosynthesis (creating an energy storage, carbohydrates), and powers the cycling of materials (water, nutrients, and organic material—weather and hydrologic cycles) distributed by gravitational forces. The ecological model illustrates the flows of energy and materials, the distribution of which is powered by sustainable energies, including the sun, gravity, and natural cycles.

Odum's model is helpful because it illustrates the simple, essential relationships and connections between natural energies and renewable resources. Since sustainability is achieved by using local renewable resources, the model illustrates the places of opportunity and connections needed for designing interfaces.

> "There is as yet no ethic dealing with man's relation to land and to the plants which grow upon it. Land . . . is still property. The land-relation is still strictly economic, entailing privileges but not obligations. Individual thinkers since the days of Ezekiel and Isaiah have asserted that the despoliation of the land is not only inexpedient but also wrong. Society, however, has not yet affirmed their belief."
>
> ALDO LEOPOLD, 1949

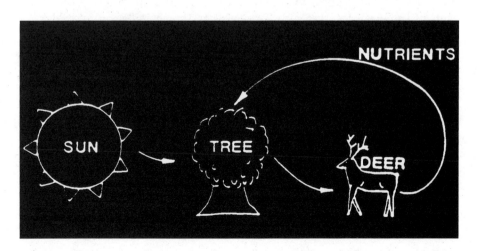

Odum's model is simple—sustainability is cycling, storing, and connecting to sustainable energies.

"We have a remarkable ability to define the world in terms of human needs and perceptions. Thus, although we draw the borders to demarcate countries, provinces, or counties, these lines exist only on maps that humans print. There are other boundaries of far greater significance that we have to learn to recognize . . . Natural barriers and perimeters of mountains and hills, rivers and shores, valleys and watersheds, regulate the makeup and distribution of all other organisms on the planet . . . We, in urban industrialized societies, have disconnected ourselves from these physical and biological constraints . . . Our human-created boundaries have become so real that we think that air, water, land, and different organisms can be administered within the limits of our designated jurisdictions. But nature conforms to other rules."

DAVID SUZUKI, *TIME TO CHANGE*
(TORONTO, ONTARIO: STODDART, 1994), 34–35.

"The earth belongs to the living. No man may by natural right oblige the lands he owns or occupies, or those that succeed him in that occupation, to debts greater than those that may be paid during his own lifetime. Because if he could, then the world would belong to the dead and not to the living."

THOMAS JEFFERSON,
ARCHITECT

Recognizing the need, understanding the importance, and designing the connections within natural-system laws will provide a framework that will produce sustainable results. In part, this is a shift in basic thinking about what is design but also what is land. For most of the history of land use and associated zoning regulations, the emphasis has been on the so-called *highest and best use* of the owner's property—now called more simply *property rights*. In the recent past, land-use issues have primarily had to do with designing solutions to solely satisfy the owner and dismiss community's rights for the greater good.

Due in part to misplaced and poorly conceived urban sprawl, considerations have shifted from only serving property owners' rights to including community interests. Today we must think about the highest and best use for the *region's health and needs* and of the *common good*, while protecting the public and private good. Property rights law is about the *rights of the property* as much as it is about the rights of its owner, focusing such laws on what Thomas Jefferson referred to as obligations. There is an important distinction between *growing*—such as weeds—and *developing*—such as redwoods—property or land. Sustainable design is about development and stewardship.

The *ecological model* illustrates the relationship between needs and things that are provided. Some examples include the heat from the sun, from the Earth, from biological processes; cooling from evaporation, from plant transpiration, from the Earth; water and waste distribution powered by gravity, precipitation, air movement, microclimates; soils and food; and the interaction between these parts.

Sun-generated power and all cycles driven by it are sustainable engines. The more connected to these sustainable engines a process or product is, the greater the potential is for it to be sustainable, as well as affordable and profitable. Humans, biota, water, wind, crops, and so on are all powered by solar energy. The more these sustainable energies are integrated into the built environment, the closer that environment will be to being sustainable.

" 'To grow' means to increase in size by the accretion or assimilation of material. *Growth* therefore means a quantitative increase in the scale of the physical dimensions of the economy. 'To develop' means to expand or realize the potentials of; to bring gradually to a fuller, greater or better state. *Development* therefore means the qualitative improvement in the structure, design and composition of the physical stocks of wealth that result from greater knowledge, both of technique and of purpose. A growing economy is getting bigger; a developing economy is getting better. An economy can therefore develop without growing or grow without developing."

"BOUNDLESS BULL," *GANNETT CENTER JOURNAL* (SUMMER 1990): 116–117.

Ecologies are adapted to the bioclimate of a region—the solar energy, soil, water supply, humidity, wind, topography, altitude, and natural events such as hurricanes, fires, floods, and droughts. Some of these energies and resources occur within the site, while some are from outside the site:

Outside energies: actions from outside the site happening to the site

- Solar (heat, light)
- Wind
- Climate

Inside energies:

- Gravity
- Soils and geology
- Microclimate
- Productivity and learning

Waste Debts

All ecologies have *wastes*, but those wastes are actually part of a cycle. They are part of the flows of energy and material within the ecology of the biome, and they are essential to the health and sustainability of the biome. Because these wastes are essential to and connected to the development and health of the system, they supply and power the system's development.

Most economies are based on the premise that their debts can be paid later—deficit spending is a critical element in a growing economy. As with all debts, waste debts must be paid, usually at a higher expense than is affordable. Nuclear power is an example of a net-energy producer (although it is not as good as fossil fuel), but it is also a producer of toxic waste that has a lethal half-life of 250,000 years. This cost is not part of the economic balance sheet. Consequently, the measured growth during the use of nuclear power is not real growth, as toxic material storage is not

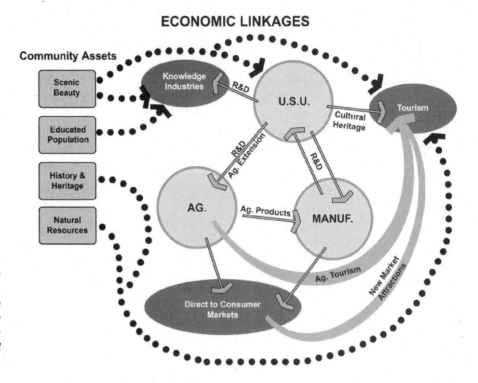

ECONOMIC LINKAGES

An ecologic/economic model. As in most places, in Cache Valley, Utah, the economy is directly connected to its ecological health and scenic beauty.

accounted for in the debt column, a debt that must be paid for over a 250,000-year period.

There are more than 1,500 Superfund sites in the United States, and the estimated cost of cleanup is in the trillions of dollars. As of 2006, storage and cleanup of nuclear waste, just one of the superfund challenges, has no permanent solution, only a temporary storage solution. The best temporary solution is to store the waste in special glass containers guaranteed to work for 10,000 years, just a fraction of the 250,000-year half-life, in which the waste will remain toxic to humans. The containers are guaranteed by a company that most likely will be bankrupt or no longer in existence long before the guaranteed and stipulated working time.

Toxic brownfields and other contaminated sites remain a significant hidden cost to the economy. The use and abuse of such land by a previous owner creates a debt to the common owners—the public, the surrounding neighborhoods, the nation, and the economy. Such abuses were allowed in part because the economic value of the polluter to the community, both local and national, was considered critical. Now the real costs are in, the profit has been spent, and the public is charged the debt. According to the NRDC, groundwater contamination in the United States is estimated to be over 40 percent.

Thomas Jefferson, in addition to being a nation-shaper, farmer, writer, and president of the United States, was an architect. He was also father of land use and

Since its inception in 1980, 1,551 contaminated sites have been put on the National Superfund Priority List; 257 sites have been cleaned up and 552 have been partially or mostly decontaminated through 2001.

ENVIRONMENTAL DEFENSE FUND, JULY 8, 2002

urban and regional design in this country. The beauty he saw in this new, developing country was integrated into the Jeffersonian grid, which was based, in large part, on ideals grounded in the greater good for the community, as well as for private good. Common space, agriculture, and a carrying capacity based on the land's natural resources were central to his vision. Inspired by the principles of freedom and community, he designed and helped to implement a community grid to be managed by the people. His plan, which was designed to express the needs and desires of the whole community, also preserved individual needs and desires. The framework of his plan, which put the community first and understood individuals as *part of the whole*, showed his ecological thinking.

Philosophically, Native Americans lived within the ecological model: There was a continuous stewardship of, tribute to, and respect for the land. Beginning with an understanding of the land's relevance to the culture of people and of place, the decisions made by the tribe were connected to the land and its inextricable connection to the long-term sustainability of the tribal community—respecting tribal history and stewarding the tribal future.

The Value of Land

As human populations expanded into the natural landscape, the relationship between the land and ownership of it became a source of conflict. Questions of

> The tragedy of the commons develops in this way. Picture a pasture open to all. It is to be expected that each herdsman will try to keep as many cattle as possible on the commons (the public areas). Such an arrangement may work reasonably satisfactorily for centuries, because tribal wars, poaching, and disease keep the numbers of both humans and beasts well below the land's carrying capacity. Finally, however, comes the day of reckoning—that is, the day when the long-desired goal of social stability becomes a reality. At this point, the inherent logic of the commons remorselessly generates tragedy.
>
> As a rational being, each herdsman seeks to maximize his gain. Explicitly or implicitly, more or less consciously, he asks, "What is the utility to me of adding one more animal to my herd?" This utility has one negative and one positive component.
>
> 1. The positive component is a function of the increment of one animal. Since the herdsman receives all the proceeds from the sale of the additional animal, the positive utility is nearly +1.
> 2. The negative component is a function of the additional overgrazing created by one more animal. Since, however, all herdsmen share the effects of overgrazing, the negative utility for any particular decision-making herdsman is only a fraction of −1.

> Adding together the component partial utilities, the rational herdsman concludes that the only sensible course to pursue is to add another animal to his herd. And another . . . and another . . . But this is the conclusion reached by each and every rational herdsman sharing a commons. Therein is the tragedy. Each herdsman is locked into a system that compels him to increase his herd without limit—in a world that is limited.
>
> GARRETT HARDIN, "THE TRAGEDY OF THE COMMONS," *SCIENCE, 162*
> (DECEMBER 1968), 1243–1248.

stewardship soon became central to the issues of freedom and ownership. For example, in the early 1900s, zoning laws started with one neighbor's land use resulting in the interruption, pollution, or denial of access to clean water and sunlight to another neighbor. At the beginning of the 2000s, there is an intriguing design problem on a regional, perhaps continental scale: the problem of designing for all conditions and needs simultaneously—maximum system value. There are no political solutions to this. The solutions lie in a design and planning that assures that the rights of the commons and the individual are both supported. Property lines do not recognize critical and contingent natural systems, and those natural systems provide an economic and environmental value to all.

Today's land-use patterns are much the same as this classic "tragedy"—using more land, more water, more soil, and more nonrenewable energy at rates that cannot be sustained. At the point where the use exceeds the supply, the standard of living is reduced and the quality of life goes down as well. Whenever nonrenewably generated electricity is used for lighting while the sun is shining, water is pumped to users while it falls (for free) from the clouds and is distributed by gravity, or materials are shipped thousands of miles to be used for a few years (or even less) and then discarded into the landfills, the tragedy expands.

Paradigm Shift

Public policy is influenced by the values and theories that are broadly held by the practitioners and researchers working in a given area of policy making. This underlying system of beliefs is referred to as a *paradigm*. A paradigm is a framework or foundation of understanding that is accepted by a professional community. Paradigms affect how professional questions are framed, research is conducted, and professional practice is changed. Paradigms are based on a *consensus* of what constitutes accepted facts and theories.

When an existing paradigm is replaced with a new one, a paradigm shift is underway. A paradigm shift occurs when the accumulation of a body of knowledge—for example, finding that design has negative impacts and can be done differently—emerges and illustrates deviations from the old paradigm. Sustainable design is a paradigm shift, where the solutions plug into natural resources, renewable energies, and place-based knowledge.

Thinking as a System: Connectivity, Not Fragmentation

In 1974, Howard Odum related the story of a project, the Crystal River Power Plant in central Florida, where he was hired to analyze environmental impacts. The challenge was to look at the comparative environmental costs of the thermal effluent, which was directly fed into an estuary, and compare the costs with an alternative approach, which incorporated cooling towers to disperse the waste heat. The Crystal River Power Plant needed a considerable number of cooling towers. These evaporative towers, constructed of wood, lowered the temperature of the thermal effluent through evaporative cooling and therefore reduced the thermal stress to the Crystal River—a crystal-clear, natural treasure. The environmentalists were convinced that the heat would degrade the estuary, and they strongly preferred treatment of the thermal effluent prior to it being introduced into the river.

Odum's analysis resulted in some counterintuitive conclusions. First, there would be considerable loss to the forest ecosystem every five to ten years to rebuild the wood cooling towers, and these huge towers would have a negative visual impact on the neighboring communities. More importantly, heat is a useful energy, and Odom was interested in employing that heat effluent as a usable energy.

Some ecosystems are perfectly adapted to heat stress; the saltwater estuary at Crystal River is one example. Oyster beds there populate the shallow waters and are capable of withstanding temperatures above 140°F. These organisms, in fact, had accelerated growth due to heat. The thermal effluent was gravity fed and distributed to the estuary, producing a prime productivity environment, with the waste heat as free energy. The analysis showed that the estuary was not only suited for the heat, but also benefited from it. In this case, the bias against the thermal effluent did not measure up.

"In *The Culture of Nature*, landscape architect Alexander Wilson observes: 'My own sense is that the immediate work that lies ahead has to do with fixing landscape, repairing its ruptures, reconnecting its parts. Restoring landscape is not about preserving lands—*saving what's left*, as it's often put. Restoration recognizes that once lands have been *disturbed*—worked, lived on, meddled with, developed—they require human intervention and care. We must build landscapes that heal, connect, and empower, that make intelligible our relations with each other and with the natural world; places that welcome and enclose, whose breaks and edges are never without meaning.' "

ADELHEID FISCHER, "COMING FULL CIRCLE: THE RESTORATION OF THE URBAN LANDSCAPE," *ORION: PEOPLE AND NATURE* (AUTUMN 1994).

BIOREGIONALISM

CLIMATE

SURFACE

GEOLOGY

AIRSHED

Quality:
- oxygen from plants
- pollution from manufacturing and industry
- gases from soil

Quantity:
- weather patterns (air currents/winds)
- location of manufacturing and industry

PRECIPITATION

Quality:
- pollution from manufacturing and industry (acid rain)

Quantity:
- weather patterns (frequency and type)
- geographic location

LAND USE

Urban Systems
Agricultural Systems
Natural Systems

SOILS

- fertility (natural and agricultural plants)
- perviousness (type, depth, and location)
- water storage capability

WATERSHED

Geographic features:
- mountains
- valleys
- lake and sea basins

SUBSURFACE

Underground features:
- tectonics (stability)
  - earthquakes
  - sinkholes
  - caverns
- underground water storage (aquifers)
- underground water transportation

Sustainable and renewable energy is best understood at the regional scale where the interactions are the spatial relationships between air (climate and essential gases), land use (water distribution, surface use, and ecology), and geology (soil characteristics and water storage potential.

BIOURBANISM

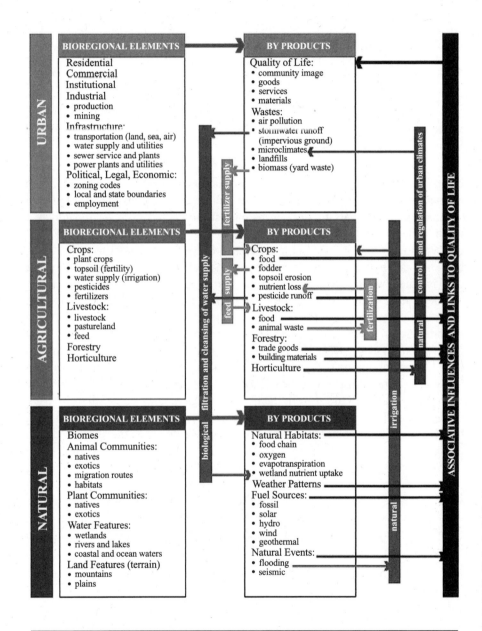

These same relationships occur at the urban and community scale. Missing are the connections back into and between the components. The location of these components is a function of the natural system character.

> "We are now engaged in a great global debate about how we might lengthen our tenure on the earth. The discussion is mostly confined to options having to do with better technology, more accurate resources, prices, and smart public policies, all of which are eminently sensible, but hardly sufficient. The problem is simply how a species pleased to call itself *Homo sapiens* fits on a planet with a biosphere. This is a design problem and requires a design philosophy that takes time, velocity, scale, evolution, and ecology seriously."
>
> DAVID W. ORR, *THE NATURE OF DESIGN*
> (NEW YORK: OXFORD UNIVERSITY PRESS, 2002), 50.

How many more opportunities are there where environmental stress and waste can be connected to the right biology and have a positive result rather than an expensive mitigation? Understanding these connections provides an opportunity for architects and designers to start developing schemes that both *fit* and *function* within the ecological system.

When ecologists study a particular system or biome, they start by defining the boundary as the next larger system. The sustainable design challenge starts similarly, studying the environmental context at the next larger scale, as a living pattern and interdependent system. In ecology the connections between systems are vital to life, whereas in conventional designing and planning only legal boundaries are used, and opportunities to integrate a site's resources and microclimate are typically left unexplored. Consequently, when designing sustainably if the project is architectural in scale, the neighborhood system must be included in the study; if the neighborhood is the project, then the city must be studied; and if the city, then the study starts with the regional scale. For this reason, the new challenge may well be to think globally, live locally, and *act regionally*. Designing regionally is the scale at which the most benefit toward sustainable living can be achieved. The need and the ability to design at this scale exist, but the will to do it does not.

Since ecology is the study of the *relationship* of plants and animals to their environment, designing ecologically requires the incorporation of sustainable relationships to power the design. The ecological model illustrates the foundation of the sustainable model and, consequently, a model for sustainable design. The resulting design will be planned to receive, store, and distribute sustainable energy and resources.

sustainable design

Follow the sun.
Observe the wind.
Watch the flow of water.
Use simple materials.
Touch the earth lightly.
   —Glenn Murcutt, architect

Architect Glen Murcutt said it succinctly when he characterized sustainable design as responding to the environmental clues of the site and region.

Where Do We Want to Go?

In Lewis Carroll's *Alice in Wonderland*, Alice asks the Cheshire Cat, "Would you please tell me which way I ought to go from here?" The cat replies, "That depends a good deal on where you want to get to."

Sustainable design creates solutions that solve the economic, social, and environmental challenges of the project simultaneously, and these solutions are powered by sustainable energies. The combined beauty and function of the design make it something that endures and is cherished; endurance and beauty are central to sustainable thinking. The underlying quest is that if the "get-to" place is sustainability, it is way past a discussion on energy efficiency.

Design Matters

How projects are designed and, more importantly, how the design program is defined, is central to sustainable design and planning. If a project does not include energy efficiency as a program requirement, there is little chance that the project will fulfill that requirement. More importantly, if sustainable design is the foundation of the program requirement, then energy, form, construction processes, materials, native place, and long life are integral to the design solution. Since design is a process, changing the process will change the product significantly. All design can be sustainable, but the change in the design process must include a change in the designers' education. Designers' expanded ability to solve problems must be grounded in ecological principles, earth sciences, and physics—all of which are sustainable models.

Why Architects?

Typically, sustainability is illustrated as three intersecting circles connecting community, economy, and the environment. But the overwhelming majority of problems, issues, and corresponding solutions are, like ecology, three-dimensional. As three-dimensional problem solvers, architects are well suited to lead the change toward sustainability. That architects are three-dimensional problem solvers is central to the resolution of nonlinear, spatial problems. Most professions do not work this way, and most people do not think spatially. The three spheres of sustainability, much like the three elements in Vitruvius' Principles—firmness, commodity, and delight—must be solved simultaneously, and spatial thinkers are best at doing that. Since these spatial relationships are essential and connected parts of sustainable design, spatial

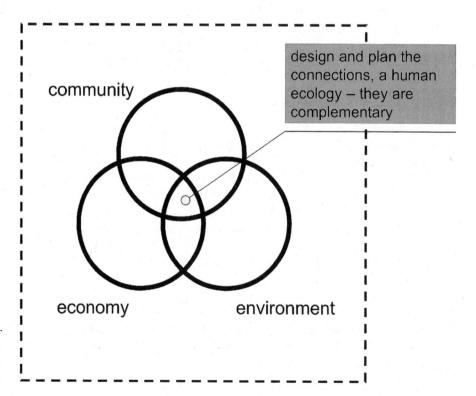

design and plan the connections, a human ecology – they are complementary

community

economy   environment

The three rings of sustainability illustrate interdependence of the elements.

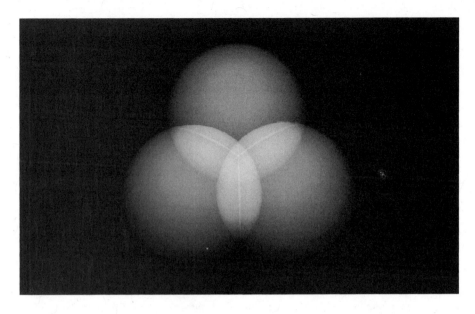

The three spheres of sustainability illustrate the spatial interdependence and connectivity critical to sustainable design. Three-dimensional problems require three-dimensional solutions.

thinkers are best equipped for the challenge, responsibility, and stewardship of multidimensional solutions.

Design is a powerful process, and as such, when it is informed by the knowledge gleaned from truly sustainable systems, design has the potential of changing how buildings, communities, and societies function. Design has the power of both satisfying a need and providing value. The unsustainable approaches to designing and building energy-consumptive structures must evolve to place-based energy and self-sufficient designs, and they need to evolve rapidly.

Design and designers are at a unique position in history within the United States and globally. Design can, within this next generation, illustrate that architects and planners are not only agents of the change toward sustainability but quite possibility the most central and effective agents for making this change happen. With upward of 40 percent of the energy consumed in the United States directly related to a building or community's location (planning), its construction (design), and maintenance (design), the reduction of negative impacts would be substantial and the benefits would be significant (AIA Architects and Climate Change, pages xvi and xvii).

Green Design versus Sustainable Design

Sustainable designs sustain—sustainable design sustains. Sustainable designs function on sustainable resident energies. Sustainable designs last; they are flexible; they are loved and cherished; they endure; they function when they are tethered to nonrenewables and also when the nonrenewables are unavailable. They can function in a blackout or a drought or natural disaster or on a beautiful day without any input from nonrenewables. The designed connection to the place affords the ability to function without nonrenewables. Sustainable architecture and design add to quality of the environment, to clean air, to water, to renewing and protecting life—all by designing the connections to what is there. The place is better because of sustainable design.

Green design is an element of sustainable design. Green buildings and communities that integrate the local climate and building resources, create healthy interior spaces with natural light, and complete recycling and reuse of materials are critical to the development of a sustainable future. Green buildings that efficiently use grid-based (nonrenewable) energy slow the energy and pollution crisis, but if the energy sources powering these buildings are unsustainable, the design is not sustainable.

Sustainable design differs from green design in that it is additive and inclusive—it includes continuing, surviving, thriving, and adapting. *Green design* incorporates ecologically sensitive materials and creates healthy buildings and processes that do not negatively affect the environment before, during, or after manufacture, construction, and deconstruction. Green design incorporates efficient mechanical systems and high-performance technologies but still functions primarily through the use of fossil fuels. Sustainable design integrates the principles of green design and goes further to become a passive *and* active structure that is designed to maximize the use of sites' natural renewable resources. When buildings are conceived as organisms instead of objects, they become part of the ecological neighborhood, and since they operate off existing site and regional renewable energies, they are sustainable.

Sustainable design improves the quality of life while eliminating the need for nonrenewable energy. When a design solution incorporates sustainable energies to power that design's functioning, that "work" is done for free. *Free work* is what natural systems provide; it powers all ecology. Human ecology, though similar, is critically different. Although largely powered by sustainable processes that provide essential needs, human settlements rely on fossil fuel for food, comfort, transportation, air, water, and security. Designs powered by free sustainable energies require no fossil fuel and are capable of providing a healthier level of comfort and a higher quality of life. In achieving this connection with local free energies, sustainable design reduces or eliminates the daily consumption of nonrenewables, reduces project costs and maintenance costs and requirements, increases user approval and user productivity, and reduces the total embodied project energy. Sustainable design is green design powered by sustainable energies—functioning unplugged.

Why Now?

Remarkably few cities or municipalities have development plans for the next 10 years, not to mention for the next 100 years. Yet any neighborhood, town, or city that wants to assure the quality of its future must actively design and plan for that quality, or it will not happen. Design and planning, in part, mean that proactive steps are being taken to assure that something necessary and desired will happen. Sustainable planning assures that the changes that occur will be desired and powered by sustainable energies and resources.

> "In any endeavor, good design resides in two principles. First, it changes the least number of elements to achieve the greatest result. Second, it removes stress from a system rather than adding it."
> PAUL HAWKIN, *THE ECOLOGY OF COMMERCE*

Most pollution problems can be abated by redesigning the source of the pollution or by distributing the pollutant to existing natural-system processes that use the pollution as part of their energy and nutrient requirement. Thinking of design as a *systems problem* challenges the designer to define the problem or scope as a process of reconnecting or looking for possible connections and compatibilities. The complexity of today's problems has increased as the population has increased, so multidimensional thinkers need to give form and pattern to multiple issues and solve them simultaneously.

As the design professions adopt sustainable design—design a chair, design a good chair, design a great chair, or design a sustainable chair—the thinking changes as well. Although the object is the same, the objective and process are considerably different. The same is true of designing a sustainable building or community. How the architect defines the problem and understands his or her responsibility to solve it dramatically impacts the design process and, consequently, the solution.

Approaching Sustainability

As architects and planners, we are taught to work on a project until it is done, then move on to the next one. But design, like sustainability, is a dynamic and living process. Sustainability is not a point that when reached, all is fine. Sustainability is better thought of as a continuum, as a calculus: **dp→S,** meaning *design and planning approaching sustainability*. A design is sustainable, or it is not. If it is not sustainable, changes can be made to make it sustainable. If it is sustainable, by necessity it will be changing and evolving. Sustainability is not static—it is iteratively changing, based on evolving knowledge that connects science and design.

A design that is considerably better than ASHRAE (American Society of Heating, Refrigerating, and Air-Conditioning Engineers) standards or is twice as efficient as the code requires or uses 50 percent less potable water for irrigating is still not a sustainable design. The design must be capable of functioning "unplugged" from the external nonrenewable energy sources and resources in order to be sustainable. There are varying degrees of green design, but sustainable design is an absolute— *the building can function unplugged*. If the building or community is highly energy efficient but cannot function unplugged, it is not sustainable. Once designers embrace the unplugged challenge, they will start to take the steps to creating sustainable buildings. If, however, the existing measuring processes and certifications continue to celebrate designs as sustainable when they are not (most are only marginally better than those required by code), there can be no real movement toward this goal. The question, again, is "Where do we want to get to?" Sustainability comes from design.

Most measurements today—such as the AIA Committee on the Environment Top Ten Measures of Sustainability, the U.S. Green Building Council LEED rating system, BRE Environmental Assessment Method, and others—are concerned with sustainability, but they measure energy efficiency instead of sustainability, and typically that measurement of efficiency is in the use of nonrenewables. Efficient use of nonrenewables is not a path to sustainability. The test is simple—be unplugged. If the proverbial plug is pulled due to drought, blackout, natural disaster, or other event, is the design still *functional?* A sustainable project would be useful under any weather condition. Ecology is bioclimatically in tune with the regional sustainable energy patterns: buildings and communities must be as well.

Place-Based Energy and Resources

Heading the list on renewable but limited sustainable resources is water. This resource also provides the most immediate and effective feedback to the question "How are we doing?" Water is also admirably deaf to political boundaries, a characteristic that renders it a highly effective common denominator. Water managers, planners, and elected officials typically get into trouble when water-supply and water-budget lines do not reflect the geographic boundaries of the users—one system, then, has to steal from the other.

Virtually all municipalities get their potable water from a watershed and groundwater storage outside their own development boundaries. The reason for the loss of supply and recharge within their own boundaries is twofold. First, demand has increased exponentially. Second, land use within the watershed has significantly increased impervious surfaces, affecting the total runoff (loss) and reducing the recharge amount, rendering the water crop polluted and insufficient. With all of the water "managed" out of the system, water-resource agencies are wondering how to provide water for communities that now exist and what to do now that this lost water is essential for additional development.

Principles for Designing Sustainably

At a time when the known nonrenewable reserves of fossil fuel are getting more costly to tap, producing less net energy and producing harmful global warming, it is prudent to start designing structures and communities that function well without them.

As energy costs soar, fossil fuel–powered comfort, water availability, transportation, and food will become less available and affordable—impacting the cost and functioning of everything. Since less net energy, coupled with the associated pollution and health issues, is the apparent future for nonrenewable-energy use, it poses a compelling challenge: how to design structures that are powered by renewables on the site and region and how to design into the project the ability to fully function without nonrenewables.

Three scalar elements should be considered in the initial design process:

1. *Connectivity*: Design to reinforce the relationship between the project, the site, the community, and the ecology. Make minimal changes to the natural system functioning. Reinforce and steward those natural characteristics specific to the place.

2. *Indigenous*: Design with and for what has been resident and sustainable on the site for centuries.

3. *Long life, loose fit:* Design for future generations while reflecting past generations.

How do the *regional, urban,* and *architectural* scales interrelate and work as a system?

Site to Region:

- What are the relevant urban, agricultural, and natural characteristics of the project site?

- What cultural and economic assets exist?

- What are the climate characteristics of the bioregional system that have formed the general attributes of the biome?

- What role do natural disasters have as part of the land use, climate, and geological region, and what impact do they have on the design and post-disaster planning?

Site to Site:

- What is the relationship between the site and its neighboring site, specifically in terms of context, scale, view corridors, materials, geometric relationships, neighborhood characteristics, and proportions that can inform your building?

- What are all the usable relationships derived from the site and environmental analysis that can be introduced into your design?

- What microclimates are present, and how do they inform design choices?

- What are the vegetation types and the soil and water retention characteristics? How do they impact temperature, air movement, and humidity on the site?

- What parts of the site's microclimate related to seasonal and diurnal changes are impacted by adjacent land uses?

Site to Architecture:

- What are the synergistic relationships between the site's climate and those of human needs and comfort?

- Is the microclimate of the site approaching human-comfort zones and meeting user needs (e.g., the air movement and humidity and temperature levels)? Chart the times of the year when special adjustments need to be made in air movement and temperature to provide interior comfort and suggest interventions to effect comfort.

- What are the areas of the site's microclimate (e.g., ground temperature for thermal-mass storage for heating or cooling the space) that can be introduced into the design solution?

A Sustainable Design To-Do List:

1. Learn and measure what exists seasonally at the region and site scale (e.g., temperature, humidity, air movement, precipitation, winds, and soils).
2. Overlay and compare measurements of what is needed by the users (comfort, water, renewable energies, and resources) to what exists on the site. List seasonal design approaches and opportunities to unplug.
3. Measure and assess effectiveness. Learn from mistakes and successes. Sustainability is a calculus; it is evolving.

Where to Start?

If the imperative is to be sustainable, the design program for buildings and communities is simple. The projects should meet the following criteria:

- Be developed within existing urban boundaries and within walking distance to transit options. New projects would preferably be built on a cleaned-up brownfield.
- Use green energy and be unplugged from nonrenewables.
- Be fully useful for intended function in a natural disaster, a blackout, or a drought.
- Be made of materials that have a long and useful life—longer than its growth cycle—and be anchored for deconstruction (every design should be a storehouse of materials for another project).
- Use no more water than what falls on the site.
- Connect impacts and wastes of the building to useful cycles on the site and in the environment around it. Be part of a cycle.
- Be compelling, rewarding, and desirable.

The following questions should be asked of designs to gauge a project's sustainability:

- Is the project accessible without fossil fuel?
- Did the project improve the neighborhood?
- If the climate outside is comfortable, does the design take advantage of this free sustainable comfort?
- If there is sufficient daylight, do the lights remain on? Do they have to?
- Does the storm water flow into an engineered underground system, or does it stay on the site for future needs while improving the natural system microclimate and pedestrian experience?
- Is irrigation done with pumped chlorinated–potable water?
- Are the toilets usable when the power is off?

"Question the assumptions. What are we doing perpetuating patterns that exist just because they have always been in place? We should be evolving our patterns into the best combinations based on accurate accounting, social patterns, and other aspects of the whole system."
     SCOTT BERNSTEIN, CENTER
        FOR NEIGHBORHOOD
             TECHNOLOGY, AT
        AIA/SUSTAINABILITY
        TASK GROUP CHICAGO,
                APRIL 28, 2006.

■ Is there sufficient natural ventilation?

■ Is comfort personally controlled?

There are limits to all resources. Technological solutions often cause problems greater than those they were intended to solve, requiring additional cleanup, storage of toxic materials, and additional taxes to pay for such services.

To achieve an interactive network of humanity and nature—a landscape that has a *place* for both the needs of humans and the functions of nature—planning and design must reorient itself from using more to the view that there are limits. It then becomes the combined mission of science, planning, and design to discover these limits and work within them, to put form to a common vision and to develop incremental steps and strategies on how to get from here to there.

regional design

Think globally, live locally, act regionally.

Sustainable design at the regional scale begins with gaining a working knowledge of the ecological system at that larger scale. At the regional scale, sustainable energies and renewable resources are measurable and have had some consistency for centuries. It is also at this scale that the relationship, interactions, and interdependencies between the three elements of sustainability—economic, social (ecological), and environmental—can be viewed.

Changes in the planning and design process at this larger scale, have the greatest positive impact on environmental protection and reduction of nonrenewable energy consumption—the greatest impact on sustainability. Urban and regional planning practices that incorporate ecological thinking are the foundation of community, economic, and environmental sustainability.

The scales of bioregionalism and biourbanism are part of the sustainable design process. This process incorporates the following three steps:

1. *Bioregionalism* involves researching and understanding the natural system at a scale larger than the project scale and applying that bioregional knowledge— in climatology, biology, pedology (soil science), and ecology—to the interaction of the urban components (i.e., the infrastructure, utilities, and neighborhood patterns).
2. *Incorporation of the free work of the natural system* includes the ecology, biology, physics, climate, hydrology, and soils of the system, using natural processes

rather than technology for water storage and cleaning, for microclimatic control, and for establishment of local and regional resource use, reuse, and recycling.

3. *Biourbanism* involves designing the connections to make use of place-based energies and resources and integrating them into the urban and community scale.

Design and planning at the regional scale have the greatest impact on sustainability—even greater than designing unplugged buildings. The layout of utilities and infrastructure has significant impacts on sustainability, such as transmission loss due to the length of lines delivering electricity. The local, regional, and national layout of highways, roads, and zoning patterns dictate whether land use is compatible with natural and sustainable patterns. When planning creates a system in which roads and highways are the only linkages to personal necessities, the planning itself creates unsustainable conditions. *Urban sprawl*, in which development extends further and further from the core business district, leads to a greater dependence on automobiles, both in the number of trips required and in the length of the trips. Highway transportation uses nonrenewables in both the vehicle and its fuel. Insidiously, sprawl increases pollution, promotes obesity and diabetes, and reduces time available for family and friends and other activities that increase the quality of life. Urban sprawl is also rapidly consuming prime agricultural land, flood protection zones, and water-recharge areas. These losses are a direct result of zoning codes informed solely by real-estate value and not the common good. This planning, or rather lack thereof, is no longer feasible with high energy costs, health hazards and associated pollution.

An infrastructure powered by natural energies—a green infrastructure—provides free sustainable services: in particular, flood protection, storm-surge coastal protection, economic value, water supply, and water quality. This is the place where the natural and free processes clean the air and water, store carbon, and establish bioclimatic conditions. The preservation and protection of these areas and their natural functions add economic value to the land. This value directly reduces taxes by performing services to the region and community while informing development patterns.

The natural processes are the foundation of every region's sustainability and are essential to all life and human settlements. Maximizing the connections between the two is essential in the development of a sustainable economy and higher quality of life at less cost. But the entire system suffers when too many resources are taken from the environment (e.g., reduction of wetlands and trees, destruction of soils, and overfishing) and too much returned (e.g., garbage, sewage, and trash) at too fast a rate to be assimilated. In the natural system, this stress is measured by decreased diversity, increased air and water pollution, and increased need for governmental controls; in the urban system, overtaxing the natural system is measured by a lower quality of life and higher taxes. The natural capital—the free work of nature—that sustains all life and creates the quality of life that humans desire is declining, and that creates a stress on the human economic and social systems. It will take tax dollars to clean it up and to get it working as freely, simply, and efficiently as it had in the past or, as the typical approach has become, we will have to rely on the development of expensive new technologies to provide the same functions that natural processes did better and for free.

Evolving from Nonrenewables

The human economy runs almost exclusively on nonrenewable, unsustainable materials and energies. The materials used in every building and every purchase made at every store rely on nonrenewables for their distribution, are derived from nonrenewables, or are nonrenewable. The fertilizers, trucks, clothing, roads, machinery, transportation, and tools—everything is inextricably linked to and dependent on the use of nonrenewables. The average food item purchased at the corner market traveled 2,000 miles before it was eaten. This is important, because when comparing organic apples to organic oranges, the distribution energy—the energy consumed transporting the product to the market—exceeds the food energy value. So even when the crop itself is sustainable, the distribution methods are not. The critical step in evolving from nonrenewables is to be powered and supplied locally.

Worldwide, *urbanism*—and all its buildings, people, and jobs—is 100 percent dependent on nonrenewables and cannot function without them. Virtually all buildings, communities, towns, and cities will have to be retrofitted for an alternative source—a source, unless it is natural renewable energy, that is not known at this time.

Estimates of oil reserves, whether growing or shrinking, are not the harbinger of a sustainable future at any scale. Design that ties its value and future to increasing efficiency of a nonrenewable energy may be reducing pollution, but the designs are not sustainable—they cannot be used for their intended purpose without nonrenewables. The design may be firm and delightful; but if it is not functioning, it does not have commodity. All major projects in the design and construction phase today, from the scale of buildings to new towns, will be powered by an alternative energy within 20 years—which is within their expected period of operation and use.

Another Weak Link: The Power Grid

The present-day urban growth and development patterns are tied to an energy source that has a worst-case and best-case availability of 40 to 200 years (assuming the air is still breathable). Electricity is produced by turbines set in motion and fueled by coal, gas, hydro, fuel oils, or nuclear power. Nationally, more than 90 percent of electricity is produced by coal, oil, and gas—all nonrenewable energies. Since power plants convert energy (nonrenewables) into power (electricity) and are located outside and away from the users (industry, cities, and neighborhoods), the power they create has to be distributed. The cost of distribution is roughly 40 percent of the total cost, so every time electricity is created, at least 40 percent of it is lost in transmission.

However, without distribution, virtually all of the consumers would not be supplied. Since electrical power use relies on a distribution system, there are other issues that are of concern. First, the power plant must have the nonrenewables; second, it must make the steam to drive the turbines to create electricity; third, it must distribute the electricity. If any part of this system is senescent or breaks down or is unsustainable, the whole system is unstable and unusable.

Perhaps the most important part of the delivery system is the grid that transfers electricity to homes, neighborhoods, town, cities, and regions. Recent blackouts such as those in the northeastern United States in 2003 are examples of failures not in supply but in distribution.

As in much of the built infrastructure in all towns, cities, and regions, the first costs and the maintained and rebuilt costs are misunderstood. A smart-growth system—for example, a gravity-based water distribution system—is relatively easy to repair. Antigravity systems that involve pumping and piping water or gas from low to high and over great distances are extremely expensive. Repairing a conceptually flawed system will not deliver anything more than a repaired but flawed system. When the power is down, the pumping, filtration, and purification of water stops.

The opportunity to rethink—to discover how to successfully design within the natural system functions—has never been more compelling or essential than now. The challenge is to integrate and reconnect regional, urban, and architectural design with natural sciences, taking full advantage of work that can be accomplished without fossil fuel.

The Regional Design

The United States Environmental Protection Agency (EPA) has identified the need for a comprehensive watershed approach to ecosystem management and protection. In cities across the United States, the results of poorly planned growth can be seen in undesirable and unsustainable conditions, which affect the regional water supply, cause a loss of habitat and a permanent loss of productive agricultural land, and lead to high costs for miles of additional roads.

The universal lack of long-term, large-scale planning is not due to a mistrust of the design and planning profession, but to the fear that people have approaching the unknowable—embarking on a process they do not understand. By working with communities, teaching the process, and creating illustrated, community-based visions, architects can help communities define their desired future and establish next steps to implement their vision. The foundation on which these visions must be built is the ecological model—specifically, water as a limit to growth and development

A new and critical challenge for architects and planners is to design entire regions at the same level of detail seen in urban and community design—literally designing regions. By designing future development patterns on a regional scale, the opportunity to connect to natural system functions is greater. Design at this scale also creates a win-win situation for business. The developer would no longer have to guess as to whether a project site is buildable or whether the environmental impacts

"The role of government is to assume those functions that cannot or will not be undertaken by citizens or private institutions . . . But forgotten is the true meaning and purpose of politics, to create and sustain the conditions for community life . . . In other words, politics is very much about food, water, life, and death, and thus intimately concerned with the environmental conditions that support the community . . . It is the role of government, then, as a political act, to set standards within the community."

PAUL HAWKEN, *THE ECOLOGY OF COMMERCE: A DECLARATION OF SUSTAINABILITY*
(NEW YORK: HARPERBUSINESS, 1993), 166.

are significant enough to cause delays or, worse, litigation. This regional planning would delineate buildable locations, water recharge areas, best transit locations, agricultural preservation zones, open space, conservation zones, soil reclamation zones, and livable, walkable communities. It would take into account the best mixes to simultaneously improve the economy, the communities, and the environment.

Designing regional-growth patterns requires the designer to have a working knowledge of the ecological communities, the regional systems' economic structure, sustainable design, and governmental policy. A design solution at this scale results in sustainable efficient development patterns, incorporating the free work done by natural systems and sustainable energy. Because these plans integrate the green infrastructure of the region, the costs for potable water, clean air, and transportation are reduced considerably. These plans are generated in design charrettes with regional stakeholders, resulting in long-term visions authored and stewarded by regional citizens. As this is a community-based vision, the permitting process is easier and the desired higher quality of life is achieved for a lower cost and little, if any, litigation.

Commuters would enjoy using a transit system or walking from their homes to work or to stores—both healthier and less expensive alternatives to purchasing another car. The natural system cycles would supply regional food, water supply, and community pride, all while the agricultural lands would be preserved and protected without taking away the rights of farmers who have accrued land value.

Regional sustainable design approaches are founded on three-dimensional, place-based criteria. This three-dimensional method is inspired by the important work of Ian McHarg, the systems integration of Howard T. Odum, and the design pattern principles of the Olgyay brothers.

Planning and design at this scale integrates natural systems principles with community design standards in a way that adds to the quality of life, even while the population increases. The information, talent, and concern exist—but not the will.

Water: A Common Denominator

Designers and planners typically get into trouble when natural-resources lines—for example, the water supply—do not reflect the users' boundaries. New York City, as

The hydrologic cycle critically informs biologic systems and urban and regional patterns. Powered by gravity and sunlight, it is a sustainable large-scale engine.

an example, has been purchasing land in the Catskills watershed for decades. It was estimated in the 1990s that if more land is not purchased to protect this water-supply area, the costs for additional treatment for their potable-water supply will range from $8 billion to $10 billion (Robert Yaro, personal discussion).

Regional watershed planning takes the approach of reconnecting isolated elements while creating more livable communities. Designing local and regional water connections that reinforce the interaction of land use and water is a first step in watershed planning and design.

The watershed design and planning objectives are (1) to build consensus among local, state, and federal interests as to the actions necessary to achieve regional water-management objectives, conservation areas, and livable communities; and (2) to use this comprehensive understanding of the relationships between land use and regional water-management objectives to create designs that reflect the vision based on these working relationships—working together as an ecological model.

With water, the challenges are simple. They focus on meeting demands of all of the components of the region—the community, the economy, and the environment. Since the resident water supply is the land area times the amount of precipitation, the determining factors are the quantity of water, the seasonal timing, the quality of water, and how the demand fits with the variability of supply. A region reliant on the precipitation that falls on its land area is self-sufficient. In ecology, the relationship of the available resources to the user needs is referred to as the land's carrying capacity—that is, its ability to sustain a population with the available resources. Carrying capacity based on watershed planning has four interrelated challenges:

1. If the water *quantity* is insufficient but sufficient precipitation exists, then the land pattern and land use must store more water.
2. If the *quality* is also insufficient, then the land pattern can be designed to store and clean the water.
3. If there is insufficient water for use and the supply is insufficient, the water must be cycled at the rate of use to make up for the lack of supply.
4. If sustainability is desired, all of the above must be accomplished.

Water sustainability requires policies and land-use patterns that promote regional self-sufficiency. The precipitation that falls on the surface of a region's watershed is the income and the budget for all water uses. Additional consumption of water *greater than* that allotted amount is deficit spending. This deficit spending eventually reduces the total capacity of the system, and because it is typically accommodating growth in population and consequently increased consumption, the problem can only get worse. In the water budgeting cycle, first the natural system and hydrological integrity should be satisfied, then the combined needs of the agricultural and urban systems can be addressed. When these priorities are not followed, the entire economic, social, and environmental system of the area is placed at risk—water is the determining factor of growth.

> "Don't import your solutions; don't export your problems."
> DONALD WATSON, FAIA

Make No Small Plans

Regional design is a map to sustainable living. Since design connects many disciplines and initiates team building, the associated impacts of the regional design process are both positive and practical. Design at the regional level is a *change-in-scale to citizens' involvement* in that it educates the value of whole systems thinking. What is most important to citizens is that their involvement can empower them to act and to plan for the long term, for the next 100 years, and help to create alternatives to the lineal trends and growth that have destroyed their land, segmented their neighborhoods, and stressed their tax bases. For example, stewards of the city of Seattle, over 100 years ago, knew that a sustainable water supply was critical to future generations. Because they knew that water was critical to the city's well-being, they purchased the entire Cedar River Watershed, providing a sustainable water supply while preserving a regional open space. Now that the population of Seattle has grown exponentially, there is a need for the purchase of additional watersheds. The original purchase has served as a case study for the regional water supply for the next century.

Short- and long-term planning visions informed by both natural and human-defined conditions will create plans and patterns that are sustainable to the public and nature. A regional-design process that informs the community-based vision while providing for an economic and environmental future is the best map for a sustainable future.

The Regional Design Process

The regional design process starts with the gathering of information on the natural and existing patterns and conditions of the biomes and natural systems. The following are maps and illustrations that are helpful in visualizing how the region works and what sustainable relationships exist.

SYSTEMS MAPS

The *natural systems map* illustrates presettlement patterns. These established patterns were created by long-standing bioclimatic conditions, and they represent thousands of years of trial and error that created the present-day sustainable patterns. Virtually everything done every day is connected and reacted to and controlled by the environmental forces that created these patterns in these particular locations, including their diversity and uniqueness. These patterns were formed by natural conditions and represent an order that occurs naturally and for free; however, any

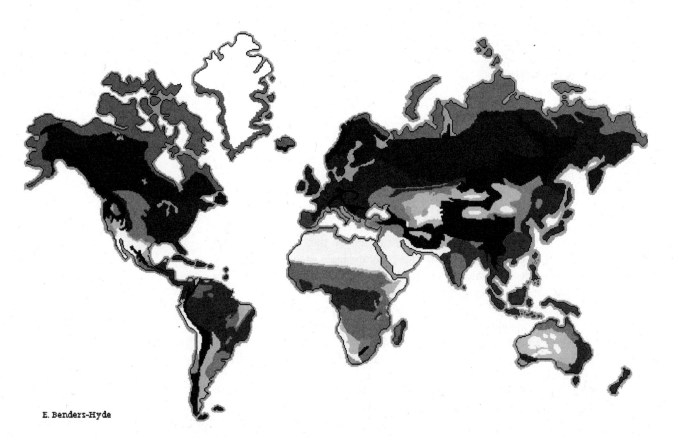

E. Benders-Hyde

The ecological biomes of the planet are well adapted to large variations in renewable energy and materials, all powered by sustainable energies.

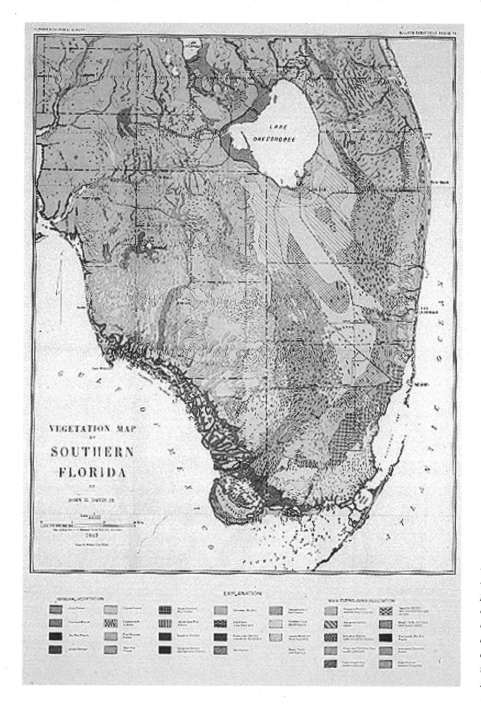

Natural Systems Map showing vegetation patterns that have adapted to changing conditions using the available sustainable energies (sunlight) and natural resources (water, soil) of the bioregion.

change to this pattern is expensive and will need constant maintenance. The order, form, and pattern is powered by sustainable free processes resident to the region.

The *natural systems map* illustrates the inherent value in understanding the tens of thousands of years of trial and error that produced the hydrologic, soil, and vegetation systems, powered by sunlight, that exist today. Combining land-use planning with knowledge of the natural sciences inspires a sustainable fit.

The following are regionally sustainable elements that inform design:

- *Climatic conditions:* Climate is a reoccurring pattern of generalities and averages that relate to temperature, humidity, precipitation, and air movement. A climate is specific to conditions driven by solar and lunar cycles in concert with water, soils, and geology. Within any climate, there are times when human comfort can be achieved without mechanical intervention and times when it cannot.

- *Precipitation:* Rain, fog, sleet, and snow supply water to the air, to the surface-water system, to soil saturation, and to groundwater storage. Water was the critical factor in starting the tremendous biological explosion that has led to today's biodiversity. Plato said that water got the least amount of care because it was so common. It is now generally agreed that water is the most critical of all resources, is in a state of decline, and is the ultimate limit to all growth and development.

- *Temperature:* Most people refer to temperature when measuring the comfort in a given setting. Their level of comfort or discomfort is often directly related to the temperature in their environment. Although there are other factors, including psychology, typically comfort is a function of temperature, humidity, and air movement.

- *Humidity:* The amount of water in the air is the culprit of many uncomfortable places. Because water is a big part of all biology and evaporating water has a cooling effect, the more water in the air (high humidity), the less evaporation and cooling. Humidity also is a factor in creating uncomfortable conditions in cold climates, because the water carries the cold temperature through clothing and building skins, finding drier interior air and then cooling it with evaporation, which is not desired in the winter.

- *Air movement:* Wind, convection, and storms all create the movement of air that changes the condition of the place. If a climate is hot and humid, the small amount of dryness in the air can still remove perspiration if it moves across the skin rapidly enough, creating cooling. This wind-cooling effect is one of the reasons people live along the breezy coast in hot and humid areas.

- *Topography:* Vertical variations in the landscape are helpful in creating potential energy storages. Gravity is one of the most significant sustainable forces. It can distribute water for free, and even stratification of microclimatic air temperature is related to its presence. Topography plays an important role in establishing patterns for smart places to develop—out of flood plains, away from coastal storm surges, and improved air circulation and movement.

- *Soils:* When asked what would be the most critical piece of equipment he would take to colonize a planet, the astronaut John Glenn answered, "Soil." Soil consists of chemical and electrical components that took billions of years to develop. Full of biology, a cubic inch contains millions of nematodes. Although food crops and plants can be grown in water alone (hydroponics), it is soil and water that are sustainable and powered by natural cycles.

The natural systems map includes regional ecology, bioclimatic conditions, growth patterns, and conflicts. The following represent challenges to be answered by the regional-system researchers:

- Learn how, when, and where the region's bioclimate is compatible with human development. Include comfort zones, location, sense of place, productive soils, disaster mitigation, and precipitation.
- Learn how the regional ecosystems function and how the climate is compatible with human settlement, including food supply and region-specific job creation.
- Learn the natural landscape, the water-management strategy, ecosystem management, and the creation, re-creation, or preservation of open space and green and blue infrastructure.
- Learn potential strategies for habitat creation and regionally appropriate conservation zones and development controls.
- Learn and map compatibilities, conflicts, and relationships between economic, social, and environmental systems.
- Learn the regional energies and resources that can be exported and whether there is a regional energy system.
- Learn the regional building, zoning, and design codes that support sustainable design.
- Learn the percentage of human-settlement energies (e.g., heating, cooling, water, and food) that is supplied by the existing regional bioclimate and soils. Include precipitation, naturally occurring surface-water flows that are due to topography, and any regeneration of soils that is due to naturally occurring nutrient cycling—determine the missed opportunities.
- Learn if the region can function during drought or blackout.
- Learn the carrying capacity—that is, how many people, plants, and animals can be supported by the existing water crop and natural resources in the region.

A map of the same scale as the natural systems map can be used to establish the precipitation and water storage patterns. This precipitation over thousands of years, combined with the soils and hydrologic periods, created the ecological systems of

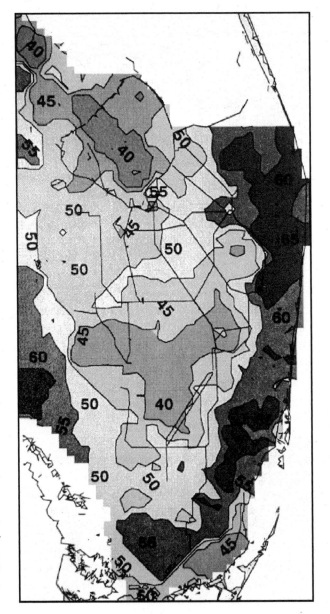

The Water Supply Map: Geohydrology. The legend shows average inches of rainfall. Precipitation is a spatially allocated supply with large variations.

that landscape and biome. Changes to this balance will cause profound changes in the system. It may take decades to see these impacts, but they will come, and they will be very difficult and expensive to correct.

This precipitation study also has topographic information attached to it. All precipitation is spatial, meaning that over the region it lands in different amounts at different locations and at different times. This map illustrates the location of the largest amount of rainfall and compares it to development patterns. When development occurs, pervious surfaces are replaced by impervious ones—the groundwater recharge is, therefore, significantly reduced and flooding increases.

Elements to be included in this map are as follows:

- Hydrological periods and seasonal quantities: highs, lows, and averages
- Drought frequencies
- Water quality
- Flooding
- Surface water and flood plains
- Groundwater storages and recharge locations

URBAN SYSTEMS MAPS: COMMUNITY DESIGN AND GREEN INFRASTRUCTURE CONNECTION

The following represents research and learning that will help promote the reconnection with green infrastructure within communities and neighborhoods:

- Learn how urban patterns promote connection to local renewable resources, to its sense of place, and to regional context.
- Learn how community (or public) space, transportation strategy, and livable-community standards are improved by connection to the regional ecological model.
- Learn how the orientation of streets and buildings helps improve comfort and reduce discomfort in towns and within buildings.
- Learn if building codes are compatible with healthy building design, material reuse, deconstruction, and green industry standards.
- Indicate the percentage of the building's users who will travel to site by public transit (either bus, subway, light rail, or train), carpool, bicycle, or on foot.
- Connect pedestrian pathways with other public systems—for example, greenways (microclimate cooling, habitat, neighborhood-edge definition) or blueways (flood control, aquifer recharge)—so that there is connectivity, efficient use of public funds, and an improved civic realm.

Establish the location of existing urban growth and development boundaries over time. The following locations should be included on the *urban systems maps:*

- Native peoples and pathways
- Early settlements
- Conservation and preservation areas
- Neighborhoods and edges
- Urban centers

- Parks and open spaces
- Rail and stations
- Highways and roads
- Urban development boundaries
- Built infrastructure

Economic system: The economy is supported and subsidized by the environmental conditions. Businesses and urban patterns that incorporate sustainable renewable energies have a competitive advantage over those that import energy.

- Learn how and where the environmental connection enhances the long-term economic benefit while creating social and environmental value. (See "Cache Valley, Utah," Regional Case Studies, page 43.)

THE REGIONAL DESIGN PROCESS ILLUSTRATED

Knowledge of the biome informs the (1) *presettlement conditions,* which inform the (2) *safe, commonsense-development locations,* and this knowledge, applied over the presettlement patterns, (3) *establishes the conflicts and sets goals* for (4) *evolving to sustainable settlement patterns.*

Combining biology and community creates a human ecology or a biological urbanism, a *biourbanism*. Biourbanism incorporates the natural-system sciences of the region into the urban and community pattern, connecting the urban, agricultural, and natural-system functioning.

The Predevelopment Pattern Illustration (page 37), which depicts areas of well-drained and poorly drained soils, is consolidated from the information on the Natural Systems Map (1943 Davis vegetation map). The dark areas, representing the elevated, well-drained soils of the coastal ridge, are more suitable for development and will remain out of harm's way and away from a rising sea level and storm surge. The lighter areas—representing the lower, saturated soils of the Everglades, the transverse glades, and the coastal marsh—tend to flood and are consequently not suitable for human settlements. Drainage of these low-lying areas reduces the regional water storages and consequently reduces the whole system's carrying capacity. Of significant importance is the loss of this area's historic ability to store water for future use and to reduce impacts from drought.

The Systems Conflict Map (page 38) overlays the 100-year flood plain on the existing development grid. As can be seen, much of the recent development in South Dade County, Florida, has occurred in areas that are flood- and storm-surge prone and less suitable for long-term development. Because these areas are becoming more impervious and more developed for urban uses, the flood criteria and impacts are changing. Once the groundwater has been lowered, there will be a significant reduction in regional storage. To combat this, new conservation areas must be designated for regional recharge. This illustration suggests that these new areas include historic Everglades wetlands, ecologically valuable coastal marshes, and crit-

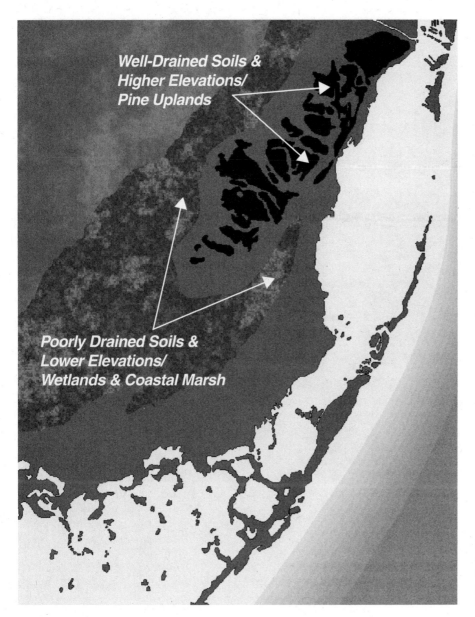

**Well-Drained Soils &
Higher Elevations/
Pine Uplands**

**Poorly Drained Soils &
Lower Elevations/
Wetlands & Coastal Marsh**

*Predevelopment Pattern.
A 500-square-mile area
informed by gravity,
geology, solar power, and
water for millennia.*

ical recharge areas for public waterwell fields. Continued development within these areas, which is the present-day pattern, will cause more local flooding, eliminate critical aquifer recharge areas, destroy valuable natural resources, and negatively impact marine health and the billion-dollar fishing industry.

The Smart-Growth Areas Map (page 39) illustrates how the land and water interact naturally in South Dade County. The lighter forms represent the areas

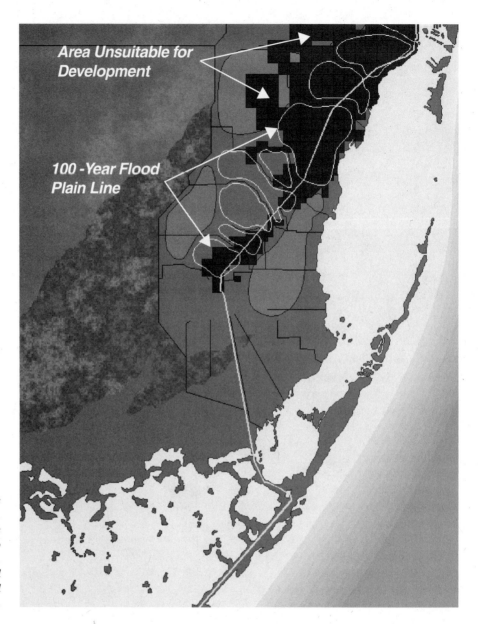

Area Unsuitable for Development

100-Year Flood Plain Line

Systems Conflict Map. As the region developed, community growth areas became less related to natural flood protection, resulting in required fossil fuel–powered pumping.

located along the coastal ridge that are at elevations above the 100-year flood plain. Storm water flows off these areas along the coastal ridge, to areas of lower land elevation and estuaries. This water eventually flows to the drainage canals and ultimately to Biscayne Bay. The areas, located on either side of the coastal ridge, are the pervious and porous areas that provide critical water recharge to the Biscayne Aquifer.

The evolving Systems-Design Approach (page 40) illustrates opportunities to recapture, over time, the free work of nature, which will efficiently collect, store,

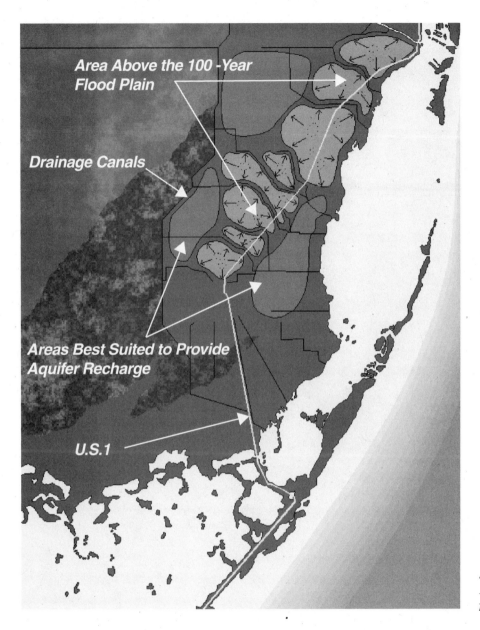

Area Above the 100-Year Flood Plain

Drainage Canals

Areas Best Suited to Provide Aquifer Recharge

U.S.1

Smart-Growth Areas Map. The natural system footprint remains.

clean up, and distribute water for all users, to urban, agricultural, and natural systems. It will also establish growth boundaries based on conservation zones, protecting hydrological-recharge zones and productive agricultural lands and improving urban and community patterns with transit-oriented development and walkable communities.

The *Sustainable Development Vision* (page 41) shows the drainage canals replaced by broad wetland systems similar to what was historically the transverse glades. These topographic low points are an integral part of the region's natural

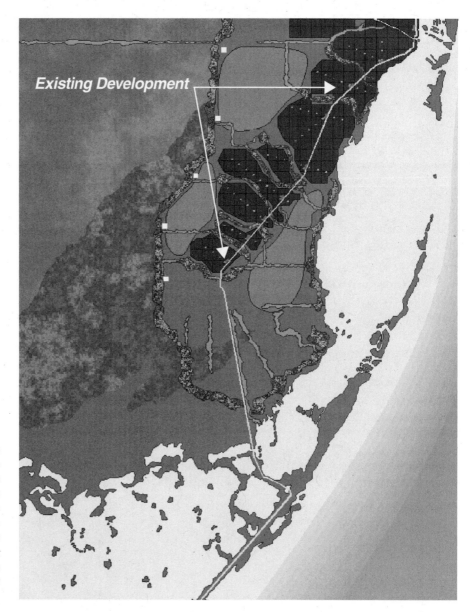

Existing Development

Systems-Design Approach. Establish plans to recreate the region's natural systems functioning and to develop community-based visions that are based on a 100-year evolution to a sustainable development model.

flood protection. The north-south canals, separating the developed part of Dade County from the Everglades, are regenerated to provide valuable storage and water cleansing.

This plan will improve the quality of water while preserving a sustainable water supply for future users. The coastal canals become *spreader* canals to enhance the distribution, timing, quantity, and quality of the water that flows to Biscayne Bay, while protecting the biological food chain and supporting the sport-fishing industry and ecotourism.

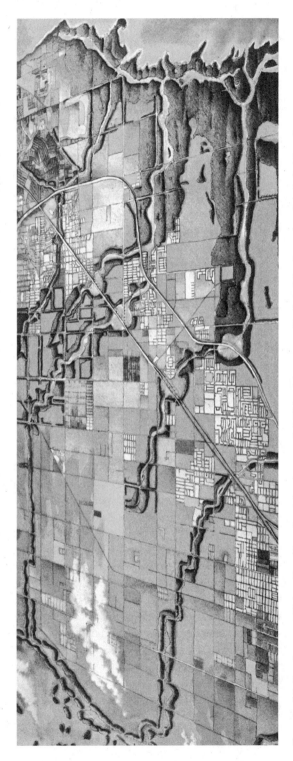

Sustainable Development Vision. Drawing the vision is essential. This vision, once developed by the regional stakeholders, becomes a dynamic map of future development, assuring the best fit between economy, community, and ecologic integrity and resulting in a higher quality of life and lower taxes.

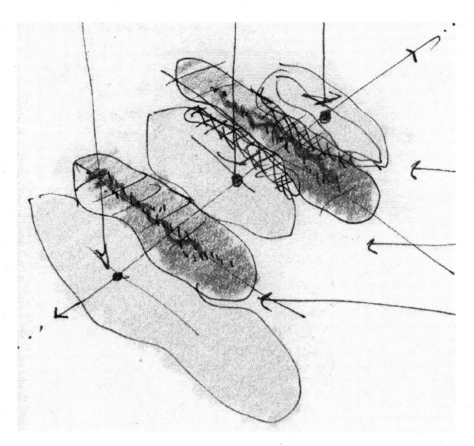

A systems-ecology sketch that connects urban development and hydrological-carrying capacity into smart growth. This simple sketch from the regional visioning charrette was the impetus for the sustainable development vision.

The light squares to the west in the Smart-Growth Plan represent subregional wastewater-treatment plants that will provide for 100 percent reuse of the waste effluent. This requires enhanced water-quality treatment, provided by natural cleansing of the water in the newly created wetland areas. By recycling this water to the aquifer, much of the water that is consumed every day will be replenished within 48 hours of use.

In this plan, open pervious land uses that provide valuable recharge to the aquifer are preserved. This will also provide for the preservation of the agriculture and quality of life that exists in the Redland agricultural area to the east today. To support this objective, development would occur on the higher ground of the coastal ridge. Mass transit and community-based transit centers would be located within developed areas. These locations will encourage the development of tightly knit communities with strong regional connections and will reinforce the opportunity to provide for future water needs.

There are four aspects to the bioregional and biourban process:

1. Bioregionalism researches and understands the system larger than the project scale.

2. The bioregional process applies regional-system knowledge to the interaction of the urban components (i.e., infrastructure, utilities, and neighborhood patterns).

3. The *free work* of natural systems—ecology, biology, physics, climate, hydrology, and soils—is incorporated by using natural processes rather than technology for water storage and cleaning, for microclimatic control, and for resource use, reuse, and recycling.

4. Biourbanism designs the connections to make use of this free work.

These process changes in planning and design can have the largest positive impact on environmental protection. Incorporating the understanding and information embodied within natural systems into urban and regional planning practices assures a valuable reconnection to historic and past lessons learned.

Regional Case Studies

The following case studies have commonalities in terms of scale, ecological analysis, and reconnection with the natural resources that reside in the region and the bioclimatic conditions. Three case studies are included:

Cache Valley, Utah: AIA/SDAT, Sustainable Design Assessment Team

Farmington, Minnesota: Building within the Community Watershed

Smart Growth: Southeast Florida Coastal Communities

CACHE VALLEY, UTAH

American Institute of Architects: Sustainable Design Assessment Team

In March 2005 local governments, business owners, stakeholders, and concerned citizens from throughout Cache Valley, Utah, requested the assistance of the American Institute of Architects (AIA) Sustainable Design Assessment Team (SDAT) program. The application for assistance highlighted many of the challenges facing the valley: improving air quality, developing transportation strategies, strengthening the local economy, sustaining the agriculture industry, preserving the quality of life and sense of place, guiding growth pressures, improving water quality and quantity, and restoring wetlands and wildlife habitat.

In June 2005, after extensive communication and a preliminary visit in May, the AIA sponsored a team of national experts to visit Cache Valley to assess its current state in terms of sustainability, including its assets, weaknesses, opportunities, and challenges, and to provide a set of recommendations to improve the sustainability of the valley.

The Team's Discovery

The team discovered that Cache Valley is really "a valley of communities [that are] connected by a system of economic and environmental factors." The most important of these desired factors are economic development and air quality—one cannot exist without the other. Cache Valley shares the same challenge most communities struggle with today: how to grow the economy and how to protect what is loved. This challenge raised several questions: Are they, the people of the Cache Valley, doing it right? And, if not, how can it be done correctly? Where can growth occur with the least negative impact and greatest value to the community? How can the beauty of the valley be preserved while development occurs? How do the valley and the communities get better, not just bigger?

The systems model shows the important relationship between the environment and the economic health of Cache Valley. In the simplicity of this model is a message the SDAT charrette participants voiced strongly and clearly: "We want a developing economy, affordable housing, great communities, a strong agricultural business, great air and water quality, and a preserved environment."

The AIA/SDAT was developed to help communities with these challenges. SDAT studies the challenges the community has defined, determines how they came to be, and delineates options that assure an economic future with ideal environmental quality. The objectives and mission of the Cache Valley SDAT were to promote a sustainable development approach to the valley by connecting the natural landscape with economic and community-based issues.

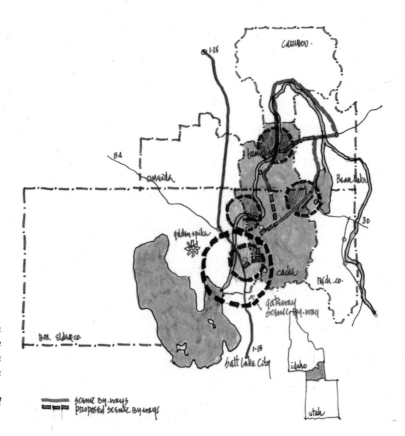

A conceptual sketch from the design charrette illustrates the design connections between livable communities, stormwater, and land use.

The objectives of this SDAT are powerful and achievable. They require

- A regional plan developed by a selected group of community organizations and interest groups that represent the economy, the communities of the valley, and the environment—both natural and human-made
- A reworking of the tax structure to create a level playing field and a spirit of cooperation between communities
- Principles and guidelines that assure changes mindful of the economy, the community, and the environment and that serve as a baseline to show that each change improves the air quality

The Valley as a Group of Communities

Regions are complex, large-scale environmental, social, and economic systems, and Cache Valley is one of the most beautiful. However, it is on the verge of having that beauty degraded to the point of limiting its future and restricting its prosperity. The elements that make up a community—the land and structures, the people and their sociocultural activities, and the business and educational institutions—are all vital and interconnected to this natural beauty. As a result, improvements to one simultaneously enhance the others, and degradation to one degrades the others. What good is it to solve an economic problem if it increases air pollution and environmental problems? What good is a solution to an environmental crisis if it wreaks economic havoc on its citizens? In either case, the community as a whole suffers.

The Cache Valley SDAT illuminated the community's stewardship of the region's ecological value and the entire regional watershed, of which many towns and communities are a part. The valley's ecology and climate are important elements in the assessment of available ecological capital. Cache Valley is clearly an example of a place where environmental protection and economic development must work together.

The sustainability of the valley depends on the stewardship of the whole valley. Future efforts that connect neighborhoods with the regionwide watershed will provide economic value and environmental protection. *Ecological capital*, which is a measure of how many resources are renewable, is very high in the valley, and development plans that integrate and connect to this natural capital provide tremendous opportunity with the least economic cost. The desire of many people to live within a parklike setting is a highly valuable factor; the availability of such natural capital adds greatly to the valley's competitive advantage to draw new business and residents. Degrade that natural capital and the advantage is gone; lose that capital and even existing businesses may leave.

Future development in Cache Valley, guided by the series of principles and recommendations from the Cache Valley SDAT, will create the best-case, win-win scenario for economic and environmental gain. These principles and recommendations spring from the valley's and the region's environmental, economic, cultural, and civic past, and they should be integrated into the valley's public policy, planning, and design decisions.

SDAT

Sustainable Design
Assessment Team

Cache Valley Sustainable Principles:

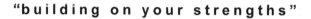

"building on your strengths"

Think Big, Act Big –To identify and preserve the beauty and economic health of the Cache Valley while improving the air quality and preserving the quality of life – a "community based" regional vision and framework must be developed. This vision will, along with leadership, insure a future that is "desired and prosperous".

action: create a regional planning council and develop a citizen-based vision that locates critical lands, view corridors and future development opportunities for the entire Valley while preserving the "sense of place".

Define the Quilt – Study the potential linkages and connections between land uses and natural resources.

action: create a map that illustrates "science-based" hierarchy of relationships between agriculture, the economy, the community and the environment. Delineate "best places" for preserving the Valley image, economic benefit and efficient growth.

Design Efficient Land Use Patterns –The "sense of place" is important on all scales. The creation and preservation of efficient regional patterns should be applied to the town plans. Focus on creating active town settings that minimize car trips and increase citizen use and a higher quality of life.

action: provide incentives to build and develop within existing towns and cities. Add life and economic vitality to existing centers.

Cache Valley principles and goals.

Principles and Guidelines

1. Build on local and regional strengths, especially the local and regional resources.
2. Understand how the whole valley works, considering economics, community, and environment; this is a valley of communities connected by a system of economic and environmental factors.
3. Grow the economy while improving the environment.
4. Grow the economy while protecting the valley heritage.
5. Guide where growth can occur: do not leave it to chance.
6. Weigh every decision based on whether *it is a value to the whole community*.
7. Each decision should make the valley and the communities better, not just bigger.

Actions Summary

Action: Create a regional planning council to develop a citizen-based vision that locates critical lands, view corridors, and future development opportunities for the entire valley while preserving the "sense of place."

Deliverable: Create a Valley Vision map that illustrates important relationships between agriculture, the economy, the communities, and the environment. This vision map will act as the *roadmap* to efficient future growth patterns while creating thriving, walkable communities and reducing car trips and, therefore, improving regional air quality:

- Locate and define the best places for economic benefit, efficient growth, and environmental protection.
- Establish development and nondevelopment zones.
- Protect the benches (i.e., the flat geological formations in the upper regions of the valley).
- Protect the agricultural and natural systems and view corridors.

Action: Create a shared economic vision of the collective communities, level the playing field, and create a cooperative atmosphere between towns and communities—individual communities but one valley!

Deliverable: A shared tax base that will establish fair and equitable competition and cooperation between communities, creating a mutual benefit to each community and to the valley.

Action: Provide incentives to build and develop within existing towns and cities. This will add life and economic vitality to existing town centers and neighborhoods.

Deliverable: Efficient land-use patterns and zoning on all scales. Focus on creating active town settings that minimize car trips and increase *peo-*

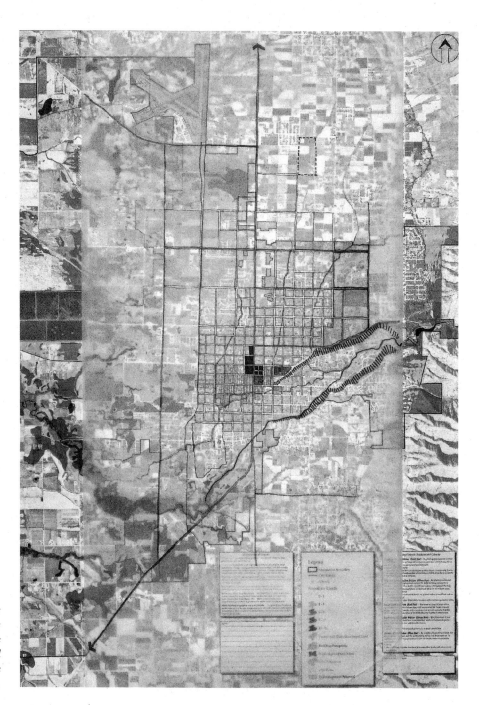

These stormwater canals create urban patterns and open space while they provide flood protection and increase property values.

ple places and a higher quality of life. Reconnect natural resources, valley image, and waterways with neighborhoods.

The regional planning council will create a regional master plan for Cache Valley. This council will be composed of individuals from each community, representing businesses, communities, and the environment. The council will advise all of the communities on plans for roads, housing, agricultural preservation, and transportation- and community-growth patterns; this will create better coordination and a more connected community vision, and will ensure an efficient use of tax dollars.

How well the plan is working will be measured by improvement in air quality, while the economy grows and quality of life improves.

Composition of the National SDAT

Daniel Williams, FAIA—Team Leader
Architect, Urban and Regional Planner
Seattle, Washington

Ken A. Bowers, AICP, PP (Economics)
Phillips Preiss Shapiro Associates, Inc.
New York, New York

E. Ann Clark, Ph.D. (Agriculture)
Associate Professor
Department of Plant Agriculture, University of Guelph
Guelph, Ontario, Canada

Elaine Lai (Water)
Office of Wetlands, Oceans and Watersheds
Assessment and Watershed Protection Division
U.S. Environmental Protection Agency
Washington, D.C.

Ray Mohr (Air Quality)
Colorado Department of Public Health and Environment
Denver, Colorado

Karina Ricks, AICP (Transportation)
Transit-Oriented Development Coordinator
District of Columbia Office of Planning
Washington, D.C.

Ron Straka, FAIA (Sense of Place)
Denver, Colorado

Ann Livingston, Esq.
American Institute of Architects
Center for Communities by Design

FARMINGTON, MINNESOTA: BUILDING WITHIN THE COMMUNITY WATERSHED

The following text was written by William R. Morrish (then-director of the Design Center for American Urban Landscape at the University of Minnesota).

Designing Waterways as an Environmental Framework for Development

Farmington, Minnesota, is located approximately 20 miles southwest of the Twin Cities on the Vermillion River outwash plain. A rural farm and railroad community founded in 1865, the city's comfortable character is due in large part to the mature shade trees gracing the city streets, the thriving downtown business district, the

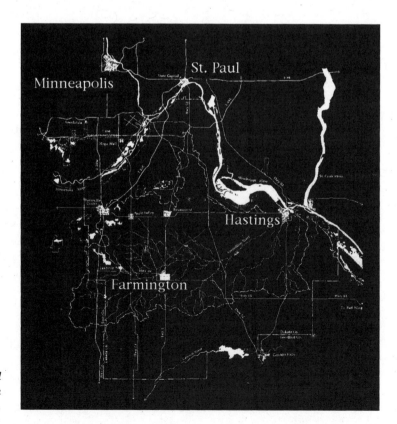

Land-use patterns and water relationships in Farmington.

community's historic architecture, and the variety of riparian plant communities along the banks of the Vermillion River.

The city of Farmington is at a crossroads. The city's question is: How can it extend its community while maintaining and enhancing the town's character and its river connections? Farmington's logo suggests a place to begin. Symbolizing the importance of the city's relationship to the river and the community watershed, the logo points to ways in which this watershed identity can be used to structure new growth and provide direction for the design of community infrastructure.

The design and planning objectives are as follows:

- To build a green space network that connects the Vermillion River corridor to the public open space of the community
- To redesign the use and function of the north-south Highway 3 corridor
- To integrate the Sienna Corporation's proposed 200-acre residential subdivision with the ecological and urban function of the city's eastern sector

Farmington is built on top of a great underground lake, whose waters drift slowly northeast to the Mississippi River. Surface water begins this slow migration, percolating through porous layers of soil into glacial deposits of sand and gravel below. Once between the soil surface and the limestone 150 to 200 feet below, groundwater from the river valley flows into a bedrock bowl beneath the city. Much of this water seeps into the limestone layers, becoming part of the region's bedrock aquifers. Groundwater under the city maintains a high water table, especially during wet weather and major storm events. Surplus water surges into the sand and gravel layers, rising two to three feet in 24 hours. Much of the outwash plain is aquifer-recharge area for the region's drinking water and the valley's agricultural irrigation. Therefore, three things must be considered when building on this sensitive hydrological site:

1. New development should be designed to minimize basement flooding caused by groundwater surges.
2. New development or city infrastructure changes should not lower the average groundwater level of the area, which is calculated by Farmington city staff and the Minnesota Department of Natural Resources to be at an elevation of 889.5 feet.
3. Storm-drainage channels and ponding areas should not be constructed below the high groundwater level unless they are designed to protect groundwater quality from pollutants.

Several developments have altered the flow of surface water in Farmington's east end and caused recurring flooding problems for area homeowners. In the 1950s, the Minnesota Department of Transportation filled a marsh to build Highway 3. In the late 1960s, a nearby wetland was covered to build the Town's Edge Shopping Center. The road, shopping center, and later construction of the Henderson Addition interrupted the natural drainage course for the fairgrounds area, which flowed northeast through these sites to the farm fields beyond. In major storms the surface water was absorbed by the wetlands or duck ponds, which served as a pressure valve to regulate the flow of excess water. However, after the wetland systems were filled and paved, the water pooled in low-lying areas, flooding city streets, basements, and sewer lines.

Any development in the eastern and southeastern part of the city must respect and maintain the ecological conditions of the area, recognizing the limitations of saturated soils, surface water, and shallow groundwater across the site. Three points should be considered when building in this wet zone:

1. Stormwater runoff from new development must be cleaned near the source before it is returned to the natural system.
2. Instead of transporting collected runoff to the Vermillion River through the traditional storm-sewer pipe and grass-pond system, construct an ecological link to the river using a *prairie waterway,* a meandering tributary planted with native wet prairie grasses and lowland forest vegetation.
3. Store stormwater during major flood events in cleaning ponds and in the prairie waterway, which will act together as a new floodplain.

Prairie Waterway Design Principles

- *City's edge:* The prairie waterway creates a transition between city and country, a permeable edge between the two land uses. Sheltering trees provide a vantage point from which to view the open croplands to the east. Views from the open country to town are defined by a horizon of vegetation.

- *Community recreation:* Seasonal changes of vegetation and wildlife can be observed from the parkway drive and from community streets, which link pedestrians to the creek channel. The parkway drive and bicycle lanes gently meander to provide changing views of the waterway and the countryside. A broad path is paved to accommodate all-weather use. A low-maintenance trail, usable for winter and dry-season walks, weaves through the prairie and lowland-forest landscape. Turf areas, maintained for active play and picnic areas, are located at the ends of city streets.

- *Rooms and views:* Tree masses, water-cleaning ponds, and low embankments define *outdoor rooms* and *views.* A variety of experiences unfold as park users move along the water corridor. Small rooms and intricate views give way to longer, wider rooms and more expansive views of the waterway and adjoining farm fields.

- *Wildlife habitat corridor:* The linear waterway and its vegetation also serve as a habitat corridor. Planted primarily with areas of prairie grass and lowland forest plantings, this wet environment affords movement, nesting, and foraging opportunities for a variety of wildlife. The patches of deciduous and evergreen woodlands that punctuate the corridor provide shelter and food for overwintering species, such as chickadees, nuthatches, and cardinals. Because this corridor links to the Vermillion River, it forms a vital connection to the region's wildlife habitat network, especially as the watershed becomes more urbanized.

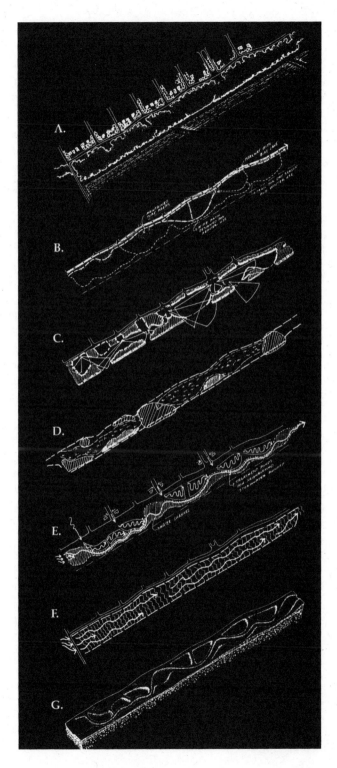

*Typology of waterways
and lineal parks.*

■ *Surface water:* The prairie waterway incorporates a water-filtration system to help clean water flowing into the Vermillion River. Chemicals, fertilizers, and salt carried by runoff from neighborhood lawns and streets first flow into ponding areas for sediment and chemical filtration. The cleaner water then joins a channel carrying water from the south end of Farmington to the Vermillion River.

■ *Floodplain:* The waterway serves as storage for excess water during major rainfalls, providing holding areas for surface water as well as groundwater that is pushed to the surface.

■ *Topography:* Low embankments separate channel and ponding areas. These earthworks are relatively shallow and do not penetrate a groundwater-filled layer of gravel just below the topsoil.

Just as the city wetlands and waterways form an important civic armature, roadways and their drainage systems can also contribute to building community networks. Originally built during the 1950s as a rural roadway, Highway 3 was designed to safely and efficiently move high-speed traffic along the eastern edge of Farmington. But because of changes in regional traffic patterns and a proposed new development to the east, in the next decade Highway 3 will be transformed from lining the community edge to being a city street. The following principles describe how the existing roadway can be redesigned as a pedestrian-scale parkway, which provides many community benefits as well as a functional and generous tree-lined right-of-way.

Community Edge to Community Street A central drainage median and frontage roads create a wide right of way conducive to fast speeds but dangerous to crossing pedestrians. Redesigning the roadway into a 35-mile-per-hour zone eliminates the central drainage median and frontage roads. Instead, this extra land can be used to create a parkway environment. This brings the new housing development visually closer to existing downtown neighborhoods. The narrower road width also encourages drivers to slow down, making pedestrian crossings safer and easier.

Pedestrian Paths and Connections The existing roadway is designed to accommodate automobile traffic. As Farmington grows to the east, the roadway will become a central community crossing. Redesigned as a parkway, the roadway now includes room for a pedestrian sidewalk and bike path. The parkway is shaded by a variety of native trees with broad canopies. Key crossings, to downtown and to schools, are signaled, and the parkway is posted as a 35-mile-per-hour zone. Sidewalks along the residential streets lead to the proposed parkway, making a new north-south recreation link for walking loops around town.

Rooms and Views The parkway becomes a long outdoor hallway linking rooms created through the consolidation of paved lanes and newly planted areas. Along this corridor, a series of openings allows glimpses of wetlands, commercial areas, residential neighborhoods, and downtown. Rooms are defined by wetland vegetation, tree-lined streets, windbreaks, hedgerows, and planted drainage systems. Use of native vegetation and enhancement of the topography create rooms and frame views of the city and rural landscape.

Plant Communities Such native trees as ash and hackberry, selected for their tolerance of periodic flooding and road salt, form the canopy layer. These trees are massed or planted in single rows, depending on the width of the planting strip. Mown turf edges the taller grasses, flowers, and cattails of the drainageway and provides unimpeded sightlines for egress from driveways and intersections. At locations along the parkway, masses of ornamental trees add seasonal color and mid-story vegetation layers. Adjoining wetland areas are more fully layered with overstory tree canopies, midstory trees and shrubs, and ground species.

Surface Water Water is collected to the east edge of the parkway for filtration in a wide, shallow channel planted with native trees, shrubs, grasses, and flowers. A wetland area is reclaimed on the site of the Town's Edge Shopping Center, providing stormwater storage capacity during floods. The shopping center is relocated to a more prominent commercial location on the corner of Highway 3 and Ash Street (City Highway 74 and Highway 50). A second wetland is constructed from saturated areas at the north end of Highway 3 to treat north-flowing road runoff and provide additional storage for excess water.

The prairie waterway and Farmington parkway design proposals offer a community framework for growth based on Farmington's stormwater and highway infrastructure. The Sienna Corporation's subdivision proposal provides an opportunity to extend the character, organization, and scale of the existing downtown residential area while exploring neighborhood-making within these new ecological systems. By structuring growth around the topography, river, and surface-water and road systems, the city can take advantage of its location in the Vermillion River watershed. The design-center scenario presents one option for future growth in the city of Farmington. The following design principles derived from the existing community landscape can be used to guide change and create a framework for new development.

Community-Design Principles

1. Use the existing city-grid pattern of square or rectangular blocks to shape the layout of new development adjacent to downtown Farmington.
2. Construct new residential streets scaled to the existing 31- to 38-foot-wide downtown-area streets. New streets should be planted with lowland-forest shade trees, which are tolerant of urban street conditions.
3. Use designated streets as pedestrian linkages between environmental corridors (or *greenways*) and civic places, especially developing pedestrian and bicycle connections between new development, downtown businesses, and local schools.
4. Rebuild State Highway 3 into a new pedestrian-oriented parkway and residential-scaled street. Use native vegetation or plant forms, combined with

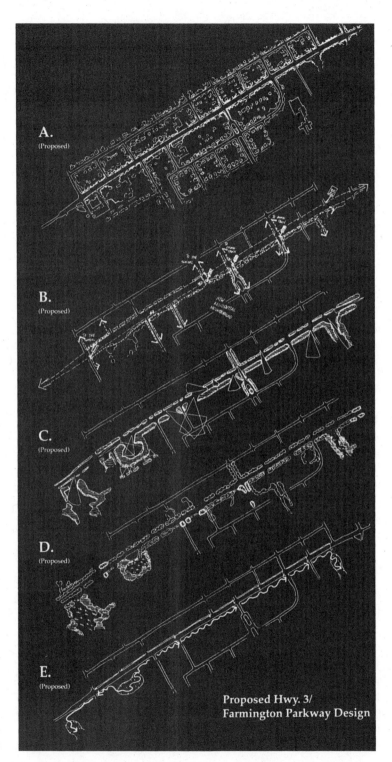

A.
(Proposed)

B.
(Proposed)

C.
(Proposed)

D.
(Proposed)

E.
(Proposed)

Proposed Hwy. 3/
Farmington Parkway Design

*Typologies of transit
and water.*

the storm-water collection ponds and drainage system, to create outdoor rooms and corridors for recreation and pedestrian activities, as well as wildlife movement and habitat.

5. Use native vegetation and highway infrastructure to design unique city *gateways,* which will distinguish Farmington from other locations in the region.

What does it mean to build community on the Vermillion River outwash plain? For starters, it means preserving and protecting existing natural resources—topography, native vegetation, rivers and creeks, surface water, and groundwater—as the backbone for community identity and developmental amenity. The proposals outlined—the prairie waterway, Farmington parkway, and watershed neighborhood—suggest ways in which the cultural identity of Farmington and the landscape of the region can be preserved and enhanced to provide future generations with a meaningful and valuable place to live and grow. The proposals also explore how communities can begin to clean up local, nonpoint-source pollution; expand wildlife habitat; and protect surface and groundwater resources. If new neighborhoods are created with respect for the ecological function of the site, the first step toward preserving the regional landscape will have been taken. The Design Center for American Urban Landscape has organized these proposals into a series of next steps, each with its own design directives and implementation strategies.

Next Steps

- Build linkages throughout the community and to the Vermillion River watershed, which preserve and incorporate the region's character and topography.

- Reevaluate the city's existing comprehensive plan. Update it to include development guidelines that are more responsive to existing natural resources. The process should begin with city leadership and staff working in conjunction with private-sector interests.

The city of Farmington and the Vermillion River watershed are now at similar crossroads. In the last ten years, Farmington has begun the transition from a small agricultural community to a small town in a large metropolitan area. The city has taken proactive measures to protect the Vermillion River as a public amenity within its own borders. It now must actively seek to develop partnerships within the entire watershed to preserve and protect the river corridor and its tributaries as community amenities around which the region's future growth can be structured.

In the future, public dollars for amenity projects will dwindle as issues of water quality, waste removal, and the repair and replacement of worn-out roads, bridges, and storm-water systems dominate fiscal budget agendas. Farsighted strategic planning that identifies and documents the opportunities for creating recreational and environmental amenities as part of future infrastructure projects will benefit both the city of Farmington and the region. Like their turn-of-the-century civic counterparts in Minneapolis, the citizens of Farmington face a historic opportunity to protect and

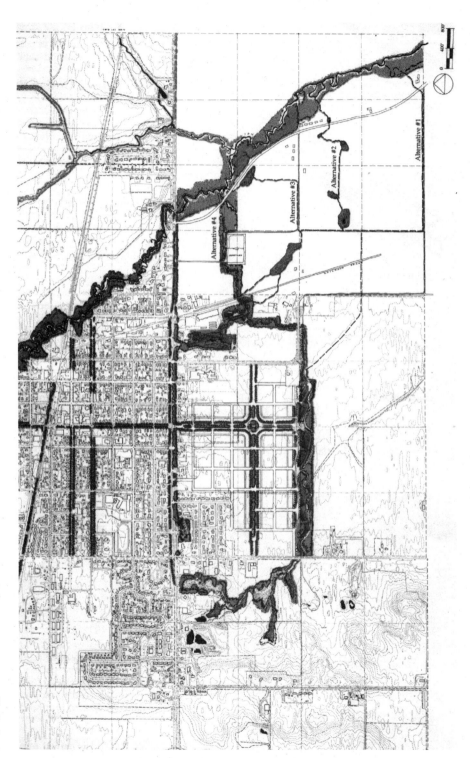

*The Farmington Regional
Systems Plan
incorporates community-
design principles.*

restore the region's natural resources and wildlife habitat while providing a framework for sound community growth.

Design Center for American Urban Landscape Case-Study Team

Regina E. Bonsignore, Research Fellow in Landscape Architecture

Catherine R. Brown, Coordinator of Special Projects

M. Elizabeth Fitzsimons, Research Assistant in Landscape Architecture

Harrison S. Fraker Jr., (former) Dean, College of Architecture and Landscape Architecture, University of Minnesota

Thomas A. Hammerberg, Research Fellow in Landscape Architecture

William R. Morrish, Director

R. G. Schunn, Research Assistant in Architecture

Hydrologists

Eugene A. Hickok, JMM, Consulting Engineers Inc.

Daniel M. Parks, JMM, Consulting Engineers Inc.

SMART GROWTH: SOUTHEAST FLORIDA COASTAL COMMUNITIES

Historically, wetlands were considered not only worthless but also a threat to human health. Estuaries were mosquito-infested mangrove swamps and in dire need of "improvement." Marine environments were considered boundless resources created for human exploitation. Thus, the last 100 years of Florida's history have been characterized by attempts to tame nature and to adapt the natural landscape to human uses. A result of these efforts, in South Florida, is a drainage- and flood-control system that is inadequate for flood control and for water supply and that provides insufficient water-quality protection. This is occurring at a time when demand for flood protection, water supply, and water-quality standards is increasing exponentially, while water losses exponentially increase due to drainage. This demand goes hand in hand with the pressures exerted on the current system by the rapid and unchecked outward expansion of urban settlement within the region.

It was not until somewhat recently that Florida's natural environment was understood as an essential and valuable natural resource with numerous vital economic functions. These functions include ecotourism, food production, wildlife habitat, flood control, climate moderation, recreation and aesthetic experiences, nutrient removal, and aquifer recharge. Most, if not all, of these functions have previously been given very little attention. Now, as we are beginning to recognize and view the destruction firsthand, the realization is that the destruction of the natural system will destroy the entire region's future chances of survival.

Water is an essential renewable resource that is in constant danger of degradation and overuse. The objective of the South Dade Watershed Project was to analyze the relationship between water and land use and to establish consensus among the diverse stakeholders. This consensus process established regional-planning crite-

"'Water, not growth-management controls, will be the ultimate factor in determining how big Florida can grow. Water management is part of the overall effort in Florida to get a handle on where this state is, and where we're headed to, and to get out ahead of our tumultuous growth, once and for all,' Lt. Gov. Buddy MacKay said. 'It gives you an idea that whatever it is that's going to limit growth in Florida, it's not going to be growth management . . . The availability of that resource is probably going to be the ultimate limiting factor.'"

"WATER LIMITS MAY HALT GROWTH," *LAKELAND (FL) LEDGER*, SEPTEMBER 26, 1994.

ria that would assure a sustainable water supply; protect of the Everglades National Park and the Biscayne Bay; and improve urban, agricultural, and natural-system functioning for the region.

Combining the knowledge missions of science and design into a vision that provides a higher quality of life, using less is to open and integrate the design process. Putting form to a common vision and developing the incremental steps and strategies on how to get from here to there assures a sustainable future.

The Process

Combining biology and community creates a human ecology or a biological urbanism, that is, a *biourbanism*. Incorporating the natural-system sciences of the region into the urban and community pattern, biourbanism connects urban, agricultural, and natural-system functioning.

The Predevelopment Pattern (page 61) compiles the information from multiple maps. The light areas (representing the elevated, well-drained soils of the coastal ridge) are more suitable for development and will remain out of harm's way and rising sea levels. The darker areas (representing the lower, poorly drained soils of the Everglades National Park, the transverse glades, and coastal marsh) tend to flood and are consequently not suitable for development. Of equal importance is this area's geological ability to store water for future use and to reduce the impact of drought.

Hurricanes (page 62) are common to this region and its coastal communities. This is a constant detriment to security and neighborhood development, but post-disaster plans, developed through community-design charrettes, can turn these disasters to opportunities.

The Systems Conflict Map also overlays the 100-year floodplain parameters on the existing development grid. As can be seen, much of the recent development in South Dade County has occurred in areas that are the least suitable for development. These areas are becoming more developed for urban uses, necessitating a change in flooding criteria. Once the groundwater has been lowered, there will be a significant reduction in regional storage. To combat this, new areas need to be used for regional recharge. This map suggests that these new areas include historic Ever-

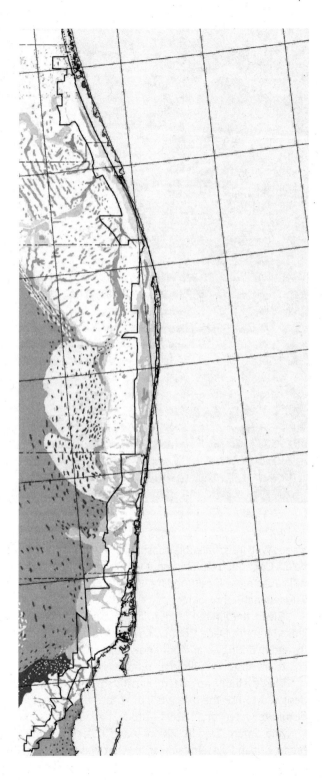

Predevelopment Pattern.
Florida presettlement
water features and
vegetation patterns.

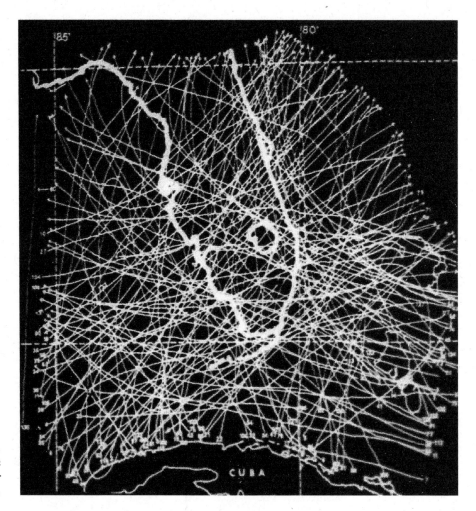

Hurricane pathways, 1889–1989 (South Florida Water Management District).

glades wetlands, valuable coastal marshes, and critical recharge areas for public well fields. Continued development within these areas, which is the present-day pattern, will cause more local flooding, eliminate critical aquifer recharge areas, and destroy valuable natural resources.

Given the limited land area suitable for development and the water resource limits of South Dade County, how do we create a system that will ensure the viability and hydrology—and our knowledge of their interactive connections? We can re-create the historic hydrologic functions of the region.

This systems approach, illustrated in the Sustainable South Dade vision, is designed to use the *free work* of nature to sustainably collect, store, clean up, and distribute water for all users—urban, agricultural, and natural systems.

The Smart-Growth Vision (page 65) shows the drainage canals replaced by broad wetland systems similar to what was historically the transverse glades. These

The 2024 built-out areas showing growth continuing the same as now. This will create sprawl, flooding, loss of agriculture, loss of potable water, and auto gridlock.

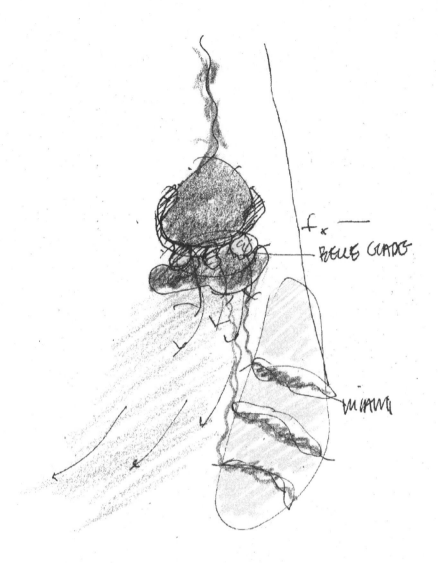

BELLE GLADE

MIAMI

A regional-systems sketch illustrating the creation of areas for agriculture, water recharge, livable communities, and transit-oriented development.

topographic low points are an integral part of the region's natural flood protection. The north-south canal, separating the developed part of Dade County from the Everglades, is expanded to provide valuable storage and cleansing of water. This will improve the quality of water while preserving a sustainable water supply for future users. The coastal canals become *spreader canals* to enhance the distribution, timing, quantity, and quality of the water that flows to Biscayne Bay while protecting the biological food chain and supporting sport fishing and ecotourism.

On the Smart-Growth Vision illustration (page 65) the light squares to the west represent subregional wastewater treatment plants that will provide for 100 percent reuse of the waste effluent. This requires enhanced water-quality treatment, provided by natural cleansing of the water in the newly created wetland areas. By recy-

EVERGLADES-AGRICULTURAL ZONE: a water storage and aquifer recharge area. Locate new sub-regional waste-water treatment plants with 100% reuse. Recharge the aquifer at the "rate of use" creating a sustainable supply of nutrients for the agricultural industry and potable water for Dade County's immediate and future needs.

COASTAL RIDGE DEVELOPMENT ZONE AND TRANS-VERSE GLADES: an urban development area. This zone receives the highest amount of rainfall but has the most amount of impervious surface. The collecting, cleaning and distributing of this water and storing it underground will increase the total available supply of water while reducing the losses to evapotransporation.

FLORIDA SOUTHEAST COASTAL ZONE: a coastal resource protection area. Provides a natural buffer from hurricane storm-surge, while enhancing the distribution, timing, quantity, and quality of freshwater flows. Improving the fishing industry while protecting the esturine values of the Bay, this plan is a win-win for economics and the environment.

LINEAR "HYDRIC PARKS" combine the recreational and aesthetic benefits of "greenways and blueways" with water resource objectives. These parks help create strong edges that define neighborhoods and communities while reconnecting habitat and increasing land value. The greatest potential for additional water storage lies within the coastal ridge. The development of neighborhood "hydric parks" increases local aquifer recharge, reduces and local flooding, and enhances community identity.

WATER STORAGE AREAS, located within communities, will recharge local wellfields, reduce the saltwater intrusion while creating neighborhood parks. The largest new storage of water for regional use would occur here in underground and surface storage. Mimicking the historic function of the transverse glades - collection, storage and biological clean-up of stormwater - these areas also restore the regions image and identity. This coastal zone stops point source loading into the bay and ocean while incorporating the free work of nature into....
a regional vision that drives the urban patterns.

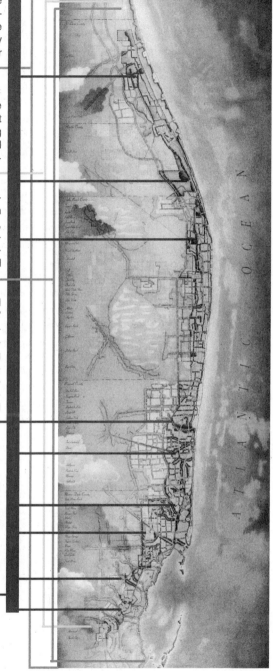

Smart-Growth Vision. This is a stakeholder-based vision that illustrates sustainable land-use patterns, agricultural protections, sustainable potable-water storages, and improved quality of life. The vision drawing, informed by the hydrology and ecology, is necessary to answer the question: What kind of tomorrow are we leaving our children?

cling this water to the aquifer, much of the water that is consumed every day will be replenished within 48 hours of use.

In this plan, open, pervious land uses that provide valuable recharge to the aquifer are preserved. This will also provide for the preservation of the agriculture and quality of life that exists in the Redland today. To support this objective, development should occur on the higher ground of the coastal ridge. Mass transit and community-based transit centers should be located within the developed areas. These locations, due to their size and strategic location for flood and storm protection, will encourage the development of tightly knit communities with strong regional connections and will reinforce the opportunity to provide for future water needs.

The bioregional and biourban processes incorporate the following:

1. Researching and understanding the ecological, social, regional, or geographical systems at a scale larger than the project scale (bioregionalism).
2. Applying this bioregional knowledge to the way in which the interaction of the urban components—specifically, infrastructure, utilities, and neighborhood patterns—are designed.
3. Incorporating the free work of natural systems—ecology, biology, physics, climate, hydrology, and soils—by using natural processes rather than technological processes for water storage and cleaning, microclimate control and resource use, and reuse and recycling.
4. Designing the connections to make use of this free work (biourbanism).

Process changes in planning and design can have the largest positive impact on environmental protection. Incorporating an understanding of the functional aspects of and information embodied within natural systems into urban and regional planning practices assures a valuable reconnection to the lessons of history.

Seize the Moment

On August 24, 1992, in the aftermath of Hurricane Andrew, the opportunity arose to use a watershed approach as a critical element in the rebuilding effort in south Florida. This *adversity-to-opportunity approach* seeks to successfully integrate future land-use development and natural-resource protection by preserving, protecting, and—when necessary—reestablishing the natural system connections on a regional scale. Watershed planning would become the conceptual foundation for the local, state, and federal planning initiatives on growth and sprawl all connected to the need for potable-water and natural-resource protection rather than arbitrary lines on a county map.

The watershed plan has three objectives:

1. Provide a comprehensive understanding of the relationships between land use and regional water-management objectives.
2. Build consensus among local, state, and federal interests as to the actions necessary to achieve regional water-management objectives.

3. Select a hydrologic basin within the watershed for future study and for the development of future demonstration projects.

Without smart planning, an additional million people will pave over an additional 21 square miles of the remaining pervious soil area. That would result in the loss of 21 square miles of recharge area that once received, stored, and distributed water to sustain the regional water budget. Use of water without recharge is not sustainable. More importantly, a region's or locale's water budget is truly defined by access to a sustainable and continuous supply. Water budgets that include use of the huge storages from an aquifer are not budgets that can be sustained. To use an economic analogy, this is similar to living off the principal rather than the interest.

Design of the area greenways will take many forms and sizes. The size will depend on the pollutant loading of the land used within the watershed draining into the canal. These greenways will also serve as habitat for various species. They will encompass diverse pathways that will be rich in function and will include lineal parks, greenways, and bike paths and will provide local flood protection. At the coastal zone, canals would no longer flow directly into Biscayne Bay but through an archipelago of sorts. Diverting the flow and creating upstream storages will enhance the water quantity and quality. Simultaneously, considerably more area for water recharge as well as for aquatic food chain nursery grounds will be created.

This new *edge condition* in the urban segment, where the canal and littoral meet in a land-aquatic transition zone, would create an identity and image for the community while increasing flood protection and neighborhood open-space amenities. The combined water-storage areas and open spaces not only help define better neighborhoods but also increase property values.

The agricultural areas remain defined by the area water regime, or rainfall pattern; reverse flooding irrigation would use less water and control nematodes and other pests while rebuilding the soil and reducing evaporation.

Conclusion

With regional and community participation, the county's urban and regional watershed plan maps out a vision for the future: to establish and protect water-recharge areas, to provide clean water, and to develop the incremental steps toward smart growth. The design calls for future development in urban infill sites in safe and appropriate locations. In this design, sewage treatment plants are strategically located to recycle and reuse water and nutrients; hydric neighborhood parks are designed to store, clean up, and distribute water, adding to potable recharge and community open space for the same tax dollars; and development is stepped back from the region's network of canals to reverse the trespass on wetlands and improve flood protection.

This vision anticipates regional population growth of an additional 700,000 people, while providing environmental stewardship, smart-growth boundaries, walkable communities, water recharge parks, sewage reclamation, an energy-conscious urban plan and design, and development that relies more on transit than on individual cars.

"My primary interest is getting everybody to understand the larger picture and have a greater understanding of how natural systems work so that they'll make better decisions. When people are actually involved, they do see the larger picture. In fact, that is how they get to see the larger picture."
ADELHEID FISCHER, "COMING FULL CIRCLE: THE RESTORATION OF THE URBAN LANDSCAPE," IN *ORION: PEOPLE AND NATURE* (AUTUMN 1994): 29.

The 20-year program is likely to cost $7 billion to $8 billion, mostly for land purchases, which is a bargain compared to engineering solutions such as pumping or desalinization.

The watershed design approach recreates many successful connections:

- Protection of natural-system functioning within regional and urban greenways increases the value of adjacent properties while providing for regional recharge.
- Storing water within these hydric green- and blueways will increase water supplies for future use and is the most effective way of increasing potable water storage while rendering the bonus of community open space.
- Preservation and protection of parks and conservation areas within the urban and regional pattern provides critical livability, health, and economy to the entire region.
- Water management is integrated with land-use decisions based on supply and population, the natural carrying capacity.
- Ecosystem management and watershed planning simultaneously address the complex issues of urban quality of life and preservation of natural systems.
- Community members and other stakeholders develop a common vision that promotes community cohesiveness.

The economic value of this smart-growth plan is quite impressive. The following savings (1999 figures) are directly attributable to sustainable regional watershed planning and design—Smart Growth:

- 67,725 acres of developable land
- 13,887 acres of fragile environmental lands
- 52,856 acres of prime farmland
- 4,221 lane miles of local roads
- $62,000,000 in state road costs
- $1,540,000 in local road costs
- $157,000,000 in water capital costs
- $135,600,000 in sewer capital costs
- $24,250,000 savings per year in public-sector service costs

(Source: 1999, Center for Urban Policy Research, Rutgers University, New Brunswick, New Jersey)

Design Team

Daniel Williams, Director

Brian Sheahan, Correa, Valle, Valle

sustainable urban and community design

The materials of city planning are sky, space, trees, steel, and cement—in that order and that hierarchy.
   —Le Corbusier

The idea of community is central to ecology. The materials and energies that constitute ecology create the *form* and *pattern* of the community, and these constituent elements are characteristics of the community's scale and size. The form and pattern are derived from the mobility of the resident organisms and their ability to feed, breed, rest, and nest within the area. A community of anything is a sum total of all elements working simultaneously. *Community*, in the truest sense of the word, is an organism—that is, "a complex structure of interdependent and subordinate elements whose relations and properties are largely determined by their function in the whole" (per Merriam-Webster's Collegiate Dictionary, 11th edition).

Much of the current thinking in urban and community design focuses on the *form* of neighborhood and community. In these projects, many important objectives are stressed: walkable neighborhoods; small-scale streets; good edge definition, design, and location of town and neighborhood centers; transportation; and community gathering places. However, long-term sustainability is not achievable in these communities, as they rely almost entirely on nonrenewable energy. No matter how charming the pattern, any biological community, including the human community, must tie its long-term development and use to the sustainable energies and resources that are resident to the *place*.

The history of settlements has shown that resources sustain communities and the people within them. When resources dry up, so do communities. A sustainable urban and community pattern comes from understanding and connecting and

> "The world is full of quaint ghost towns. The history of urban settlements has shown that renewable resources sustain towns and communities—and the creation of a sustainable neighborhood pattern is a function of understanding, connecting, and adapting to those renewable resources."
> **CONGRESS FOR NEW URBANISM, NATIONAL CONFERENCE 1999, PANEL ON SUSTAINABLE DEVELOPMENT**

adapting to local sustainable resources. As fossil fuel dries up, what do these new communities look like? What is the pattern of sustainable settlements?

A Matter of Place

Each *scale,* or *level,* in the sustainable-design process is informed by what exists at the next, larger scale. Understanding the relationship between the local use and the regional supply of sustainable energy, for example, is a critical element in the sustainable design process. There is great diversity within regional systems, although the system characteristics fall under a specific classification.

A *desert biome,* for example, in the Southwest region of the United States may have small pockets of water, but it is always a desert. The Pacific Northwest may have areas that receive considerable sunlight, but it is generally an *evergreen biome* with clouds and moisture. Urban design that approaches sustainability incorporates the bioclimatic conditions of the region, and the patterns of the community are informed by the microclimate of that location.

A region's bioclimate is its character. This character includes soil, vegetation, and animal life, which all operate on sustainable resident energy. Urban design that approaches sustainability works by maximizing the use of this kind of resident energy and local resources. This biological urbanism, or *biourbanism,* incorporates natural systems and green processes into the urban design. Examples of these processes are oxygen production, water storage, water purification, water distribution, microclimate cooling and heating, flood protection, water treatment, food supply, climatically derived walking distances, and job creation.

Barcelona Declaration on Sustainable Design
Adopted at the Construmat Fair in Barcelona, Spain, May 28, 2003

1. Whereas the design of cities and buildings is responsible for the urban metabolisms that can give rise to serious consequences for the quality of life for human inhabitants;
2. Whereas the complexity of global ecological problems should inspire change in the course of uncontrolled growth of the human habitat;
3. Whereas urban phenomena of crisis produce conflicts that must be studied with new criteria, using new tools and providing new approaches;
4. Whereas the architects represented by the presidents of UIA, AIA, RIBA, and CSCAE defend and endorse the conclusions of the World Summits of Rio de Janeiro, Istanbul, and Beijing, in favor of the world's sustainability;
5. Whereas the best architecture is the one that fits with the environment and place;

6. Whereas it is essential to maintain a culture of architects, planners, engineers, technical agents, and economists charging them with the stewardship of cultural and ecological values;

7. Whereas urban projects should offer ideas and visions that yield holistic solutions to problems incorporating social inclusion, mobility, health, welfare, and quality human settlements for citizens all over the world;

8. Whereas Barcelona—among other cities in the world—is a useful example of this new sensibility and the Universal Forum of Cultures 2004 will be the perfect opportunity to accentuate this thinking and to spread it globally;

9. Whereas architects and presidents of the professional institutions represented hereby are contributing with several programs to present in the UIA Congress in Istanbul, in 2005, the best examples of architectural biodiversity and to create a "Bazaar" of world architectures, illustrating a position of responsible behavior with the future of humanity and its built environment;

In conclusion, the undersigned support the present BARCELONA DECLARATION in the forum of the Construction Fair, CONSTRUMAT 2003, as a starting point for strategic actions, aiming toward a fuller understanding of environmental projects related to sustainable design in architecture, encouraging cities to develop their own identity of environmental culture and architectural values underpinned by the collaboration between architects and the construction sector for a humanity in peace and assuring through design stewardship with the natural resources and their ecological values. OPTING FOR A HOLISTIC ARCHITECTURE AS AN ENVIRONMENTAL RESOURCE FOR THE EARTH AS A WHOLE SO:

In appreciation of the work of Construmat 2003 and in recognition of the important role that architects have in pursuing ecologically responsible solutions to the design of buildings, towns, cities, and regions in the context of improving environmental conditions and quality of life for all, we the undersigned confirm our support through the Barcelona Declaration for

- The widest cooperation between architects and all other members of the construction teams of all nations in research, knowledge acquisition, and knowledge distribution;
- The promotion and sharing of innovative architectural solutions that will lead to a global architecture that complies with the Brundtland definition of sustainability; and
- The ongoing endeavor to educate, equip, motivate, and inspire architects, construction professionals, the wider development and construction industry, and the widest public—especially those not yet involved—so that they may contribute with ever greater effect to the delivery of a built

and natural landscape which is safe for children and the children's children of all species and communities.

For the UIA (International Union of Architects)
Jaime Lerner

For the AIA (American Institute of Architects)
Daniel Williams

For the RIBA (Royal Institute of British Architects)
Paul Hyett

For the CSCAE (Consejo Superior de los Colegios de Arquitectos de España)
Carlos Hernández Pezzi

Principles for Sustainable Communities

The ecological model, when applied to urban and community design, guides the form of the urban pattern. The elements of that pattern will help to maximize the use of existing resident renewable energy and resources. All of the designed components act as linkages, collectors, and concentrators of local resources and energies. Sustainable urban and community design connects these natural elements so that the community works together as an organism, creating interdependent patterns that sustain each other.

The resident renewable energies and their relationship to urban and community design are described in the following section.

Regional Ecology and Biourbanism

NATURAL SYSTEM

If the region is compatible with human development, it will include the following elements:

- A bioclimate with compatible comfort zones
- Close proximity to other places, an ideal location
- A compelling sense of place and connection to nature and natural resources
- Buildable land and smart-growth patterns
- Adequate precipitation
- Regional and local public transportation
- Productive soils and agriculture
- A diverse employment base, as well as job-creation capacity
- Plans to heal and reconnect natural-system functions to urban patterns and green infrastructure needs

To re-create communities that are sustainable, the approach must incorporate the use of sustainable energies, those forces and resources within the region. To retrofit existing communities and to create higher-density communities with a higher quality of life is a significant challenge. The resulting community plans and designs will retrofit and integrate the biological systems and incorporate a green infrastructure that is resident to the region.

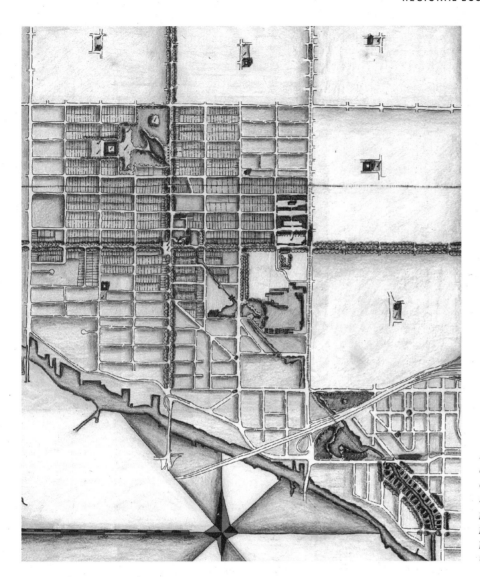

Integrating stormwater and natural drainage creates urban open spaces—improving property value while protecting residents from flooding—with public utility funding.

In a natural landscape, water- and ecosystem-management strategies and the creation, re-creation, and preservation of open space and green infrastructure are integrated into the urban pattern. The strategy for habitat creation and regionally appropriate conservation zones and development controls is to connect them to useful tasks within the urban pattern. This practice illustrates how the relationships between social, economic, and environmental systems are improved in this urban design. In this pattern, water, transportation, growth control, and flood protection are accomplished by reclaiming the pathways delineated in the regional design analysis. These elements should inform regional building, zoning, and design codes so that they support sustainable design.

The AIA Principles for Livable Communities

1. *Design on a human scale:* Compact, pedestrian-friendly communities where residents can walk to shops, public services, cultural resources, and jobs reduce traffic congestion, benefit people's health, and provide a sense of community.
2. *Provide choices:* People want variety in housing, shopping, recreation, transportation, and employment. Variety creates lively neighborhoods and accommodates residents in different stages of their lives.
3. *Encourage mixed-use development:* Integrating different land uses and varied building types creates diverse, vibrant, and pedestrian-friendly communities.
4. *Preserve urban centers:* Restoring, revitalizing, and infilling urban centers takes advantage of existing streets, services, and buildings and avoids the need for new infrastructure. This helps to curb sprawl and promotes stability for city neighborhoods.
5. *Vary transportation options:* Giving people the option of walking, biking, and using public transit, in addition to driving, reduces traffic congestion, protects the environment, and encourages physical activity.
6. *Build vibrant public spaces:* Citizens need welcoming and well-defined public places to stimulate face-to-face interaction, collectively celebrate and mourn, encourage civic participation, admire public art, and gather for public events.
7. *Create a neighborhood identity:* A sense of place gives neighborhoods a unique character, enhances the walking environment, and creates pride in the community.
8. *Protect environmental resources:* A well-designed balance of nature and development preserves natural systems, protects waterways from pollution, reduces air pollution, and protects property values.
9. *Conserve landscapes:* Open space, farms, and wildlife habitat are essential for environmental, recreational, and cultural reasons.
10. *Design matters:* Design excellence is the foundation of successful and healthy communities.

URBAN SYSTEM: COMMUNITY DESIGN AND GREEN INFRASTRUCTURE CONNECTION

Urban and community design and its approach to sustainable land-use patterns provide connections to local renewable resources and a sense of place within a regional context. Public spaces for the community, transportation strategies, and efforts to establish a livable community are improved by reconnecting to the ecology of a place. An important strategy is to develop plans that progress toward reclamation of natural-system functions, creation of better flood-control and water-recharge areas, and establishment of livable communities.

The orientation of streets and buildings helps to improve comfort within structures and within the civic realm, because it reduces discomfort in buildings as well as in civic spaces by providing shade and sunlight at appropriate times of the year. The building codes must be compatible with healthy-building design, material reuse, deconstruction, and green industry standards. In addition, they should be based on regional and urban bioclimatic conditions. The typology of streets and sidewalks, when informed by natural conditions (such as the position of the sun in winter), will improve the neighborhood and the real estate value. Water, for example, can be integrated into neighborhood amenities as water-friendly, hydric streets.

Conflicts in urban patterns become opportunities for reconnecting to the natural processes. Old drainage canals evolve to healthy urban aquatic systems: value + flood protection.

When the process takes time, plan for iterative steps.

The plan can be fast-tracked when a natural disaster occurs, moving from adversity to opportunity. Large-scale urban and regional changes are funded by post-disaster funding.

The traditional black-and-gray infrastructure— illustrating roadways creating heat islands, uncomfortable microclimates, and scaleless nonpedestrian streets—is not compatible with livable community standards.

Same-size right-of-way as the traditional (see above) but less pavement, more natural drainage, nicer scale, and microclimate cooling, resulting in a real estate value that is 40 percent higher and less costly to build and maintain.

SUSTAINABLE-DESIGN METRICS

The following questions framed as challenges will help to evaluate how successful a design is in terms of the sustainable design principles:

- What percentage of human-settlement energies (heating, cooling, water, and food) is supplied by the existing regional bioclimate and soils? The percentage should include precipitation and naturally occurring surface-water flows due to topography and regeneration of soils that are part of naturally occurring nutrient cycling.

- Does the community pattern express the bioclimatic conditions? Are natural disasters considered in the pattern and material? Are amenities—for example, flood control—integrated into the civic spaces?

- Can the community function during drought or blackout? For how long? How does the design cause or resolve drought or blackout?

Pattern and form mitigate wind damage while creating a livable scale—that is, an urban pattern in which the form itself protects the buildings and occupants.

Wind shadows (Olgyay) illustrate the potential value of buildings to create protected space and provide passive ventilation.

■ How many people can be supported by the existing resident-water crop? When in drought or blackout, does the water supply meet the demand? How does the design and planning solve this dilemma?

Urban- and community-design metrics, or evaluative measures to be used as tools, are just beginning to be developed. Although buildings can be made quite energy efficient, if their location requires car trips for shopping, education, civic involvement, and fulfillment of basic needs, the resulting fossil-fuel consumption quickly dwarfs what is saved in building energy efficiency. When it comes to movement of anything, a central location is very effective and can be measured as follows:

1. What percentage of the community residents travel by public transit (bus, subway, light-rail, or train), carpool, bicycle, or on foot?
2. Are pedestrian and vehicular pathways part of another public system—such as greenways that provide microclimate cooling, habitat, neighborhood-edge def-

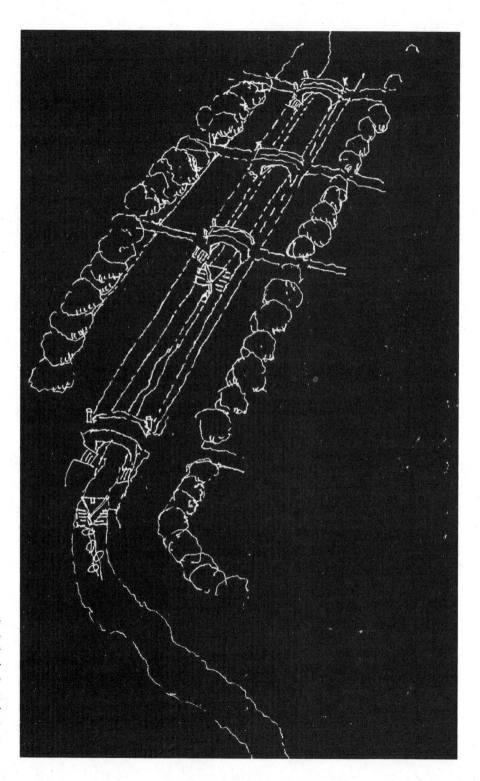

When areas flood, there is an opportunity to develop open spaces that store floodwater for recharge while they create civic amenities; in this way, solutions for local issues may satisfy more than one agenda with the same funding.

inition, or blueways, while also providing flood control, aquifer recharge, and habitat—thereby creating connectivity? Are there connections to natural-system connections? Are public funds used efficiently?

3. What percentage of consumed materials and resources are locally provided? In particular, is the amount of water that lands on surfaces sufficient for community needs? Are jobs and food available locally?

Sustainable Urban and Community Case Studies

The following case studies detail three urban, community-scaled projects. They have in common *scale*, *ecological analysis*, and *biourbanism*. These case studies address design and planning that reconnects to the natural resources within their respective urban microclimates. The bioclimatic characteristics and analysis of natural systems at the regional scale inform the planning and design process and enables the reconnection to sustainable resources on the urban and community scale. The three projects presented here are located in Belle Glade, Florida; Tucson, Arizona; and St. Paul, Minnesota.

Lessons from Belle Glade: Can We Save the Everglades and Sustain Agriculture?

Rio Nuevo Master Plan

Growing the Great River Park

LESSONS FROM BELLE GLADE: CAN WE SAVE THE EVERGLADES AND SUSTAIN AGRICULTURE?

Glades Community Development Corporation

The negative impact of the agricultural industry on the Everglades National Park, Florida, is well documented. The question is whether opposing natural and economic systems can be redesigned to make them compatible. Can connections be developed between agricultural and natural systems? Water in the Everglades watershed is both abundant, due to considerable precipitation, and scarce, due to lack of long-term storages. This design connected water-pollution abatement with smart-growth patterns while restoring healthy, natural-system functions and civic amenities.

Sustaining agriculture while protecting the quality and quantity of water distributed to the Everglades is illustrated in this charrette vision. Various ideas were debated for months, creating a healthy atmosphere of the awareness that plans must be built on consensus, knowledge, and the union of diverse community agendas.

The creation of regional open space has a value to communities as parks and recreation while also acting as a regional recharge site for potable water. Conflicts between urban and environmental needs are a constant issue. The Belle Glade plan was developed by integrating environmental science with urban and regional design

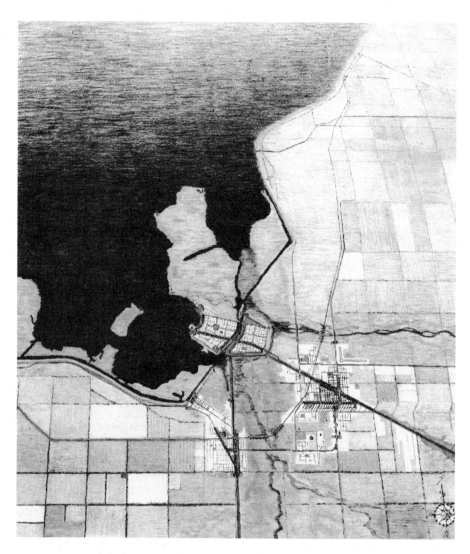

The town of Belle Glade, Florida, is inextricably connected to Lake Okeechobee, the regional lake system. There is a complex relationship between water, soil, and the existence of 800 square miles of agriculture and the Everglades National Park.

principles. The County Natural Resources Division used the plan to create a regional network of *hydric parks* that eliminate flooding while storing and recharging the potable water supply.

This regional design would be a win-win situation for the economy, the community, and the environment. The natural system, in this case the Everglades National Park, would receive cleaned-up sheet flow from the lake. The agricultural system, degraded from the past 100 years of abuse, would be revitalized by using a gravity irrigation-distribution system, reducing fossil-fuel dependence while rejuvenating the historic town image.

The conceptual base for this project included the regional hydrological patterns and historic flows of surface water in Everglades National Park. The application of

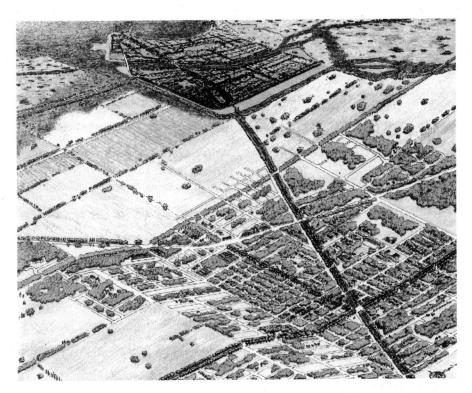

New Belle Glade visually reconnects with Lake Okeechobee, while the lake's hydrological system rebuilds the soils and creates an opportunity for ecotourism.

Connecting the new town to the historic town with urban canals and a celebration of the agricultural heritage.

this knowledge generated a plan that included protection of the natural system and provision for a new agricultural economy based on seasonal hydration and rebuilding of depleted soils.

The creation of the community's well-being starts with the education and action of its citizens. The Belle Glade charrette began with precharrette meetings—called the Citizen Planner Series—intended to educate the community in basic planning and design concepts (and what constitutes good planning and design), as well as hydrological and ecological concepts necessary for sustainability.

The removal of the 120 lineal miles of levee that surround Lake Okeechobee would create an industry for selling much-needed fill while reclaiming the valuable lakefront and marsh edges that contribute to the health of the upland and aquatic systems.

Design Team

The Glades Community Development Corporation—GCDC

The MacArthur Foundation

Center for Community and Neighborhood Design, University of Miami, Miami, Florida

Team: Daniel Williams, Harrison Rue, Chris Jackson, Jamie Correra, Estella Valle, and Eric Valle

RIO NUEVO MASTER PLAN

The following text was written by Mario Campos of Jones & Jones of Seattle. Jones & Jones was the urban design consultant for Rio Nuevo, with Hunter Interests, Inc., as prime consultant for the City of Tucson.

Tucson, Arizona

Tucson evolved as a community of cultures intimately connected with the Sonoran Desert and its mountains and rivers. Water was paramount to the development and establishment of these cultures, and careful understanding of desert ecosystems contributed to their successful use of water resources. As the city of Tucson has grown, the pace of its development has threatened its historic identity and livability. The original connections to these desert ecosystems have become tenuous, and the community is now working to reestablish them, based on the city's own multicultural roots and natural heritage. The redevelopment will begin with the downtown area and, at its core, the Rio Nuevo corridor along the Santa Cruz River and the adjacent neighborhoods. The Rio Nuevo Master Plan is Tucson's comprehensive development plan. It is designed to turn the city around, give it a livable center, and return it to a present-day livability. The master plan encompasses two plans that coincide: a ten-year development plan and a long-range vision plan that incorporates projects that may be implemented within the ten-year life of a new Tax Increment Finance District (created in 1999), as well as projects that may extend well into the future.

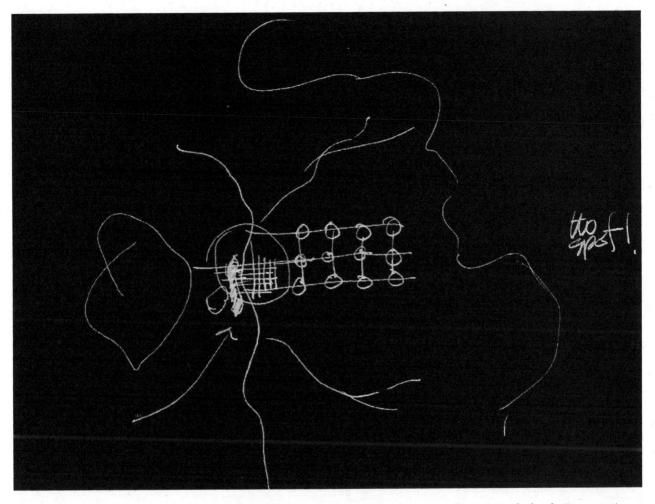

Long-established communities have a pattern based on the natural energies and resources that exist in the locale. Reconnecting with that pattern starts with an analysis of the past integrated into the desires of the future.

Because the Rio Nuevo plan covers several important areas of the city and beyond—for example, much of the downtown, a landfill at the site of significant archaeological and historical elements (e.g., Native American pit houses and a Spanish mission and gardens), several old Hispanic and historic neighborhoods, the Santa Cruz River corridor, and the adjacent Sentinel Peak park—master-planning development required extreme sensitivity to cultural and environmental issues.

The Rio Nuevo plan provides a unique and flexible vision that is bold, innovative, and unifying. The plan approaches the project from an economic, cultural, and environmental sustainability perspective by healing and restoring the natural systems and cultural heritage of the disrupted areas and bringing them back from the periphery to the heart of the city. It will be a celebration of nature and culture in the streets, public squares, and open spaces of the city. Moreover, Rio Nuevo shows that

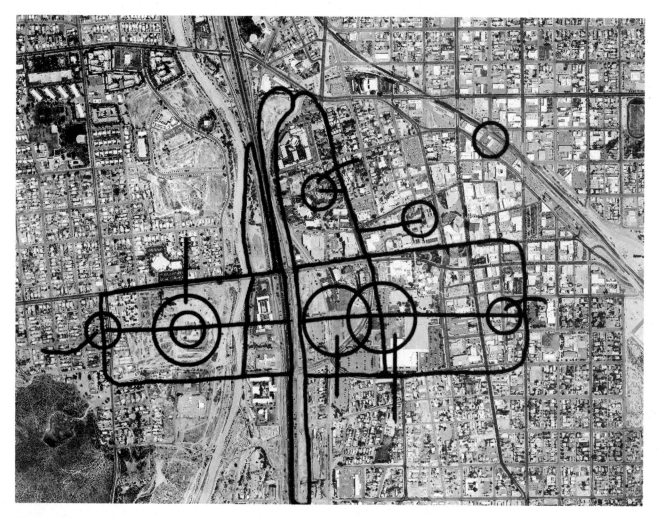

Conceptual reconnection of east and west communities that have been socially, economically, and environmentally fragmented for years.

a plan centered on natural systems and the acceptance and inclusion of diverse cultural values is one that can bring a divided citizenry together.

Designers recognized that the plan had to be innovative from an economic development perspective as well, with a unique emphasis on market analysis, financial feasibility, and strategic leveraging of public investment to gain significant commitments from both private and public investors. The Rio Nuevo plan thus represents a pragmatic blueprint for development based on market realities and current development trends that are in harmony with environmental and cultural goals. It can be implemented as a sustainable effort with achievable and measurable first steps and actions that can be initiated immediately. More than a short-term blueprint for development, the plan is a long-term healing strategy for a city that has been torn apart.

'river walk'

Recovering natural water patterns that were part of the region 100 years ago requires stormwater reclamation, storage, and redistribution—to regenerate a flowing river that stopped 100 years ago.

Disturbances to the original harmony of the city have come in several waves. A freeway severed the city through the middle and disenfranchised neighborhoods and residents, separating people and historic settlements from downtown and the commercial center and separating the Santa Cruz River—now controlled and heavily channeled—from the downtown and its plazas, the Presidio, and other historic neighborhoods. Several blocks of traditional low-income but well-established Hispanic and minority neighborhoods were cleared for construction of a convention center. Most of the material left over from the excavation was dumped on the other side of the river, burying important archaeological sites.

Urban sprawl, strip malls, isolated condominium clusters, auto-dependent housing developments, and other ubiquitous models for development challenge the city and continue to take over the surrounding Sonoran Desert. Memories of lost places and displaced neighborhoods, the loss of usable active open space, the prevalence of massive walls and inert facades, the ubiquity of empty streets in the evenings, and the scale of projects such as the 1960s urban renewal convention center are daily reminders to citizens that top-down planning and isolated megaprojects are unsuccessful approaches to revitalization.

The Rio Nuevo Master Plan is the result of an extensive public-outreach program that encompasses many environmental, historical, economic, and culturally diverse points of view. It brings together successful grassroots preservation efforts and arts investments and consequently builds a commitment to cultural diversity and the renewal of public life, as it provides a new look at water and water resources and creates a new paradigm for development and civic revival.

Rio Nuevo creates a network of interconnected places—such as a museum; housing; mixed-use and commercial development; a unique system of parks, recreational open spaces, cultural parks, plazas, and public urban places; entertainment

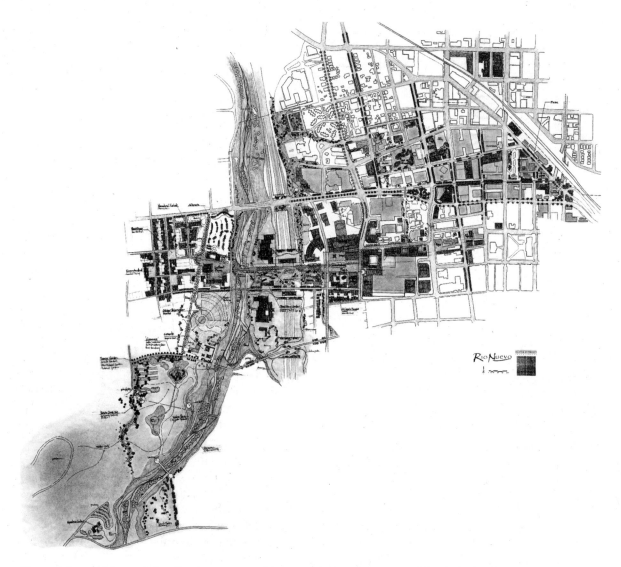

Tucson's larger vision reclaims the stormwater and integrates it into the pattern of the city's social, economic, and environmental future.

areas; and sites for multiple business uses—all interwoven and in harmony with history, living natural systems, and cultural heritage throughout the Rio Nuevo District. The plan builds on the early successes of local preservation efforts and a commitment to diversity and the preservation of natural resources—water, in particular—in an inclusive way, weaving ecology, history, architecture, and art into a vision for the future. The core of the plan, as its name suggests, lies in the reclamation of the Santa Cruz River as an environmental and cultural icon. The vision is of a restored riverbed, with terraces and cottonwoods strewn along a corridor of public trails and pathways

The east and west connection is a celebration of past and future.

that provide public access to the river and amenities, as well as to cultural and recreational opportunities.

The vision of new cultural and natural landscapes for the city comes together on the floodplains and riverbanks of a restored riverbed, along with plants and animals and a better understanding of how generations of desert inhabitants and dwellers sought life-giving water, cooling comfort, sustainable living endeavors, and the company of others along the banks of the braided streams of river water. The water—now a permanent, gentle flow that serves as intermittent storm-water management—provides evidence of the river's rich ecology and healing power and, so too, the memory and imagination of the geography, history, and culture around the river.

A restored Santa Cruz River would integrate the necessary technologies needed for flood control and water management with a vision of the unique landscapes and places that sustained life in the area for thousands of years. A series of workshops with local residents and diverse constituencies, with barrio and long-time city residents, uncovered the memories and the vision. Long-time residents of Tucson told stories of visiting the river on holidays and during important cultural ceremonies. Although many argued over economic development, the need for flood control, residential development models, and the location of cultural facilities, plazas, and streets, they all agreed on the need to connect with the river and the natural world in and around the city, with the extended goal of reuniting the healed river with the city and the western barrios, reconnecting Sentinel Peak and the natural areas to the downtown and commercial areas, traversing the highway intermittently, and creating a network of interconnected places and landscapes, of scenic corridors, and of protected view sheds. The heart of the Rio Nuevo plan is a healing landscape and a living flow of water that is intimately linked with the history of Tucson.

The Rio Nuevo Master Plan incorporates 19 or more cultural projects, 10 residential projects, 12 commercial and mixed-use projects, and several infrastructure projects, resulting in a total capital investment need of approximately $750 million, and the effective revitalization of the downtown area. The implemented master plan will result in an average of $300 million-plus in direct impact annually, as well as creating more than 4,000 jobs.

The vision begins with restoring the river and reweaving the eastern and western neighborhoods together. Reconstructed islands, sandbars, and natural terraces slow the water to a more even and natural pace, providing resting places for fish, birds, and other wildlife. Carefully planned and designed weirs contribute to water retention and habitat reclamation, accelerating the process of healing the river. Banks and restored terraces support new plantings of indigenous cottonwoods, willows, Arizona ash, and other riparian trees and shrubs.

Sentinel Peak is a meaningful landmark also known as Shook-Shon Mountain, which rises out of the banks of the river and its original settlements and evokes the city of Tucson's name. Rio Nuevo brings the mountain and river together; a restored cienega (a desert marsh and watering hole) anchors a natural park habitat for endangered amphibians and birds and provides interpretive and learning opportunities for visitors and residents. Situated in a mesquite shrubland with saguaros and paloverde, an upland habitat that once served as an Indian burial ground, the peak itself is restored as a functioning wilderness park connected to the river. A network of trails provides access to the park for visitors and residents.

The natural park at the foot of Sentinel Peak connects the mountain to the river, providing a continuum of habitat for wildlife and plants as well as an extended park. Through careful reconstruction, the park design interprets important historical and cultural elements. An elevated walkway along a recreated cienega illustrates the value and role of important microhabitats in the desert and serves as a refuge for birds and migratory fowl. Reconstructed acequias, or irrigation troughs, as first built by the native Hohokam farmers for growing corn on the flood plain more than 1,000 years ago and then by Spanish settlers along the river, contribute to the understanding of cultural landscapes and how careful use of water contributed to sustainable life in the desert. Recreated foundations of the round dwellings of the Pima Indians are interpreted for contemporary residents and visitors. Although nothing remains of the late-eighteenth-century adobe Mission San Agustin del Convento, the plan calls for a visitor center adjacent to the archaeological dig to interpret the mission and its gardens, which are seen as the birthplace of Tucson.

A restored Santa Cruz River runs throughout the district, through strands of restored arroyos, extending into the larger watershed to nourish a renewed environment. Strands of vegetation, terraces, and functional arroyos contribute to storm-water management by slowing down the flow to the Santa Cruz; they provide connectivity by serving as wildlife corridors along the new urban landscape, cutting across the freeway and flowing into the streets, parks, and plazas of Tucson. This natural extension of the river environment to the city supports the basic stated goal of the redevelopment effort: to reconnect the east and west sides of the city and the Santa Cruz River to Tucson.

In the same manner, multiple penetrations and connections under and over the freeway weave the urban fabric of the city with a cultural plaza and *alameda* that extends farther west to the old barrios and brings new cultural and economic vitality to the west side. Major investments are directed to the construction of a plaza and a new center on the west side that includes a farmers' market, or open-air *mercado*, as well as homes for the Arizona State Museum, an American Indian Cultural Center, and a Regional Visitor Center.

Connecting lids and tree-lined pedestrian bridges link the entire plaza complex to a new civic plaza in downtown Tucson. Additional pedestrian and vehicular crossings penetrate the freeway to reconnect the new developments and older barrios of the west side with the entertainment district of downtown Tucson.

A large lid over the freeway supports the new Science Center and connects to the civic plaza, anchored by the Arizona Sonora Desert Museum, theaters, hotels, retail, a new conference space, and art galleries. A reflecting pool and fountains underline the character of the plaza, welcoming residents and visitors with a reference to the river. Additionally, a new streetcar line along an urban boulevard links the civic plaza to the existing Plaza de Armas next to City Hall and the Tucson Museum of Art.

All of the elements work together to get people out into a new network of open-air plazas, pedestrian streets, trails, and parkways with the life-giving presence of the Santa Cruz River in the form of restored natural landscapes and carefully planned water features. The plan brings hope to Tucson and has activated the community to rally around a new form of development that makes a connection with its past and its natural setting, with the Santa Cruz River at its core.

GROWING THE GREAT RIVER PARK

The Saint Paul Riverfront Corporation

The Great River Park is the defining image of Saint Paul, Minnesota. Although this currently emerging Great River Park vision is not yet a plan and, further, is not just about parks, it has profound implications. It is about the city straddling the remarkable Mississippi River valley, a green corridor of enormous dimension and breadth, stretching as a continuous green spine through the length of Saint Paul, linking it to Minneapolis. It is about dozens of thriving (and emerging) neighborhoods, commercial nodes, and corridors. It is about the downtown's residential, commercial, cultural, and entertainment center embracing the river. It is about a singular fusion of city and river, as Saint Paul is endowed with 26 miles of shoreline with a unique bluff line and valley topography, 3,500 acres of parkland (more than four times the size of Central Park), and more than 25 miles of trails. This is the Saint Paul advantage.

The concept of the Great River Park is at the leading edge of a new paradigm—the city in the park, the park in the city. In the heart of the city of Saint Paul you can (or will be able to) see an inspiring and increasingly green natural setting, watch the sunrise or sunset over the Mississippi in unbounded nature, or view the downtown towers lit up at the water's edge. People will be able to stroll, cycle, jog, hike, cross-country ski, watch birds; be alone or with people; get out on the water (on excursion boat, rowboat, kayak, canoe, powerboat); fish; live or work on or near the river; participate in active recreation; have a family picnic; watch a concert; take in a series of great annual events; and eat a meal and enjoy a drink.

The proximity of urbanity and nature is one of the most valuable qualities in contemporary life. And in Saint Paul's case, much of this is already there—it simply comes with the territory! The city now has the opportunity to exploit this incredible natural advantage and become both more urban and more natural. It has the opportunity to develop a great park in the heart of the large and varied city. With the greatest length of river on both sides of any city on the Mississippi, the city can become a resort for its inhabitants, workers, and visitors.

The Great River Park Is about Economic Development

Supporting and developing this unique and valuable resource is the key to Saint Paul's future prosperity. The economic case for the Great River Park is rooted in a new paradigm for economic development—competing on value and not on price—that emphasizes quality of life over the traditional focus on factor costs. At the heart of this new paradigm is the insight that cities and regions that compete with each other primarily on the basis of cost are engaged in a losing game, and such competitive policies inevitably lead to a race to the bottom and impoverishment of the public realm and public services. This game is particularly unproductive for cities, as the cost playing field is invariably tilted toward the suburbs, with their larger expanses of cheaper land, emphasis on privately rather than publicly owned amenities—large private yards as opposed to urban parks—and heavy governmental subsidies for roadways and other infrastructure.

An economic development strategy focused on value is furthermore sustainable over the long term. Unlike the cost strategy, which is ever at risk of being undercut by the competition, the value strategy has these advantages:

- Builds on localized assets that endure over time, including the city's natural setting, its historic fabric, and its cultural institutions
- Does not starve revenue-essential public services, such as education, parks, infrastructure maintenance, policing, and so forth

■ Nurtures businesses whose leaders and employees are vested in the civic life of the community

The Great River Park is the quality-of-life distinguisher for Saint Paul. As a valuable resource unique to Saint Paul, providing multiple benefits to the city, the Great River Park is the cornerstone of a value-based economic development strategy.

Resource for Neighborhood, Business, and Tax-Base Development

The Great River Park will be a great recreational resource for the residents of Saint Paul and the region. In general, cities and regions that are desirable places to live tend to do well economically. As much as people follow jobs, businesses follow people to take advantage of local markets for skilled labor and consumer dollars—the *place* in itself is a value.

The Great River Park has the potential to draw large numbers of visitors from outside the city. If Minnesota is like most other states, the number-one attraction for out-of-state visitors is not the Mall of America but visits with friends and family. This is true for regions as diverse as Napa Valley, where friends and family outweigh the wine country as the primary draw, and the state of Connecticut, where such family visits outnumber those to the nation's largest Native American casinos. Therefore, as was discovered in Napa Valley, the most effective way to market local attractions to out-of-state visitors is to market them to in-state residents, who then recommend them to their visiting friends and family members, seeing the *place* as a value.

This is already the case for special events, and in the future this will become increasingly the case for the year-round recreation and leisure-time resources and activities the park will offer. Like anything that generates visitation, be it a museum, theater, or a park, there is the potential for Saint Paul retailers, restaurants, and bars to capture the ancillary spending of these visitors. A two-pronged strategy for increasing the capture rate for potential visitor spending includes making the downtown the main gateway for park visitors and increasing linkages between the park and adjacent commercial areas.

The Great River Park will help elevate Saint Paul's profile for all manner of site location decisions. As a unique resource, the park has great marketing value and can be used as a cornerstone for promoting the city to prospective businesses and investors. But it also offers real value to employers. In creative- and knowledge-based fields, where success depends on the ability to attract, hire, and retain talented employees, local amenities and quality of life become important competitive advantages. Talented employees are less likely to relocate away from places they enjoy living. Further, locations that offer ample opportunities for outdoor recreation tend both to attract active people and to promote healthier lifestyles, which minimize lowered productivity and time lost to poor health or illness. All these considerations are as important to the retention of existing companies as to the attraction of new companies.

Neighborhoods as Systems

Neighborhoods and regions are complex physical, social, and economic systems. The elements that make up a community—land and structures, people and their sociocultural activities, business and educational institutions—are all vital and interconnected. As a result, improvements to one simultaneously enhance the others. What good is it to solve an economic problem if it causes environmental degradation? And what good is a solution to an environmental crisis if it wreaks economic havoc on its citizens? In either case, the community—the system as a whole—suffers.

Urban stormwater is a pollutant, but it can also be an important resource and help to irrigate lawns and open spaces, to recharge groundwater, and to improve surface-water flow. When stormwater is viewed as an amenity, the path from the upland areas to the river can be a lineal park that will do the following:

- Increase access to the river (a neighborhood goal)
- Improve stormwater quality (a city and regional goal)
- Improve real estate value (a public and city goal)

In this way, problems regarding stormwater control, additional clean-water supply, and the addition of open space can all be addressed simultaneously and with the same funding. In addition, the primary natural forces and conditions relied on in this strategy—gravity and surface porosity—occur without the need to expend fossil fuel. This solution is inexpensive, sustainable, and adds real value to a neighborhood.

Saint Paul's Great River Park charrette illuminated the community's stewardship of the river ecology and the entire regional watershed of which Saint Paul is part. The river and the natural climate are important elements in the assessment of available capital—ecological capital—and Saint Paul is clearly an example where environmental protection and economic development are complementary.

Sustainable development in Saint Paul is connected to stewardship of the river and future efforts to connect neighborhoods with the regionwide watershed. Ecological capital is very high in Saint Paul. Development plans that integrate and connect to this natural capital provide tremendous opportunity with the least economic cost. The vision of living within a setting ("just out your door and you are in a park") is a highly desirable factor and adds greatly to Saint Paul's competitive advantage to draw new business.

Cities and communities are about their regional place. Saint Paul has not forgotten that, and this present effort to connect and draw image and identity from the river and its land is an environmental, economic, and cultural win-win. Sustainable design is critical in the rebirth of Saint Paul and its region. In the field of urban and regional design, sustainability is achieved by connecting the environmental capital with the sociocultural capital and with local economics. Sustainability itself suggests a state in which a system or process can successfully continue over a long period of time. The new urban model is one that integrates the great urban diversity of people and places with natural settings.

Cities must evolve out of their reliance on fossil fuel. To understand the magnitude of the change required, it is important to note that no city could function without it—no food, no water, no transportation, and no electricity without the use of fossil fuel. Their total reliance on a nonrenewable resource underlines the critical need for cities to begin initiating changes in how they function, what they use for energy, and how the basic services can be accomplished with the simple reconnection to natural-system functions. The development challenge of sustainability presupposes that cities desire to develop alternatives to their reliance on nonrenewable resources, and that the sooner these alternatives are in place the sooner those cities will have a competitive advantage over cities that do not offer alternatives.

Implementing Sustainable Practices

The city of Saint Paul *exists* because of the river. Future planning moves in the city and region can be informed by a series of principles developed by regional and his-

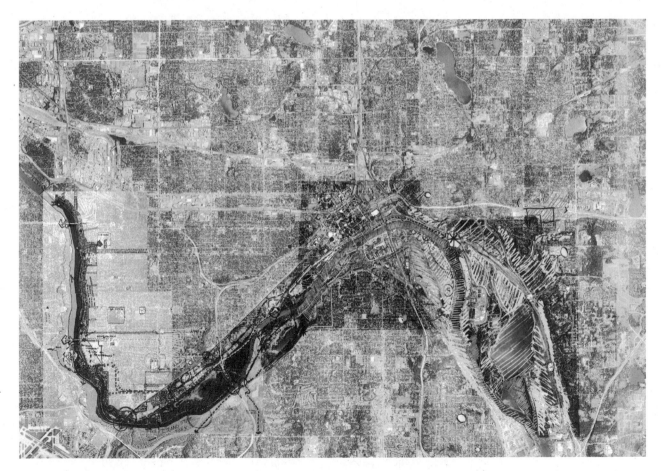

The charrette sketch reconnects the river, the community, and the city while restoring wetlands and buildable infill property.

Legend

Saint Paul Topo
Elevation

- 357 - 384
- 330 - 357
- 303 - 330
- 275 - 303
- 248 - 275
- 221 - 248
- 194 - 221
- 167 - 194
- 140 - 167
- 113 - 140
- 86 - 113
- 58 - 86
- 31 - 58
- 4 - 31
- -23 - 4

Great River Park Master Plan
Saint Paul Topography

This image of Saint Paul, Minnesota, illustrates the geologic substrate that locates the historic and natural connections to the river from the upper bluffs.

toric references to the cultural and civic past. The following suggested topics can be used to build city- and river-development principles.

Land Use Future land-use decisions must integrate with public transportation, livable- and walkable-community design, and civic amenities. With regard to urban development, the most beneficial land-use strategy is to choose a development site within an existing community. It is especially helpful if it is a brownfield that requires remediation. This enables the existing services, such as police protection, roads, sewer and water, open space, transportation, schools, and libraries, to be used.

Site Ecology All designs passively fit the regional ecosystem and bioclimatic conditions.

Community Design and Connections Efforts to promote community, including respect for historic attributes, and the development of regional- and local-transportation strategies, are central to efficient development. It is smarter, healthier, and cheaper to develop within the existing city pattern.

Water Use Connect the river to the city with the use and reuse of water. The pathways that water takes in its journey from neighborhood to river can illustrate conservation and clean up water prior to it reaching the river. These blueways can connect people, neighborhoods, river, and commerce.

Energy Performance Energy-efficiency strategies that capitalize on the local climate—use of sunlight, ground temperature, orientation of structures, and transit—are important push factors to efficient development. These efforts range from the more standard approaches, such as improving local energy codes, to more creative options, such as establishing alternative green power use and regional transit systems.

Energy Security Analysis of energy security highlights those issues that directly affect local energy independence, including the use of (and designing in) renewable energy and the ability of buildings and the city to function under emergency conditions. (The frequency of blackouts is increasing, so the ability for a community to continue to function without access to the utility grid has the interest of all leaders in all communities.)

Materials and Construction The selection of local, healthy, and environmentally safe building materials enables green construction practices. Local communities can look to local suppliers for materials and servicing of these materials, equipment, and systems. In this way, a city helps to retain its local, unique character while supporting its local labor force and renewable building resources.

Light and Air A focus on light and air addresses indoor and outdoor environmental quality, including daylighting, natural ventilation, and seasonally comfortable public spaces. Through sustainable zoning and building codes, urban designers can ensure livable and walkable communities. Improving the outdoor air (by supporting public transit), city leaders can go a long way toward improving the indoor air that occupants breathe.

Bioclimatic Design Designs should be appropriate to the project's region and climate. Orientation of streets and buildings, selection and location of indigenous landscape materials, and the celebration of regional and natural characteristics are inexpensive to accomplish and highly valuable to community and neighborhoods.

Long Life, Loose Fit The adage "Long life, loose fit" advocates design flexibility. Development should be planned and designed to allow for dynamic adaptation of buildings and streets as new opportunities and needs arise.

Projects and Development Potential

- Regional interpretive center—this is a cultural, geological, and ecological educational center.
- Water-treatment and community-education facility—rework treatment plant and use gravity feed to terraced treatment areas with biological (living

The environmental analysis informs the vision by recreating the connection between the urban form, the economy, and the health and vitality of the river.

machine) uptake and appropriate nutrient loading to wetlands within the floodplain. Improve flow from the north floodplain into the river or lake body; this flushing will improve habitat, birding, and community use.

- Ecotourism and mixed-use housing development—connect this parcel to the upper community through walkways in geological formations. This parcel will act as a case study of how to connect and steward the river with ecosensitive design and planning.

- Pedestrian-cross connections—make pedestrian paths over and under tracks and highway, and extend to upper neighborhoods. Stormwater to be day-lighted, cleaned up through bioremediation and holding pools and intro-duced as blueways along pedestrian paths.

- Restore native habitat—use floodplain as a garden for regional connectivity and a national model of city and river relationship.

- The working river—continue with the working river but with the needs of the natural river and its positive impacts on the city accounted for. The working river theme is both local and regional and should be part of the interpretive center.

The sustainable-cities movement reaches far beyond what its name alone would imply. This approach to growth encourages thoughtful development that not merely maintains but actually improves the quality of community life. In Saint Paul the opportunities are many—from restoring critical ecosystems and city fabric and supporting local labor forces to taking advantage of cost-saving efficiencies by connecting to natural processes. The Great River Park and the city within the park are powerful and economic engines that connect people to river to place.

Each part of this varied setting has different environmental characteristics, distinct vegetation and habitat, a particular carrying capacity, adjacencies to surrounding neighborhoods, and access challenges. Many portions of the park have been planned as individual parks, taking their specific characteristics into account. Weaving these designs together into a larger and connected whole opens up some new challenges and opportunities to do the following:

- Work with and enhance natural watersheds and hydrology
- Build on cleanup and river-valley restoration efforts currently under way
- Enhance and strengthen unique natural features and landscape types (bluffs, plains, valleys, and vegetation)
- Create a great range of park landscapes from civic to recreational to natural

Developing the Program for the Park

The Great River Park is Saint Paul's Central Park. It has enormous potential for community building, uniting citizens regardless of race, ethnic background, age, gender, or socioeconomic status, because the Mississippi is a resource central to all. With a shared sense of vision anchored by a comprehensive community-participation model, the people of Saint Paul can "rally round the river." The key element in planning programming, whether for grand ideas like festivals and civic celebrations or quiet retreats in a beautiful, protected reach of the river, is to plan locally. If the locals are happy, visitors will come. It will serve a range of needs: active or passive, residential or visitor, and seasonal or year-round.

It is important to match program to resources. Understanding the larger pattern of geology and ecology gives us the opportunity to match programs and activities with the river's unique ecological, geological, or historical aspects. We can tailor the experience of the Great River Park, using programming to highlight the unique stories (geological, geographical, ecological, historical, cultural, and recreational) found along the Mississippi River and in Saint Paul.

The Great River Park becomes a major reason to live, work in, and visit Saint Paul. It is open all year, with periodic special seasonal events. There is a big picture, but it is also intensely local and neighborhood specific, with relationships to what happens on its edges. As a key part of a healthy active community, it meets a broad range of active and passive recreational needs. It serves residents and visitors of all ages and mobility levels. It has both temporary and permanent facilities and programs. Ecotourism and cultural and heritage tourism, both local and national, are major components of the park vision.

Developing and Improving Connections

Successful economic development, as well as park use, safety, and stewardship, will be greatly enhanced by strong neighborhood, river, and park connections. All manner of connections—pedestrian, vehicular, visual, and thematic—are called for. Connections are of unique importance and value; they have to be carefully planned to advance broader goals. Current connections are limited; new ones will be expensive. The strategy must therefore work to capitalize on existing connections and to develop additional connections.

Conclusion: Realizing the Vision for the Great River Park

Saint Paul has an exceptional opportunity to build on its momentum and past successes and move decisively forward with the creation and connection to the Great River Park, building on its unique competitive advantage—the Mississippi River valley.

This is a clear case where good environmental stewardship, effective economic development, and successful community building are intimately linked and mutually supportive. The combined effort, which is already underway, must be grounded in a clear and compelling community vision in a form that everyone understands and can embrace. The project involves a multiyear program of carefully linked initiatives at the scales of the whole (including the larger regional scale) and of the parts. These incremental moves can lead to dramatic results.

Promoting a more holistic approach to city building, the Saint Paul Development Framework reflects a fundamental shift in thinking, represented in ten principles:

1. *Evoke a sense of place.* Create a physical setting for new development that says, "This is Saint Paul."
2. *Restore and establish the unique urban ecology.* Look for opportunities to restore those parts of the natural environment that have been lost over time due to development, such as trees, native habitats, and clean water.
3. *Invest in the public realm.* Create a network of streets, sidewalks, and parks that are safe, vibrant, and pedestrian friendly.
4. *Broaden the mix of uses.* Create a downtown and riverfront where people live, work, and play.
5. *Improve connectivity.* Provide people with safe, attractive, and convenient ways to move between neighborhoods, downtown, and the river.
6. *Ensure that buildings support the broader city building goals.* Design new buildings to fit into their surroundings and help to make adjacent public spaces active.
7. *Build on existing strengths.* Start with what residents already treasure—the historic buildings, the parks, the tree-lined streets, and the Mississippi River.
8. *Preserve and enhance heritage resources.* Preserve historic buildings and public spaces.

9. *Provide a balanced network for movement.* Design city streets to accommodate pedestrians, cars, buses, bikes, on-street parking, landscaping, lighting, and signs.
10. *Foster public safety.* Increase the number of people in public spaces downtown, along the riverfront, and in the neighborhoods.

Design Team

Ken Greenberg, Greenberg Consultants, Inc.

Ken Bowers, Phillips Preiss Shapiro Associates, Inc.

Mary Jukuri, JJR

Daniel Williams, Daniel Williams Architects and Planners

Charlotte DeWitt, International Events, Ltd.

architectural design

The ecological model is powered by energy and resources resident to the site and bioregion. Ecology is place-based, connecting form and biological function as a system. When this kind of systems thinking is applied to architectural design, it suggests that the design acts as the collector and concentrator of those resident energies and resources. The connection, collection, and concentration of these energies can provide comfort, value, and delight. Sustainable design accomplishes the most with the least energy consumption and in a connected and comprehensive manner.
—Dan Williams

The historic roots of architecture lie in the connections between the natural place and its inherent ability to provide comfort and security to the inhabitants. Architecture up until 100 years ago had to be ingenious in providing comfort by integrating passive elements of the natural place into design solutions. Passive elements include warm air rising, prevailing breezes, ventilation chimneys, floor plans proportioned and oriented to provide daylight and fresh air to all users, unique methods of construction, virtual elimination of waste, a symbiotic relationship between the structure and the materials needed to build it, and the reuse or return to the earth of the materials after their use. These elements were the very foundation of the architectural and planning profession, grounded in sustainable principles before they were called such. Even though regional and urban design is the scale that will have the greatest impact on sustainability, it is the architecture, the daily experience, that provides the best direct opportunity for the public to learn and embrace sustainability.

The Site: Challenges and Opportunities

The site is more than an address. It is the sum total of the economic, environmental, and social attributes of its location. An in-depth and comprehensive analysis of the site will help determine the following:

Historically, architecture created communities that provided civic spaces for economic opportunities, cultural settings, protection from the elements, and security.

- Optimum form and size of the building footprint
- The building's orientation
- The glazing location, orientation, and size necessary for natural and passive daylight
- The glazing location for heat gain or to reduce heat gain
- Locations of openings for natural ventilation

- Building materials and finishes appropriate to the impacts from the climate and the weather
- Landscape type, size, location, and variation
- Low-maintenance strategy for the upkeep and operational costs of the structure

The term *place-based design* refers to designs that include, integrate, and connect the site's natural characteristics and resources into the design. In sustainable design, *site means place*—it Includes all aspects of the region and microclimate. A study and analysis of the site and regional environmental conditions, the ecology, biology, geologic history, anthropology, and climate provide significant information that informs architects and planners in their designing for sustainability.

A sustainable site analysis begins with study of the sun and its impact on the region, the community, and the site. This impact includes its climate and ecological niche and how the sun angle, intensity, and duration establish the bioclimate and microclimate. Solar, soil, and water patterns and flows have been sustainable resources on the site for many years; these are the free generators of the natural character and form of the site. Working against those natural patterns is expensive, requires significant mechanical intervention, and is, therefore, not sustainable. The natural patterns and characteristics are unique to each region and site, and understanding and connecting to them will benefit the design.

The sustainable site analysis also includes the study and understanding of the "next system larger." The reasoning for this is as follows: The region has a bioclimate, a series of biological functions specific to its climate. The site's bioclimate is similar to the region's, but the site has a specific microclimate unique to its location. It is impacted by its surroundings: the soil, slope, precipitation, temperature, humidity, air movement, and direction, as well as impacts from surrounding buildings. The site, as the smaller scale of study, is impacted more significantly by changes such as storms or fires or earthquakes. The region, however, has characteristics that will only change with global changes. Although a warm-humid region may be severely impacted by hurricanes, it will remain warm-humid, whereas coastal developments, in the extreme global change case, may lose the land and need to move.

There are also considerable impacts from surroundings, such as prevailing winds that can create different microclimates within 100 feet of one another or in urban settings, when the reflective skin on a building face concentrates energy onto neighboring buildings. This reflected light and heat energy is an annoyance to the residents of the neighboring buildings, as it changes the temperature within the spaces, adds to cooling bills, and creates considerable glare. Every piece of architecture changes the microclimate of its site and its neighbors' site, sometimes requiring considerable changes, associated costs, and potentially litigation.

The site and environmental analysis is three-dimensional. These dimensions are illustrated and are called out as air shed, watershed, and geologic shed. A site is much more than a surface on which to build; a look at the patterns of the site can provide information on how resident forces shaped it over time. By observing and researching these patterns and forms, the designer can mimic these free-energy patterns and include them in the building design. Sustainable design acknowledges these forces as potential energy to power the building and makes a commitment to utilize them.

Site Design and Environmental Analysis

Upon this gifted age, in its dark hour,
Rains from the sky a meteoric shower
Of facts . . . they lie unquestioned, uncombined.

Wisdom enough to leech us of our ill
Is daily spun; but there exists no loom
To weave it into fabric . . .
　　　—Edna St. Vincent Millay

The sustainable designer's process can be seen as a loom. This metaphorical loom is the thinking process and the resulting solution that captures and connects the renewable resources. The loom links the facts of the site in a manner that preserves and protects both site and building, creating uniqueness. In the twenty-first century, energy scarcity and the transition to alternative energy sources is a prime design parameter. Site design begins with the analysis of the site and environmental conditions and integrates them into the program and design solution. Integrating the natural attributes of the site can reduce energy consumption considerably.

The natural resources of the site are the renewable energies and materials residing on the site. Conceptually, a sustainable-design solution creates the form and skin of the structure in a manner that captures, stores, and distributes the resident energies. The simple capturing of these energies with the function and form of the structure is basic to sustainable design. Sustainable design is an expression of understanding and connecting with the site and the environmental conditions, connecting with the place.

Ecology has seasonal changes—it is dynamic. Some ecologies, like those in the hurricane-prone states, have vegetative patterns that have adapted to this stress. Inherent in the form and pattern of these ecological communities is the process of morphing to the changing energy and dynamic existing conditions. An example in architectural design would be to design architectural and planning forms and patterns that change to reduce, redirect, and mitigate destructive wind forces. After the recent hurricanes of Andrew, Katrina, Rita, and Wilma, it is obvious that current building locations and building forms illustrate that the construction industry has learned little when it comes to designing for wind mitigation.

Postdisaster design and planning is an opportunity for local officials and design professionals to create architectural and urban-planning patterns, where the very form itself creates a more secure place. This approach not only provides for rebuilding community but also expresses the very real connection to place and makes a dif-

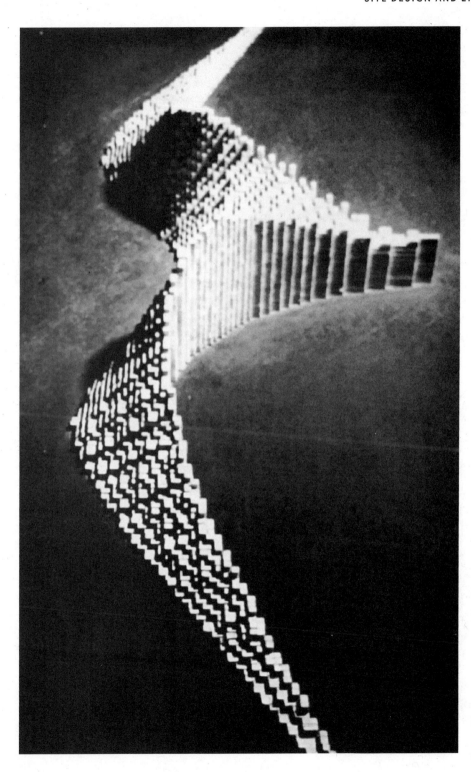

As illustrated in this model by R. Knowles, today's architectural challenges accommodate large populations—both new and existing—in patterns that can maximize the natural energies resident to the place.

ference to a community's sense of security and well being. It is also an opportunity to reconnect to sustainable patterns.

In his book *Energy and Form*, Ralph Knowles illustrated the design value of sunlight on form. This is a powerful example of the potential value that sustainable design has on form. The challenge to designers is what has been learned and how that science can be applied to form. H. G. Wells stated the lost opportunity this way: "Civilization is always a race between learning and disaster."

On August 24, 1992, Hurricane Andrew, carrying winds between 145 and 200 miles per hour, reached landfall. South Florida, in less than three hours, was changed for all time. The 33 communities that were damaged or destroyed incurred over $30 billion in structural and building damage, and 250,000 people were displaced. Out of the ruin there stood, for no readily apparent reason, structures minimally damaged, while others next door were completely destroyed. There is evidence that the reason for this lies within the mitigating aspects inherent in some architectural and urban planning patterns. This leads to the question: Can form itself mitigate wind damage?

Form is knowledge expressed. The form of an object evolves from the knowledge and technology that the designer possesses when the design process starts. When the designer has new knowledge, the design process changes and change in the form is the result. Aerodynamics affords an excellent example. In the last ten years the design process has incorporated new criteria and new tools, along with computer

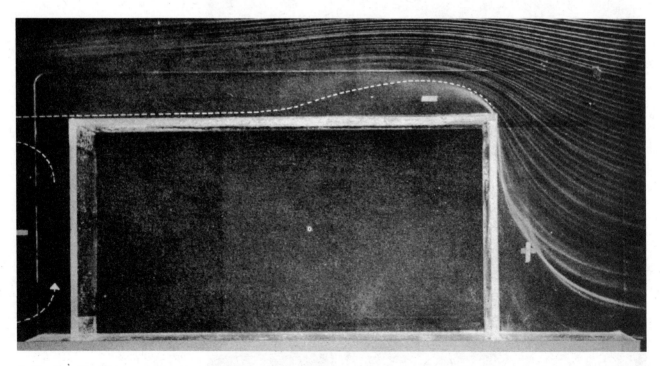

As illustrated by Olgyay, wind energy acts on forms in varying ways.

Sustainable architectural and urban patterns can mitigate wind forces, protecting the structures of home and community.

analysis, to create designs that reduce wind resistance. This knowledge has changed the designer's creative baseline, and this change has resulted in new, more efficient forms in planes, trains, and automobiles.

Using form to mitigate wind damage is not a new or untested idea. In Mikonos, Greece, gales from the sea often blow from 50 to 75 miles per hour, yet one can walk 20 feet inside the town and light a match. What is happening here is that the form itself is acting as a labyrinth, creating a back force—dampening the wind velocity and mitigating its force. In comparison, Chicago, where the buildings tend to reinforce and concentrate the winds, requires chains to assist pedestrians so that they will not be blown into the street. Architectural and urban form can be designed to baffle the wind forces and reduce wind damage—something known in Mikonos for hundreds of years and missed in Chicago, Florida, and the Gulf states.

A house in south Florida was in the west fringe of Hurricane Andrew and sustained 100-plus-mile-per-hour winds. A courtyard wall, creating the entry space,

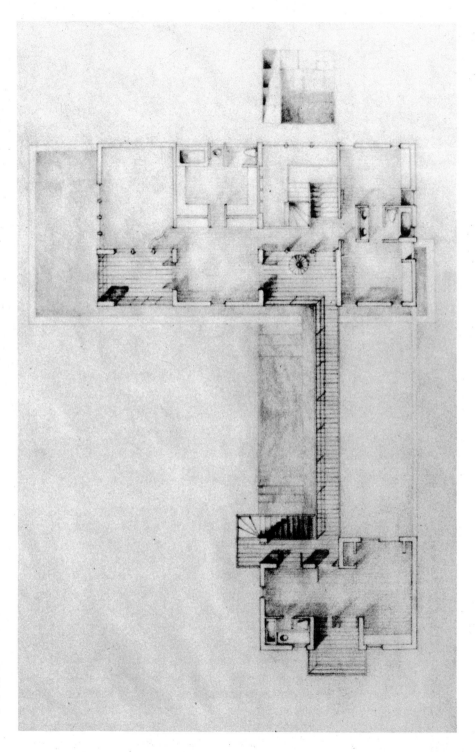

This site plan responds to solar and wind orientation to create usable spaces and protect the structure.

Courtyards baffle the winds, create family spaces, and mitigate wind damage.

was oriented askew with the front of the house. This wall was the same shape as the 16-foot-long, 7-foot-high window system. After the storm, the front of the house was covered with leaves and debris three inches thick. The window system, which corresponded to the *wind shadow* created by the courtyard wall, was without even the slightest debris. A negative pressure, created by the wall, mitigated the wind force.

Using wind as an informer of form is largely overlooked during the creative process due to the scant and difficult-to-absorb scientific nature of the data. It is especially difficult for designers to effectively interpret and apply the data that do exist. A low-rise coastal architectural form typically does not relate to wind force at all. Structures are often sited perpendicular to prevailing wind forces; this is diametrically opposed to what the orientation would be if wind force were to be mitigated (at 45 degrees). The rule has been to increase the structural sizing to withstand the force, rather than understanding the force as a design parameter and partner. Adding structural size is not cost-effective and, in many cases, due to the extreme forces of tornado-force winds, is not effective at all. After Hurricane Andrew, a 16-foot-long section of 8" × 14" concrete tie beams was found several blocks from its original location. The same was true after Hurricane Katrina, which scraped entire communities down to their footings and even to bedrock.

Consideration must be given to the creative use of form to mitigate storm energy, but location on the coastal "hot spot" makes it not just difficult but almost impossible. Designing wind mitigation is effective, but only if the development location is out of the main force of the wind; the lesson here is to build in smart places. Strong winds have deconstructive impacts, but they also have potentially important positive impacts on energy consumption—the forms and patterns can be designed to provide for passive ventilation and cooling (Olgyay, 1992).

Existing studies of wind energy can be reduced to the simple principles of surface-to-volume ratios and frictional surface qualities. The conditions, however, become more complex with the unpredictable behavior within a hurricane system (for example, in one instant a wall surface can receive the wind vector perpendicular to its surface as a positive pressure and reverse to a negative pressure as the storm moves). Working with these forces would suggest that the structural form should relate to the forces, not just withstand them. Examples in nature were all around after these hurricanes—even palm trees on the beaches remained. But there were other examples: an AirStream trailer in the middle of debris from everything else that had been destroyed; housing protected by certain types of vegetation; and single-family houses on interior lot sites where the corner structures were destroyed, yet they remained relatively unscathed. There is logic to the siting of architecture, and researching, understanding, and applying that knowledge to the design will have measurable positive results.

There are many examples of design responding to considerable force. Tents can be designed to withstand 200-mile-per-hour winds. Can architecture? The spoiler on a race car helps keep the car from being airborne at speeds up to 600-plus miles per hour—this thinking can be applied to the design of a spoiler on a roof parapet, resulting in the wind forces actually pushing the roofing membrane onto the roof, protecting the roofing membrane and consequently protecting the structure.

The opportunities to create an architecture specific to the site and its resident energy are significant. The following relationships suggest a process to study the site and its regional characteristics. It is helpful to organize the site issues and opportunities and view how one affects and connects with another.

Site to Region:

- Determine the relationship between the site and the regional environment and climate; chart how that climate corresponds to human comfort and natural resource needs.
- Determine the urban, agricultural, and natural characteristics of the region. How do they inform the design's context, and how is the natural and historic value of the place integrated into the design?
- Determine the cultural and economic assets that exist regionally. How do they impact the site? What is their relationship to the site?
- Determine the climate characteristics of the bioregional system. How have they helped form the general attributes of the biome?
- Determine the role that natural disasters have as part of the form and pattern of the land use, the climate, and the geological region. What impact do they have on the pattern and form, the designs, and postdisaster planning?

Site to Site:

- Determine the relationship between the site and its neighbors. Context, scale, view corridors, materials, geometric relationships, neighborhood character, and proportion can all inform design.
- Determine the compatible relationships derived from the site and the environmental analysis that can be introduced into design.
- Determine the microclimates that are present. How can they help inform the design decisions and eliminate nonsustainable methods?
- Determine the indigenous vegetation types. What are their potential uses for cooling, shading, storm protection, flood protection, soil improvement, and water retention? How do they adapt to the climate? How do they impact temperature, air movement, and humidity on the site?
- Determine the site's microclimate and how it is impacted by adjacent land uses.

Building to Site:

- Determine the synergistic relationships between the site's climate and human needs, comfort, and building layout. For example, use bubble diagrams (or a similar method) to show attributes of the site's natural characteristics (temperature, wind, water, contours, noise, solar pathways), and evolve the building's bubble diagram (functional layout) to integrate those attributes.

■ Determine the microclimate of the site. When does it approach human comfort zones—that is, temperature, air movement, and humidity and building-user needs? Chart the times of the year when the microclimate and human comfort zones are incompatible—when the microclimate is too hot, too cold, too humid, too dry, too windy, too still, and so on. These times need special attention.

■ Determine when adjustments need to be made due to humidity, air movement, and temperature. Design the interventions necessary to make those adjustments.

■ Determine the locations of the site's microclimate and native vegetation (e.g., prevailing breezes, mosses, wetlands, impacts from off-site surroundings, ground temperature for thermal-mass storage for the heating or cooling of the space), and introduce them into the design solution. The living roof illustrates the use of a vegetation system natural to the climate; if the design adopts this vegetation, it will grow naturally with no maintenance—design the fit.

Connected thinking, in these terms, is important at the start and throughout the project—both the questions and the answers have an impact at significant points in the design process. The site analysis informs the design solution but, more importantly, informs the design program and any problem(s) to be solved. Sustainability is

Resident vegetation is the choice for natural energies and sustainable growth. This living surface *presents the regional material for living roofs and walls.*

Using the local, indigenous moss created a self-maintaining living roof at no cost. Learning what sustainable systems exist in the region of the site and creating the environment for that to happen can create free and sustainable living roofs.

not an add-on to the project; it is thoroughly integrated into the program and solution. An in-depth environmental analysis of the site informs the design in ways that do the following:

- Eliminate the need for the use of nonrenewables-based grid energy
- Increase the efficient use of the site's and the region's renewable resources
- Improve overall energy efficiency
- Improve the building envelope's longevity
- Inform the design of the skin and envelope in order to be appropriate to the climate
- Reduce maintenance cost
- Improve quality of life
- Are essential to the larger community
- Improve the healthy environment of the users
- Act as a steward to the environment and the community

The knowledge gained from an in-depth analysis of the site, when integrated into the design, can solve the design program without unnecessary mechanical and environmental costs. Building designs that use the site energies are typically less expensive to maintain, are better for the environment, and offer a higher quality of experience for the user.

Sustainable Infrastructure

Buildings and project sites contain a considerable amount of infrastructure—for example, structure, stormwater controls, sewers, water supply, heating, ventilating, and air conditioning (HVAC), lighting, electrical circuitry, and data management, among other elements. As a community ages, the infrastructure and utilities require considerable retrofitting, as do the buildings. Because of this, the building itself can be looking toward new approaches to solving the problems without using the old infrastructure—for example, use of green roofs instead of new stormwater piping or additional operable glass for ventilation and daylighting instead of new lighting or mechanical ventilation.

Renovating and reusing existing infrastructure and infilling the urban grid are two of the most effective sustainable design approaches. Much of the infrastructure required for development already exists within senescent communities. Once renovated, the buildings already have connections to transit, neighborhood context, schools, libraries, civic center, police and fire protection, and utilities.

The Skin

The three elements of a building skin are floor, wall, and ceiling. The corresponding structural elements are the foundation, column (wall), and roof. Each has a finish, a

Infill development reuses infrastructure and builds density within existing urban cores.

material composition, and a structure; each impacts the flow of energy from one point to another within the structure. The energy required to make and transport the material from its raw state to the manufacturing and processing plant and then on to the construction site is considerable. Therefore, any time a local material source can be used or reused from a local stockpile, the construction practices are less wasteful and the design better approaches sustainability.

The word *envelope* is often used when referring to a building enclosure. This word, by chance or intent, contributes to the problem. An envelope is functionally large enough to hold the required contents, and the contents, once folded or manipulated, are sealed securely. But a building, if it is to act as a biologic entity, must be wrapped in something more like real skin. These skins or layers should breathe, let water out (or in for evaporative cooling), cool by evaporation, be closed to moisture and cold—the skin should have a loose fit and be anchored for reuse. It is functionally layered rather than relying on one material to do it all.

A good example of a skin relating to temperature changes is in the way one layers clothing. A soft, comfortable, and easy-to-clean layer is placed next to the skin; a next layer contains an air-confining weave or composite; and the final layer is a moisture-, wind-, or solar-protective or -responsive layer. Each of these layers brings to the composite a specific solution that, combined with the other layers, creates an extremely effective, flexible, and symbiotic system.

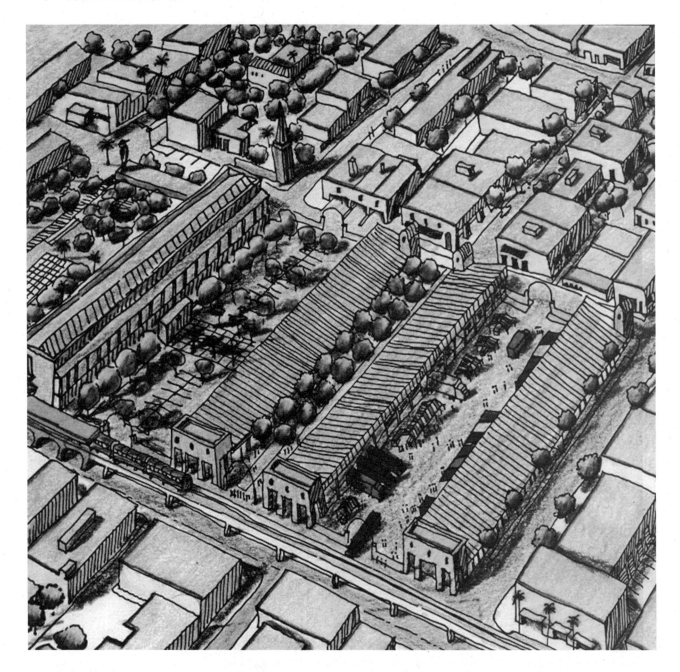

The character of a place is greatly increased by retrofitting existing structures for reuse and community pride. Funding infill and brownfield sites is a local and national opportunity.

Layering is the most effective way of dealing with diurnal and seasonal changes in weather conditions. Can buildings have skins rather than envelopes and can they be dynamically layered to suit changing conditions?

Consider the forces on a wall: contraction, expansion, heat, cold, moisture, rain, sleet, snow, wind, ultraviolet light, humidity, sunlight—they are benign to the structure at certain times, sometimes helpful, and detrimental at others. If one material is chosen to do it all, that material also excludes the desired to keep out the undesired. The function of conditioning the air has become to keep everything out that is out and everything in that is in, and then ventilate just enough to keep the air quality within the OK range.

For example, if a wall is required to isolate the outside temperature from the inside temperature and humidity, it must be insulated to stop the flow of energy (temperature variation) from moving inside to outside, or vice versa. The penguin uses this layered method and survives quite well in temperatures from minus 40 to plus 40 degrees Celsius. The layered method also suggests the interior surface be a renewable/reusable material that reflects light and sound, and carry the desired aesthetic. It should not be drywall or plaster or other single-use material.

The most powerful climatic events of regions—such as hurricanes, rainstorms, temperature swings, and tornadoes—are often not used as design criteria, just as engineering criteria. Yet these reoccurring disasters are normal conditions of the coastal region and are, consequently, important to the sustainable design solution as 90 percent of the population lives within 10 miles of the coast.

The art of architectural planning has always had as its goal the combining of the aesthetic and the functional. Architectural form today can be directed to provide protection from natural disasters while providing for better, energy-efficient structures and communities.

Evolving a Sustainable Design Practice

- Become ecologically literate by gaining a working conceptual knowledge of biology, ecology, and the earth sciences that is locally and regionally specific to the project site.
- Evolve your professional practice to incorporate ecological literacy and pursue at least one sustainable design project.
- Select a staff member dedicated to sustainability issues.
- Address economic, community, and environmental issues simultaneously while designing.
- Develop feedback loops to your own projects—learn and grow knowledge with each project.
- Establish a *best resources list* for research on sustainable materials and methods of construction.
- Evolve sustainable issues into your project specifications.

Information that guides the architectural design practice is extremely dynamic. With hundreds of new materials presented each week, it is little wonder that designers are often overwhelmed with data. Practicing sustainable design adds still another layer, and the information is growing rapidly. Fortunately, Web sites can supply constant updates, and any office can create their own favorites and even add them as an addition to home pages.

The foundation for creating a personal office database for sustainable design can start with the following example acting as a foundation. This example suggests the layout of the information following the "AIA B141 Owner / Architect Contract" document outline. The categories are arranged in a manner that will allow the user to move through the information in a logical and seamless manner that conforms to the AIA contract criteria between owner and architect. The designer should research

Web sites and references and filter them to give the most direct and informative result for the type of work. Keeping up with this trail of information proves to be a daunting task, but over time it becomes an effective method of research that is easily updated, cross-referenced, and hyperlinked. The most successful searches are those that begin with a list of links obtained from a recognized Web site or from works cited at the end of a periodical or book pertinent to the project type. Regular visits to these sites for updated links and other information will produce the most successful dynamic knowledge base.

Environmentally responsive sites that contain good information explained in a simplified manner are more valuable than having a large number of nondescriptive sites. For example, EBN (Environmental Building News, www.buildinggreen.com) has a simple and well-defined search engine based on CSI, Sweets, and basic consumer subjects. This information is constantly updated by research that is not ethically conflicted by the presence of trade groups provided funding.

An additional suggestion in creating an office database is to keep it simple: for example, find 3 materials that solve your problem rather than 30. This list can grow with each project and your experience, but it is not necessary or possible to find *the* answer, as that point is constantly changing.

Sustainable Design and Existing Buildings

Existing buildings, communities, towns, and regions are a considerable challenge to sustainability. Virtually all of the built structures in the world need considerable design renovation work to make them approach sustainability or even be marginally energy efficient. In each existing structure, there is an opportunity to introduce sustainable design principles, and in so doing, accomplish the following:

- Introduce natural ventilation and daylighting.
- Eliminate consumption of nonrenewables.
- Provide a healthier, more participatory environment for users.
- Redesign so existing structure can function unplugged.

In September 2003, the AIA Committee on the Environment (COTE) hosted an intensive sustainable-design charrette. The meeting evaluated the AIA headquarters building in Washington, D.C., developing a range of short- and long-term strategies that would ideally integrate green design while improving the community link and economic opportunities. These strategies were developed for consideration by the AIA Board of Directors, and greening the AIA Headquarters became an AIA150 project.

The AIA leadership recognizes the importance of sustainability in "the culture of innovation" that underpins its mission. In his introductory remarks to the team, Chief Executive Officer Norman Koonce, FAIA, articulated the visibility and profile of the AIA headquarters building to the nation. Enhancements to the facility can embody the "AIA's commitment to history, while addressing the economic, environmental, and social opportunities that define sustainable development."

The AIA headquarters building shows the challenge of adapting existing architecture to sustainable principles. The redesign of the national and international stock of existing buildings is by far the greatest opportunity for carbon reduction and retrofitting for sustainability.

A multidisciplinary charrette is an effective way of establishing goals and next steps for retrofitting for sustainability.

The discovery of unused space—the roof of the AIA headquarters—leads to opportunities for additional uses and recovery of urban stormwater for irrigation.

The opportunity to green the AIA headquarters has many multiplier effects:

- It enriches the urban and community pattern, making connection to the larger system.
- It creates business opportunities and revenue-generation sources.
- Buildings can be rejuvenated with "good bones" that exemplify historic stewardship and reinforce the urban street.
- The environmental quality and energy savings can be improved.
- Employee health, productivity, and retention can be increased.
- There is support for the creative nature of collaborative work.

Projects with the greatest promise for enhancing community and revenue potential are outlined as follows:

- Create an environmentally rich conference center where the building will *teach*.
- Link the AIA into the green processional spaces of the city.
- Improve the plaza to create a new front door to the Institute and incorporate natural light for underground spaces, increasing usable and rentable space.
- Create a high-performance and collaborative work environment for staff.
- Develop roof and plaza spaces to include a living roof, photovoltaic cells, and an architects café.
- Incorporate smart and green infrastructure, such as improving free cooling and ventilation opportunities.
- Develop green operations and maintenance protocols.

These initiatives build on previous studies and ongoing improvements to a building that continues to be a source of pride to AIA members everywhere and a representation of the value of design to the world at large.

Summary of Opportunities for AIA Headquarters

Passive Opportunities

- Create an environmentally rich conference center building that teaches.
- Promote smart and green infrastructure.
- Improve free-cooling opportunities.
- Showcase green technologies.
- Integrate daylighting.
- Use green materials.
- Incorporate innovative and efficient water-plumbing strategies.
- Use living roof on boardroom.
- Link the AIA to the green processional spaces of the city.
- Link into the Michael Van Valkenburgh plan for Pennsylvania Avenue.
- Create native perennial landscape in front of the Octagon Museum.
- Enhance street tree-planting areas and utilize for stormwater management.
- Create a connection to the National Park along E Street through coordinated landscape and paving design.
- Explore opportunities to partner with the National Park Service to develop educational exhibits about architecture and the environment in the park along E Street.
- Improve the plaza to create a new front door for Institute headquarters and to draw the public in to experience the gallery, bookstore, library, and the historic Octagon.
- Enliven the plaza space with furniture, displays, environmental art, and a new café in the Pump House.
- Enhance garden areas with native plantings, integrated stormwater management, and water features that celebrate rainwater collection.
- Integrate plaza skylights to daylight the lower level of the building.
- Develop a collaborative, high-performance work environment for staff.
- Develop new collaboration spaces with indoor and outdoor space.
- Improve the visual environment with integrated daylighting and task and ambient electric lighting.
- Create test bed for window-wall innovations in two orientations.
- Light shelves for enhanced daylight distribution.
- Develop *roofscape* with a living roof, photovoltaic array, and a new architects café.
- Use architects café to enhance conference center.
- Develop living roof for stormwater management and rainwater harvesting.

- Solve "1,000 points of energy drain."
- Develop a protocol for green operations, cleaning, and maintenance.
- Make the comprehensive recycling and composting program more visible.
- Provide visible recycling containers.
- Establish a policy for construction waste.
- Develop a travel and greening of conference venues policy.
- Provide educational information and display sustainable strategies.

Active Opportunities

- Increase marketability through enhanced flexibility, collaboration opportunities, and improved comfort in existing meeting rooms.
- Develop additional indoor-outdoor collaborative conference spaces on roof and in library.
- Use high-performance lighting and controls and LEC and LED (light-emitting diode) exit lighting.
- Integrate photovoltaic powered night-lighting strategy for public areas to enhance image, reduce energy usage, and create a public education opportunity.
- Incorporate a high-performance building envelope to eliminate the need for perimeter fan coils.
- Use a demonstration-scale photovoltaic array as part of the concept of letting the *building act as a teacher*.
- Enhance dehumidification.
- Enhance HVAC controls to improve comfort control and energy effectiveness.
- Optimize boiler efficiency.

The AIA headquarters can be a national example, helping to develop principles that architects can use for retrofitting buildings internationally. Through this greening of the AIA headquarters charrette and the subsequent actions that will improve the headquarters facility, the AIA will demonstrate the value of design and the role of the architect in making positive change in their communities, while developing a process that can be used by architects to help them green the existing buildings of their clients.

"You must be the change you wish to see in the world."
MAHATMA GANDHI

Design Team

Chair, Daniel Williams, FAIA

Vice Chair, Mark Rylander, AIA

Joyce Lee, AIA

Vivian Loftness, FAIA

Sandy Mendler, AIA

Don Nall, AIA

John McRae, FAIA

Although the headquarters is not a truly historic building, it is an example of the opportunity for existing and historic buildings to be used to study the *long-life, loose fit* aspect of sustainable design while analyzing energy consumption reduction as a step toward being unplugged. These buildings also exhibit an enduring connection to the community's view of itself.

Sustainable Interior Architecture

Although interior designers have been at the forefront of green materials and indoor air-quality standards, the place-based aspects, specifically integrating sustainable energy and orientation, have been missing. Interior design traditionally has been design of the interior realm of an existing space within a building or of a building under construction. As in architectural design, the opportunity to connect to sustainable energies has not been addressed. With little or no regard to the orientation and location of the functions within the space, the relationship to other spaces within the same building, or the impacts from neighboring buildings, the opportunity for the space to function sustainably is lost.

An important opportunity lies in analyzing the space and functional components as they relate to the solar and exterior conditions and available sustainable resources (e.g., light, heat, and ventilation). Orientation of the functional design layout to solar- and exterior-based elements (e.g., reflectance off other buildings, view corridors, prevailing breezes, solar-heat gain, and daylighting) can have positive impacts on user performance and well-being while reducing or eliminating use of nonrenewables.

As in sustainable architectural design, interior architecture that addresses the natural context of the project site has an opportunity to improve sustainability for the user. To this end a project was given to a second-year design class at Cornish School of the Arts in Seattle, Washington. The project program was to design a personal live-work studio. The site was their classroom, where they had already spent the better part of four months. The program was set up to learn the relationship between solar energy (light and heat) and the functional needs of the design program—a space for study, sculpture, computer-aided-design (CAD) work, food preparation, eating, sleeping, and entertaining.

The challenge was to understand the relationship between orientation and location of the functions within the space and to design using dynamic solar angles to determine the location of specific functions that had special relationships to light, glare, heat, and seasonal changes. The program challenged the students to decide—with the given orientation to the sun at the equinoxes and at summer and winter solstice—what is the best location for the elements of the design program:

1. A sculpture workspace
2. A computer
3. A dining room
4. A bedroom

The students were to analyze and diagram how the spatial requirement would be impacted by the changing solar incidence and adapt their designs to those solar

Like all design, interior architecture has an opportunity to be connected to natural energies. Using daylight, light shelves, orientation, and location of functions specific to solar access and natural-ventilation opportunities is critical to the programming and location of spaces. The challenge here was to bounce in enough natural light—all year— to read at any point in the room and make that free light available through the extreme seasonal changes in sunlight and reflectance.

changes in the summer and winter. The spaces were to be 100 percent daylighted, and the students had to work out how enough light for reading and sketching would get back into the space 30 feet from the windows.

They had to address the following challenges:

- Bouncing, enhancing, and/or filtering the natural light to a usable light level throughout the space and to every function
- Letting in light without heat
- Letting in heat without light
- Achieving functional layouts that respond to specific user needs (i.e., elimination of glare on monitors, wake-up natural light, use of light bounced from the outside surfaces)
- Researching water use and reuse
- Researching green materials usage
- Modulation of building materials, anchoring systems and components to enable reuse of all building materials
- Analyze how the space can function without using nonrenewables (function unplugged)

Through this assignment, the students were able to recognize the importance of integrating site design analysis into interior architectural programming and design and expand their knowledge of problem solving to include energy efficiency and passive interior architecture.

PART TWO

CHAPTER SIX

The AIA/COTE Top Ten Green Projects Program

In 1997 American Institute of Architects Committee on the Environment (AIA/ COTE) instituted the AIA/COTE Top Ten Green Projects program, in partnership with the U.S. Department of Energy, in 1997 to recognize and commend the best exemplars of green and sustainable design. The AIA/COTE announces the winners annually on Earth Day, and recognizes the projects and the architects annually at the AIA National Convention and Expo. To learn more about the awards program, visit http://www.aiatopten.org or http://www.aia.org/cote.

The winning projects address significant environmental challenges with designs that integrate architecture, technology, and natural systems. They provide positive contributions to their communities, improve comfort for building occupants, and reduce environmental impacts through strategies such as reuse of existing structures, connection to transit systems, low-impact site development, energy and water conservation, use of green construction materials, and design that improves indoor air quality.

The range of building types and sizes of projects among the submissions to the Top Ten program in the past decade have varied greatly. Architects and other design professionals are beginning to address sustainability in increasingly sophisticated and effective design solutions. Whether reducing greenhouse gas emissions to mitigate climate change, reducing peak energy loads to lessen demand on the power grid, using stormwater on site to eliminate runoff, conserving building water, or preserving wetlands, these buildings also promise to enhance the level of comfort and amenity for the people who inhabit them.

Chairs of AIA/COTE

1990	Bob Berkebile, FAIA
1993	Kirk Gastinger, FAIA
1994	Greg Franta, FAIA
1995	Harry Gordon, FAIA
1996	Donald Watson, FAIA
1997–98	Gail Lindsey, FAIA
1999	Muscoe Martin, AIA
2000–01	Sandra Mendler
2002	Joyce Lee, AIA
2003	Daniel Williams, FAIA
2004	Mark Rylander, AIA
2005	Vivian Loftness, FAIA
2006	James Binkley, FAIA
2007	Kira Gould, Assoc. AIA

This portion of the book, developed in cooperation with the AIA, presents the winners from the program's inception through 2006 in chronological order. The summaries of the projects either are based on interviews with the architects (particularly those that note Lessons Learned by the Architects) or have been adapted with permission from the AIA's project descriptions, with additional research.

1997 AIA/COTE Top Ten Green Projects

Body Shop, U.S. Headquarters, Wake Forest, North Carolina

Center for Regenerative Studies, Pomona, California

Durant Road Middle School, Raleigh, North Carolina

Herman Miller "Greenhouse" Factory and Offices, Holland, Michigan

National Public Radio Headquarters, Washington, D.C.

Natural Resources Defense Council Headquarters, New York City

New Canaan Nature Center Horticultural Education Center, New Canaan, Connecticut

Prince Street Technologies, Cartersville, Georgia

Way Station, Frederick, Maryland

Women's Humane Society Animal Shelter, Bensalem, Pennsylvania

At Body Shop's U.S. Headquarters by Design Harmony, the entry features indigenous vegetation and solar-based orientation.

The interior of Body Shop's U.S. Headquarters provides simple, flexible space with natural light and ventilation.

Herman Miller "Greenhouse" Factory & Offices was designed by William McDonough + Partners to consider the health of the workers inside as well as the integration of the building into the landscape.

The Natural Resources Defense Council Headquarters (NRDC), completed in 1988 by Croxton Collaborative Architects, stands today as the seminal project that turned the tide toward green architecture in America by addressing the full ecology of the building: light, air, energy, and human health and well-being.

Sustainable design goals and the selection of resource-efficient building systems and materials were encouraged for the National Public Radio (NPR) building, provided that these features contributed to a healthy, productive working environment, and did not significantly add cost.

The NPR Headquarters by Burt Hill required major renovation of a 25-year-old former commercial office building.

The Way Station, located in the heart of the Frederick Historic District, was designed by The ENSAR Group, Inc., to complement the neighborhood. It is organized around a central light court with a large garden where the primary building circulation occurs.

1997 AIA/COTE Top Ten Winner
CENTER FOR REGENERATIVE STUDIES
Location: Pomona, California
Architect: Dougherty + Dougherty

This project originated as a multidisciplinary graduate student environmental design project and was then brought to reality through a series of private grants. The team leader was the late John T. Lyle, who was a fellow of ASLA and a professor at the Center for Regenerative Studies. The project has been renamed in his memory. The client representative was Marvin Malecha, FAIA, who was then dean of the College of Environmental Design at California State Polytechnic University, Pomona.

The mission of ecological regeneration was integrated into the planning and design of the Center for Regenerative Studies.

Building Performance, According to the Architects

Regenerative Studies is home to an environmental program of study at the university that is faculty- and student-driven. The site is subject to heavy use, and this was initially a concern to university trustees. They predicted a slowly deteriorating site, with mosquitoes in the aquaculture ponds and unkempt grounds. The reverse has been true. There is a distinct sense of place, opportunity, and community at the center. Students and faculty are using every available approach to explore alternative solutions to environmental problems. Many students are inspired to study ways to design and construct such projects as solar panels, solar ovens, composters, and irrigation systems and to conduct agricultural experiments. In this way, the environmental performance has been enhanced, just as it was envisioned. This project has taken on a life of its own, and it continues to evolve as an academic setting for environmental research.

1997 AIA/COTE Top Ten Winner
DURANT ROAD MIDDLE SCHOOL
LOCATION: Raleigh, North Carolina
ARCHITECT: Innovative Design

At the time this school was designed, the firm had specialized in energy design and had experienced considerable success with daylit schools in the adjacent county.

Durant Road Middle School is the first school in the county to comply with ASHRAE's 15 cubic feet per minute (cfm) per-person guideline.

Daylight illuminates the gym during the day.

Their energy performance, as well as the indoor environment, was excellent, and the schools were used as a regional benchmark. This was a major factor in Wake County Schools' decision to hire the architectural firm. Client and architects adopted the then-current version of North Carolina's High Performance Guidelines (very similar to Leadership in Energy and Environmental Design, or LEED, but with more state-appropriate variations).

Building Performance, According to the Architects

Durant Middle School was completed in 1995 for use as a year-round school (with the resulting increase in energy and operating requirements). It was the first school in the county to comply with ASHRAE's 15 cubic feet per minute (cfm) per-person guideline. In 1995 the school consumed $0.84 per square foot per year in energy bills. This compared at that time to $1.34 per square foot for the typical year-round school in this area of North Carolina that also complies with the 15 cfm ASHRAE standard. Since that time, a considerable number of mobile classrooms have been added to the campus, and Sunday church services within the school have increased; but the energy costs, excluding the mobiles, have been maintained and actually have improved, ranging from 10 percent below the first-year (1995) usage to $0.73 (2003–2004). Performance in some classrooms has been reduced due to lack of maintenance and lack of use of the operable shades in those classrooms. Such maintenance details and staff operational practices have to be continually addressed.

1997 AIA/COTE Top Ten Winner
NEW CANAAN NATURE CENTER HORTICULTURAL EDUCATION CENTER
LOCATION: New Canaan, Connecticut
ARCHITECTS: Donald Watson, FAIA, and Buchanan Associates Architects, in joint venture

In 1981, when the program was formulated, the client established that the building should be a prototype to demonstrate and promote energy-efficient greenhouse design, and it would be combined with classrooms and offices. The program and design concepts were subject to extensive research, including a survey of similar projects internationally, computer and daylight modeling, and consultations with experts in mechanical systems, construction, and horticulture. One of the early green demonstration projects of the 1980s, the project received numerous awards for design and energy innovation. For more information about the center, visit its Web site at http://www.newcanaannature.org.

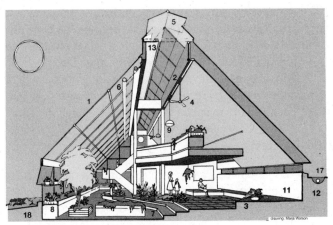

Energy design techniques

1 South-facing greenhouse
2 Solar collectors
3 Thermal storage elements
4 Ceiling fans
5 Roof monitor
6 Operable sun-shade
7 Earth-contact floor
8 Root-bed heating
9 Grow-lights
10 Composting bins
11 Wood stove w/ heat recovery
12 Well-insulated structure
13 Operable insulating curtain
14 Automatic temperature controls
15 Energy-efficient lighting
16 Water-saving plumbing
17 Roof-water collection
18 Earth-berms

Design goals   HELPS PLANTS TO GROW
USES SOLAR HEATING (winter)
USES NATURAL COOLING (summer)
USES NATURAL LIGHTING
SAVES NON-RENEWABLE RESOURCES

drawing: Maria Watson

New Canaan Nature Center Horticultural Education Center

The program and design concepts of the New Canaan Nature Center Horticultural Education Center were subject to extensive research, including a survey of similar projects internationally, computer and daylight modeling, and consultations with experts in mechanical systems, construction, and horticulture.

The passive aspects of the design (i.e., thermal mass and earth berms) have proven both economical and durable in the New Canaan Building.

Building Performance, According to the Architects

Completed in 1983, the project has been in operation for more than 25 years. Energy consumption was documented for several years, and revealed that actual utilization exceeded the energy reduction anticipated by computer simulations. The building has been evaluated in a series of postoccupancy studies, at two, five, and ten years after inauguration. These evaluations offered a number of lessons. Some features originally installed for energy conservation are no longer operated: for example, a solar hot-water system installed in 1983 was little used and has been disconnected; a large, insulating shade (70 ft. long × 40 ft. high) originally installed to operate automatically now runs by operator switch controls. Other features have proven durable. One of the innovations used was *root-bed heating;* innovative at the time, it now has been adopted widely in greenhouses in the northeastern United States as an energy-efficient technique to maintain healthy planting environments.

Lessons Learned by the Architects

- The building circulation is designed as a visitor tour, with movement through the building providing sequential openings and views, as in a forest. Interactive exhibits that explained the energy features of the design were innovative at the time of the building's opening. These were removed after a decade to make room for gardening programs.

- The nonmoving aspects of the design (i.e., passive design, thermal mass, and earth berms) have proven both economical and durable. The moving parts, such as the insulating shade, have proven to be a challenge. The long-term lesson is "Keep It (Very) Simple."

- Our firm adopted solar energy and environmental design as a primary focus of a teaching and research-based practice beginning in the mid-1960s. We continue this focus still. Great emphasis is given to the programming and preschematic phases, in establishing parameters of performance and reducing liability and costs, seeking double- and triple-use opportunities and natural fit with the given climate and context. In this project, the large greenhouse is essentially a multiuse atrium space for plants and people, serving as a horticultural greenhouse, a reception area for events, a place for exhibits, a garden gift shop, and an educational classroom.

- Design architect of the project, Donald Watson, FAIA, sums up lessons as: "Delve diligently into all design options. Test carefully, and adopt new approaches with vigilance. Seek advice from a wide range of experts. Be ever patient with the client. Use the process to educate yourself and others. Follow up with [a] thorough evaluation. Be honest about mistakes and lessons learned. Be modest before the complexity and wonder of nature."

1997 AIA/COTE Top Ten Winner
PRINCE STREET TECHNOLOGIES
LOCATION: Cartersville, Georgia
ARCHITECT: Thompson, Ventulett, Stainback & Associates

The architects' approach to design draws from the client's needs as well as an understanding of site opportunities and constraints, in addition to budget and time considerations. The client is an innovative manufacturer of high-end custom carpet. To select an architect, it sponsored a design competition for its new corporate office, showroom, and manufacturing facility. The client established that the new facility

Activity is shared visually at Prince Street Technologies through the generous use of glass, from the plant, design studio, offices, and conference rooms to showrooms on the outside radius.

The Prince Street Technologies facility provides a work environment that conveys a sense of family and emphasizes teamwork. It is a marketing tool for its products, while reflecting the client's commitment to the environment.

should provide a work environment that conveyed a sense of family and emphasized teamwork; be a marketing tool for its products; and reflect the client's commitment to the environment.

To facilitate the close sense of family and teamwork that employees of Prince Street shared, the design incorporates open architecture to accomplish the client's goal of "flattening" any perception of corporate hierarchy. Activity is shared visually, through the generous use of glass, from the plant, design studio, offices, and conference rooms to showrooms on the outside radius. The primary visitor to this facility is the design community. The design solution was to create a framework for tours that tell the story of the product and the company, which includes an environmental message. Many aspects combine to optimize energy efficiency and the health and well-being of employees and to respect the natural environment. Daylighting is prevalent, sun shading reduces heat gain, and air ducts are built into precast concrete floor panels for maximum energy efficiency. Other environmental concerns are addressed by the use of low-maintenance landscape and simple building materials that are underfinished.

Building Performance, According to the Architects

The facility was used less than five years. After only a couple of those years, Prince Street combined its broadloom-manufacturing processes with Bentley, the company's other top-tier carpet line. All of the production was moved to an existing Bentley facility in California.

1997 AIA/COTE Top Ten Winner
WOMEN'S HUMANE SOCIETY ANIMAL SHELTER
LOCATION: Bensalem, Pennsylvania
ARCHITECT: Susan Maxman & Partners, Architects

This was the first sustainable project that Susan Maxman & Partners, Architects undertook, and the client was new to sustainable design when they started the project. In the early stages of the project, Maxman met Amory Lovins and decided to undertake an energy-efficient, green building. Maxman convinced the client, who agreed to pay an additional fee to simulate the performance of the design and deter-

The energy performance of the Women's Humane Society Animal Shelter has been tracked, and its performance is better than was anticipated in the computer modeling.

mine energy-efficient strategies for it. When it came to budget cutting, the client did not eliminate any of the energy-saving strategies.

1998 AIA/COTE Top Ten Green Projects

Cambridge Cohousing, Cambridge, Massachusetts
Energy Resource Center, Downey, California
Environmental Showcase Home, Phoenix, Arizona
Florida House Learning Center, Sarasota, Florida
Interface Ray C. Anderson Plant, La Grange, Georgia
Patagonia Distribution Center, Reno, Nevada
Ridgehaven Green Demonstration Project, San Diego, California
SC Johnson Wax Commercial Products Headquarters, Racine, Wisconsin
Thoreau Center for Sustainability, San Francisco, California
Wal-Mart Environmental Demonstration Store, City of Industry, California

Cambridge Cohousing by The Green Village Co.represents an innovative and promising model of collaboration for community residents and green-thinking professionals.

The overall environmental achievements at Cambridge Cohousing are a good precedent for multifamily housing.

The Energy Resource Center by WLC Architects acts as a showcase building, integrating not only top-quality energy strategies but also environmental material choices and indoor environmental quality elements.

Energy efficiency, indoor air quality, and resource conservation were all key goals in the design of the Energy Resource Center.

Environmental Showcase Home by Jones Studio was designed to introduce a full range of environmentally responsible design ideas, systems, and products to mass-market production housing builders.

At the Environmental Showcase Home, water conservation, waste reduction, and the evaluation of materials through a life-cycle assessment were integrated into the design solution.

A unique aspect of the Patagonia Distribution Center by The Miller\Hull Partnership was Patagonia's environmental philosophy and corporate culture, and the connection between its products and the environment.

Interface's Ray C. Anderson Plant, a manufacturing plant and customer center for the carpet manufacturer, was designed by Thompson, Ventulet, Stainback & Associates.

The SC Johnson Wax Commercial Products building designed by Zimmerman Design Group and Hellmuth Obata + Kassabaum (HOK) serves as a benchmark for environmentally responsible design and construction.

The challenge for HOK was to create the most advanced, environmentally responsible building possible without adding to the overall cost.

1998 AIA/COTE Top Ten Winner
FLORIDA HOUSE LEARNING CENTER
LOCATION: Sarasota, Florida
ARCHITECT: Osborn Sharp Associates

The primary goal was to create a *state of the shelf* demonstration of sustainable design and development. The firm wanted the public to adopt the thinking and to take action by using the right design and by making the right purchases. The architect was also the president of the nonprofit learning center. This helped to simplify the communication and decision making. The firm used a collaborative process between all professionals and stakeholders.

The design process had to be more collaborative with the required integration of the building systems. The firm developed a *taxonomy of system layers* to integrate whole-system thinking into the process, termed "natural, built, economic, and social layers." The firm uses the LEED (Leadership in Energy and Environmental Design) and the Florida Green-Building systems as metrics. More importantly, however, they use them to involve, communicate with, and educate the client.

Building Performance, According to the Architects

This project is unique as a public and private partnership for a sustainable model home and yard for the public to visit. The public may also attend classes on how to make their lifestyle in Florida more sustainable.

Florida House Learning Center is unique as a public and private partnership for a sustainable model home and yard for the public to visit.

The firm uses the LEED (Leadership in Energy and Environmental Design) and the Florida Green-Building systems as metrics in the Florida House Learning Center.

We have remodeled the finish materials and landscaping, adding storm shutters as well. The building is doing better than expected and has been improved over the years through upgrades. A public and private volunteer advisory board maintains the demonstration home and yard and keeps the curriculum up to date. More than 10,000 people visit each year, verifying the strong demand for credible information on sustainable designs of homes and yards.

The firm also learned the importance of educating everyone involved in the construction process on the different sustainability goals. The contractors, their subcontractors, the subcontractors' employees, and down the line, all need to know what must be done and avoided to accomplish a sustainable design.

Lessons Learned by the Architects

We have learned that there is a new language of sustainable design and construction, that an integrative design process takes much more time and fees, and that there will be hurdles in local codes and construction practices to overcome.

We incorporate sustainable issues into our entire project specifications by using (1) a separate specification document that addresses only the sustainable-design issues and (2) separate notes and notices on our plans. We rely on our consultants for the specialized information.

Furthermore, we would also

- Expand the design-charrette process to aid in the discovery of auxiliary community needs and stakeholders for a center of this type
- Build in more hurricane resistance and technology
- Add more photovoltaic solar cells
- Add more offices and meeting rooms or classrooms for a center of this type
- Incorporate and feature more varied glass types and window technology, especially the use of "second-surface" low-E glass for Florida's climate

1998 AIA/COTE Top Ten Winner
RIDGEHAVEN GREEN DEMONSTRATION PROJECT
LOCATION: San Diego, California
ARCHITECT: Platt/Whitelaw Architects

Building Performance, According to the Architects

The project was originally designed as a green demonstration project. The city of San Diego has continued to add demonstration elements such as leaf composting, photovoltaics, and recharging stations. The building has exceeded expectations for a number of reasons: extensive commissioning allowed the building to exceed the design energy-efficiency goals. Responsible maintenance and operations by the city (based on a green-maintenance manual provided by the design team) has resulted in maintaining the interior environmental quality.

The client (the director of the city's environmental services department) and his team were visionary in creating a green demonstration project. An integrated design team was assembled that included members of the local utility company as well as experts in energy efficiency and sustainable design. Charrettes were used to pursue a process of visioning as well as detailed modeling and cost analysis. The client never lost sight of the overall vision throughout the process, even during periods when the budget and schedule were severely challenged.

Lessons Learned by the Architects

The project was an adaptive reuse of an existing building. The budget was extremely limited. Priorities were set based on payback benefits. Certain envelope improvements were excluded from the project due to longer payback benefits. Since the existing building has limited floor-to-floor heights, underfloor distribution was not feasible, but subsequent work we have done with wind scoops and vertical ducting, down to displacement ventilation outlets, has shown promising application for buildings with large floor plates such as this.

Working through a charrette process with an integrated client and design team was a stimulating, successful process that we try to apply on other projects. We learned the true value of energy modeling as a design tool. As a result, we introduced the resources and ability to model energy performance into our practice; although we usually still use consultants for this task, we are able to better understand and challenge that process. The awareness we gained of the impact of the built environment on human health and performance has become an integral part of our firm's design philosophy. This brings with it the responsibility to keep expanding our knowledge base. We have developed the appropriate resources in the office and have "greened" our office operation. An understanding of and commitment to sustainable design is an important criterion in the selection of new staff members.

We use the LEED system as a design tool, because it is a useful, comprehensive checklist. Like any other tool, it is only as good as the user's ability to apply it. We have several LEED-accredited professionals on staff; the training is one important component in developing a full understanding of the practice of sustainable design. We do maintain a healthy skepticism of the LEED (and any other) rating system, since its blind application (shopping for points) can be detrimental.

1998 AIA/COTE Top Ten Winner
THOREAU CENTER FOR SUSTAINABILITY
LOCATION: San Francisco, California
ARCHITECT: Tanner Leddy Maytum Stacy

The client was critical to the vision and success of the Thoreau Center. The client team and the design team shared the same goal—to make the Thoreau Center a model for practical integration of a sustainable building within the context of a national historic landmark. The client was involved in the design decisions and sup-

Thoreau Center for Sustainability is a model for the practical integration of sustainable building principles into the context of a national historic landmark.

ported the entire project process. The firm has continued its relationship with the client team and has completed several other projects with them.

The firm currently uses the LEED-rating system, with one gold-rated project complete and several others in the works. Having LEED-accredited professionals on staff is very important and encourages other staff members to become accredited.

Building Performance, According to the Architects

The Thoreau Center has been very successful on a number of levels. The project has continued to be a model for sustainable design within the context of historic preservation. The methods and materials selected ten years ago still perform very well; they have been easy to maintain and operate; and they still look great. The other aspect of the design and original concept of the project was to create a community of nonprofit organizations to share the buildings and share resources. This has been extremely successful. More than 50 nonprofit organizations are now located in the Thoreau Center, with a public gallery, shared conference center, and a lively café where the community comes together.

Lessons Learned by the Architects

The design team learned many lessons from this project in the design, documentation, and construction process. An inclusive process, with the client group and reviewing agencies, was critical to the success of the project. The importance of product research in materials selection and the incorporation of sustainable-building requirements into the project specifications were also critical to the construction process. Finally, incorporation of operation and maintenance procedures and tenant standards was vital to the ongoing success of the Thoreau Center over the last ten years. The lessons learned from this project have been incorporated into the firm's office practice and into our projects over the last ten years.

1999 AIA/COTE Top Ten Green Projects

CCI Center, Pittsburgh, Pennsylvania

Denver Drygoods, Denver, Colorado

Duracell Headquarters, Bethel, Connecticut

Georgia Institute of Technology Olympic Aquatic Center, Atlanta, Georgia

Kansas City Zoo Deramus Pavilion, Kansas City, Missouri

Malvern Elementary School, McKinney, Texas

Missouri Historical Society Museum, St. Louis, Missouri

New York Life Building, Kansas City, Missouri

Real Goods Solar Living Center, Hopland, California

REI Seattle, Seattle, Washington

1999 AIA/COTE Top Ten Winner
CCI CENTER
LOCATION: Pittsburgh, Pennsylvania
ARCHITECT: Tai + Lee Architects

Building Performance, According to the Architects

Successes of the building with respect to initial goals include the following:

- The green building design reinforces the organizational mission.
- The building design combines renovation and new construction in an urban office building for green organizations.
- Project uses salvaged materials extensively.
- The project building is a model of energy- and resource-efficient design.

The design of Malvern Elementary School by SHW Group, Inc. illustrates multiple elements for a pilot sustainable school.

Simple industrial components for the Malvern Elementary School helped to create a fit with the fabric of the community.

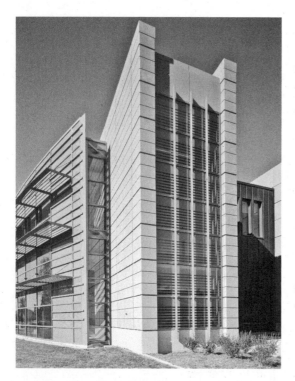

The Missouri Historical Society Museum expansion by Hellmuth Obata + Kassabaum (HOK) preserves the integrity of the historic structure, while substantially increasing the exhibition area.

High ceilings and contiguous open space accommodate a variety of exhibition and artifact configurations in the Missouri Historical Society Museum.

Center for Regenerative Studies. *Architecture as teacher. This design explores alternative solutions to environmental problems. Students are inspired to study ways to design and construct such projects as solar panels, solar ovens, composters, and irrigation systems, and to conduct agricultural experiments.* From Milroy McAleer Photographers.

Women's Humane Society Animal Shelter. *In the early stages of the project, Amory Lovins was consulted, which led to undertaking an energy-efficient, green building and a simulation to determine energy-efficient strategies.* From Catherine Tighe.

Interface Ray C. Anderson Plant.
Sustainability has become an important consideration in every business decision at Interface, a floor-covering manufacturer based in Georgia.. Photo by Brian Glassel/TVS.

Thoreau Center for Sustainability. *The Thoreau Center is a model illustrating the practical integration of sustainable design within the context of a national historic landmark.* Copyright Richard Barnes Photography.

Kansas City Zoo Deramus Pavilion. *This design supports and symbolizes the mission of the zoo and exemplifies a sustainable design for a civic structure. This design clearly expresses the aesthetic of natural materials and use of daylighting. It is constructed from salvaged or sustainably managed wood and got its design clues from the ecological site planning process.* Copyright 1998 Mike Sinclair.

New York Life Building (right). Under the long-life loose-fit sustainable design challenge, this design combines historic preservation and environmentally sensitive design. The design takes advantage of inherent green qualities of the original nineteenth-century building (infill, daylighting, natural ventilation, and long-lasting materials). *Copyright 1997 Mike Sinclair.*

REI Seattle Flagship. Coop members were polled for their environmental priorities, which were used as design criteria. The project balances environmental and cost accountability with retailing needs. Energy efficiency, use of resource-efficient materials and recycled-content materials, and the recycling and reuse of construction and demolition waste were central to this design solution. *Copyright Robert Pisano.*

Bainbridge Island City Hall. Recycled content and reused materials are integrated throughout the design as a public message. The city's stormwater management system was significantly upgraded as part of site preparation. Daylighting, optimized natural ventilation, and nontoxic finishes provide a healthier and safer indoor environment. *Copyright Art Grice Photography.*

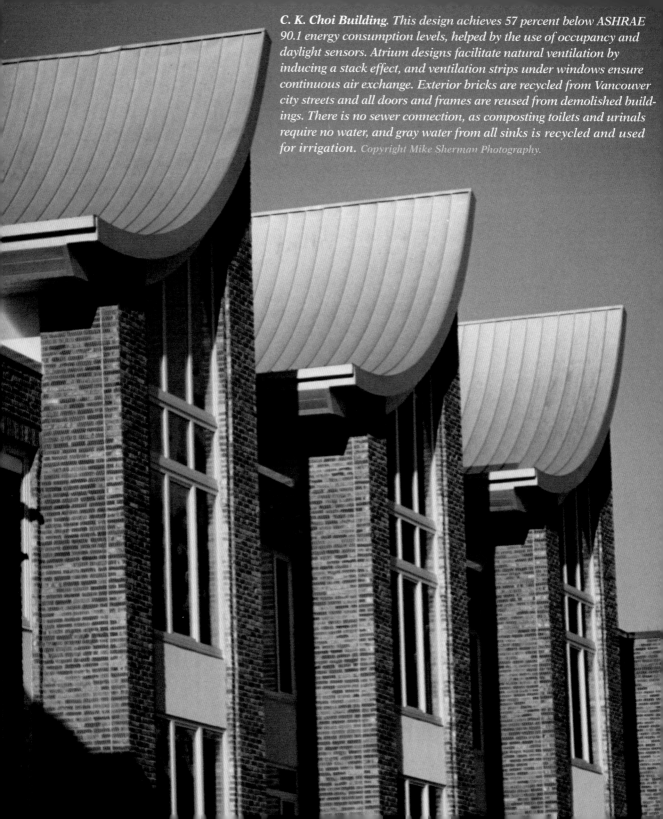

C. K. Choi Building. *This design achieves 57 percent below ASHRAE 90.1 energy consumption levels, helped by the use of occupancy and daylight sensors. Atrium designs facilitate natural ventilation by inducing a stack effect, and ventilation strips under windows ensure continuous air exchange. Exterior bricks are recycled from Vancouver city streets and all doors and frames are reused from demolished buildings. There is no sewer connection, as composting toilets and urinals require no water, and gray water from all sinks is recycled and used for irrigation.* Copyright Mike Sherman Photography.

New South Jamaica Branch Library. *The energy performance of the library is integral to the basic architectural design, supported by a sophisticated mechanical and electrical control system. The building's relationship to the sun drives the architectural form, and the changing effects of natural light are significant to the quality of the interior space.* From Stein White Nelligan Architects.

Adeline Street Urban Salvage Project. *Integrating a sustainable attitude to an urban neighborhood infill project. The concept is compact, simple, and responsive to recycled materials and unique uses.* Copyright Ethan Kaplan Photography.

Chesapeake Bay Foundation Headquarters. *Chesapeake Bay Foundation is dedicated to protecting and preserving the environment. Its mission and its dedication to that mission drove the design and inspired the design team.* Copyright 2001 Prankash Patel.

PNC Firstside Center. *Energy costs at PNC Firstside are 50 percent lower than the conventional building's and employee retention has improved 60 percent.* Photography by Ed Massery.

Sleeping Lady. *The project endorsed integrated design—simplicity, placeness, climate-responsive design, and enhancing the relationships of social and natural systems. From Jones & Jones Architects and Landscape Architects, Ltd.*

Zion National Park Visitor Center. *Indigenous and long-lasting materials, coupled with the use of passive ventilation towers, characterize this landmark building.* Courtesy of Lisa Ogdon, Zion National Park.

Camp Arroyo. *This environmental education camp, which serves middle-school students as well as critically ill children and other guests, was designed to demonstrate a series of ecological design principles as part of the curriculum.* Copyright J. D. Peterson.

Edificio Malecon. This 125,000-square-foot office building was built on a reclaimed brownfield site at Puerto Madero, a redevelopment area in Buenos Aires. Its garage was built within the foundations of a nineteenth-century warehouse.
From Daniella Mac Adden.

Pier 1. This adaptive-reuse project transformed a dilapidated warehouse on San Francisco's waterfront to 140,000 square feet of class A office space and an acre of new public open space. Water flows through radiant tubes in floor slabs for heating and cooling. This system moderates the interior climate according to each zone's location and orientation. Generated heat is rejected into a submerged condenser water loop under the building.
Copyright Timothy Hursley.

Colorado Court. The 44-unit, five-story building is the first affordable housing project in the United States to be 100 percent energy neutral. This project provides an excellent model of sustainable development in an urban environment and promotes diversity through strategically placed affordable housing. *From Pugh and Scarpa; photo by Marvin Rand.*

Fisher Pavilion. This is one of the first buildings in Seattle to be designed and constructed under the city policy requiring all public facilities over $5 million to achieve a LEED Silver rating. Burying the building and using the high-mass thermal capacity of a concrete roof decreases envelope loads on the building. *Photo from Steve Keating.*

Steinhude Sea Recreation Facility. *The theme for EXPO 2000, "Man, Nature, Environment," led to the goal of an artistically intriguing structure that was fully self-sustaining with minimal impact on the surrounding ecosystem. This small recreation facility is located on an island at the south shore of the Steinhude Sea. The island ecosystem consists of a beach area, green fields, nature walk, children's play area, and a bird sanctuary. The new 3,057-square-foot facility accommodates, with minimal ecological impact, a café, lifeguard facilities, boathouse, storage, public toilets and showers, and an exhibition area and observation deck. Prefabrication of the building in a nearby factory resulted in waste minimization and ecosystem protection.* Copyright 2000 Peter Hubbe.

20 River Terrace. *The Solaire is a 27-story, glass-and-brick residential tower in Battery Park City, Manhattan, directly adjacent to the site of the former World Trade Center. The design meets both the recently enacted New York State Green Building Tax Credit and Gold LEED Certification. The 357,000-square-foot, 293-unit building is estimated to require 35 percent less energy than conventional code-complying design; reduce peak demand for electricity by 65 percent; and require 50 percent less potable water.* Copyright Jeff Goldberg/ESTO.

City of White Rock Operations Building. *Daylight light shelves provide balanced daylight and reduce electric lighting needs. A green-sod roof reduces runoff from impermeable surfaces, while a pervious parking lot allows infiltration of water into the ground. The facility also uses stormwater rather than potable water to wash city vehicles and for toilets, and waterless urinals and low-flow faucets throughout the facility further reduce water consumption. Extensive use of materials produced within a 500-mile radius of the site also reduced transportation effects on the environment. Photo by Colin Jewall.*

Genzyme Center. *The sustainable design in this building is fully integrated into architecture, space, and light. Sustainability in this sense is not an extra you could add or not. It is interwoven with the vital parts of architecture.* Photo by Anton Grassl.

The Plaza at PPL Center. *An eight-story glass atrium brings natural light deep into the core of the building, while extensive perimeter glazing provides panoramic views and abundant daylight, filtered through*

The Barn at Fallingwater. This is an adaptive reuse of a nineteenth-century heavy-timber bank barn and its twentieth-century addition, framed in dimension lumber. Salvaged fir, new sunflower-seed composite panels, and sound-absorptive straw panels complement the palette of original materials while underscoring the structure's connection to farming. A zero-discharge wastewater-reclamation system, gray-water flushing, and low-flow fixtures reduce potable water use. *Copyright Nic Lehoux Photography.*

Evergreen State College Seminar II. A central open volume allows daylighting, natural stack ventilation, and visual connections between the academic programs. To safeguard the site's forest ecology, the building is fingered into the landscape. Planting features a mix of native species organized according to their natural setting and replaces the forest disturbed by construction. To reduce the impact of the project on Thornton Creek and its native salmon, a 20,443-square-foot vegetated roof was installed. *Photo by Lara Swimmer.*

CATALYST PROJECT

vertical axis wind turbines

vegetated roof

PV or SHW panels

solar control at south facade

solar shading

cafe/Living Machine

rainwater storage (opt)

rainwater storage (opt)

district thermal loop connect to building

district thermal loop connect to building

rainwater storage (opt)

to subsurface irrigation at landscape areas

district thermal loop connect to Lloyd Center Tower

wastewater
reclaimed water
rainwater collection

Note: This concept plan is not intended to represent specific planned or required development proposals.

Lloyd Crossing Sustainable Urban Design Plan. Lloyd Crossing is a sustainable neighborhood design and a unique COTE Top Ten entry. Rather than the typical building or building complex, it illustrates sustainable design as an urban solution—past the building object. This study has generated extensive discussion internationally and has created a methodology for expanding the scope and criteria for urban and city infrastructure design. Copyright Mithun.

1999 AIA/COTE Top Ten Winner
DENVER DRYGOODS
LOCATION: Denver
ARCHITECT: Affordable Housing Development Corp.
and Urban Design Group

Building Performance, According to the Architects

The building is performing as well or better than expected. The use of evaporative coolers in the apartment portion of the project has dramatically reduced the amount of electricity used for air conditioning of the apartments in the summer. The use of low-E double-pane glass has also reduced energy consumptions for the apartments. We are now replacing the retail storefront (as needed) with low-E double-pane glass. Another developer developed the final four floors of the building as residential, for-sale loft condominiums, utilizing conventional approaches. This does, however, provide a basis to compare our energy-saving investments with their (lack of) investment.

The architect, engineers, and first-phase developer were committed to energy efficiency and sustainable development from the very beginning for Denver Drygoods.

Rocky Mountain Institute assisted throughout the design process for Denver Drygoods.

Lessons Learned by the Architects

The architect, engineers, and first-phase developer were committed to energy efficiency and sustainable development from the very beginning. Early in the design, we engaged RMI, the Rocky Mountain Institute, to help us through the design process. Evaporative cooling enabled downsizing of mechanical equipment and cost savings. The developer also worked with the architect to specify the most sustainable materials possible. We required the contractor to recycle materials during the construction as well.

1999 AIA/COTE Top Ten Winner
DURACELL HEADQUARTERS
LOCATION: Bethel, Connecticut
ARCHITECT: Herbert S. Newman and Partners

Building Performance, According to the Architects

The building has fulfilled the client's objectives for an environmentally responsible corporate headquarters. Energy-efficient mechanical systems have been reported to have saved more than a million kilowatt-hours (or $121,000 annually) and qualified for nearly $250,000 in utility incentives, reducing the incremental cost of premium efficiency equipment needed to achieve those savings. Additionally, the building has gained praise as a flagship of corporate responsibility. Employees show enthusiastic acceptance. The facility is supported by local nature and youth groups, who maintain the surrounding nature paths and habitat, which support features such as bluebird-nest boxes and bat boxes.

Duracell established an internal Green Team to work alongside design and construction professionals to establish and meet environmental goals. Thus, client involvement positively impacted the sustainability of the site design, natural planting and landscaping, habitat and wildlife, stormwater runoff, architectural design, construction-waste management, building materials, energy conservation, water conservation, preparation for move-in, waste management, and employee safety.

Lessons Learned by the Architects

- We would take advantage of the wider range of readily available and less-expensive sustainable building materials.

- We learned of the importance of the earliest possible involvement of engineers and subconsultants, green-design charrettes at every phase of design, and the development of a *green budget* to account for energy savings.

- Our firm has consistently worked to apply sustainable principles to the design process, and therefore we have not modified our professional practices as much as we have supplemented them by sponsoring the continuing education of our staff, utilizing design tools, and if necessary supplementing our project teams with expert consultants in the field of ecology and green design.

- We use a number of design tools that enable us to achieve sustainable-design objectives. Computer software allows us to make informed choices by evaluating the relative environmental merits of comparable materials. We keep current on developments in sustainable-design practices by using the latest versions of these software packages and maintaining subscriptions to periodicals specializing in the field. In particular, the Women's Network for a Sustainable Future helps us to learn about cutting-edge technologies and materials and how to communicate with our clients more effectively, gaining their support and endorsement for green endeavors.

- We work with engineers and contractors who understand and share our sustainable-design principles. We hold a *green workshop* with all disciplines on the design team, including client representatives, to ensure that each entity understands these objectives and to brainstorm ways to improve the process.

- We specify construction-waste management procedures, material reclamation and recycling, materials, mechanical equipment, finishes, and lighting that do not need to produce waste in production.

- We use LEED and GreenGlobe as guidelines for environmental performance, and often we design for LEED certification. The decision to pursue LEED certification is still, ultimately, client driven. A rapidly increasing number of prospective clients require identification of LEED-accredited staff and firm experience with LEED certification.

1999 AIA/COTE Top Ten Winner
KANSAS CITY ZOO DERAMUS PAVILION
LOCATION: Kansas City, Missouri
ARCHITECT: BNIM Architects

The Deramus Pavilion project does the following:

- It supports and symbolizes the mission of the zoo.
- It clearly expresses an aesthetic of natural materials.

The client and architect were united to create a Kansas City Zoo Deramus Pavilion that would be at once loved, efficient, durable, and pedagogical.

- It shows exemplary use of daylighting.
- It uses structure built completely from salvaged or sustainably managed wood.
- It uses ecological site planning.

Building Performance, According to the Architects

The performance is still as projected. Staff and community love the building, with the possible exception of the IMAX Theater, now one of three in town and thus not attracting full use and capacity.

Lessons Learned by the Architects

- Beauty is as important as performance.
- The client and architect were united to create a facility that would be at once loved, efficient, durable, and pedagogical.
- More emphasis on integrated design and less on controls.
- We spent a lot of time doing materials analysis and resource mapping, because very little information was available at that time. In response, we have created Elements, a subsidiary group of seven professionals primarily responsible for our research, resource mapping, and daylight and energy modeling.
- Biology and earth sciences play a critical role in our design work, some of which is accomplished by Elements, some by our in-house landscape architects and some by outside consultants.
- We have developed high-performance sustainable specifications over the last 20 years. We use LEED and have accredited professionals, but we also create custom design and measurement tools to define and measure "triple bottom-line" performance beyond LEED Platinum.

1999 AIA/COTE Top Ten Winner
REAL GOODS SOLAR LIVING CENTER
LOCATION: Hopland, California
ARCHITECT: Van der Ryn Architects

Projects goals are as follows:

- Support mission and business philosophy of Real Goods Trading Co.
- Design climate-responsive building and site.
- Make extensive use of solar and daylight.
- Maintain aesthetic of original building form.

The form of the Real Goods Solar Living Center by Van der Ryn Architects is similar to a sundial.

Building Performance, According to the Client

Real Goods founder and president John Schaeffer states:

> The building is performing famously and even exceeding expectations. Still never gets over 78°F in summer even when 110°F outside, and in the winter we only need one small woodstove to take off the chill even when it is 25°F outside. The thermal performance is superior to that predicted due to the added thermal mass of the 2 to 3 inches of soil-cement applied in addition to the 1-inch base coat, as modeled. This extra mass enables the building to "bridge" extremely hot or cool periods.
>
> Original projections were to attract 50,000 visitors per year. Since opening in 1997, the site has consistently been visited by over four times that number. The Solar Living Center has inspired over a million visitors. Now as home of the nonprofit Solar Living Institute, we hope it will continue for many years to come. For more information, see http://www.solarliving.org.

Lessons Learned by the Architects

- Changes would likely include greater use of building-integrated photovoltaic options and a few finish materials that weren't available ten years ago. Otherwise the project stands as a good example of *second-generation ecological design,* well suited to its climate and program.

The building and outdoor plan are fully integrated at the Real Goods Solar Living Center.

■ A most important lesson is the importance of collaboration in creating integral, ecological design. We also have learned that straw-bale construction is well suited to passive-solar design, as it features high levels of insulation while supporting ample thermal mass on the interior surface. Testing confirmed that there is a perfect 12-hour diurnal transfer of heat from the surfaces to the center of the bale walls.

■ Operating costs of maintaining the landscape have been expensive, so ongoing fund-raising for the Institute is always a priority.

■ Our approach to "ecological design" is on a much more intuitive, holistic level than that captured by LEED or any of the rating systems. That's not to discount them, only to say that we have our own systems that are not targeted to "points" so much as they are at achieving higher levels of integration, balancing these with the overall design goals and relationship to the greater landscape.

1999 AIA/COTE Top Ten Winner
REI SEATTLE
LOCATION: Seattle, Washington
ARCHITECT: Mithun

The REI flagship store's green building design supports REI's conservation ethic. Coop members were polled for their environmental priorities, and these were used as design criteria. The project balances environmental and cost accountability with retailing needs.

The architect and REI considered a number of design choices based on the environmental-priority information collected from their members. The top priorities were as follows:

■ Energy efficiency

■ Use of resource-efficient materials and recycled-content materials

■ Recycling and reuse of construction and demolition waste, keeping materials out of the waste stream

Other priorities mentioned included the following:

■ Alternative transit options

■ Water conservation

■ Building operations that include recycling

The design utilized a number of sustainable-design strategies:

■ Energy efficiency

■ Interior zoning with floating temperature conditions to reduce the areas where full heating, ventilating, and air-conditioning (HVAC) controls and strict temperature set points are required

REI Seattle by Mithun balances environmental and cost accountability with retailing needs.

- Natural daylighting used extensively throughout the building
- Carbon monoxide sensors that activate garage exhaust fans only when needed
- No escalators
- High-efficiency metal halide and fluorescent lighting used within the building
- Computer-controlled energy-management system
- Building layout for solar use and control, with the morning sun used in the building warm-up stage and solar sunscreens to control summer sun
- Low-E glass used at optimal locations

- Extensive bike racks for customers and employees, with employee showers to encourage bike use, and covered bus stop provided by REI

Material Efficiency

- Stone used involved no active quarrying; waste stone from closed nearby quarry was used.
- Limited use of internal coatings; steel inside the building is left raw; no stain or coating on structural wood and much of the wood paneling.
- Wood structure uses engineered lumber, thereby eliminating need for wood beams and columns from large-diameter trees.
- Engineered wood-panel products from postindustrial waste (medium-density fiberboard, or MDF, and oriented-strand board, or OSB) are used for wall elements, cabinets, and merchandise fixtures.
- Roof water is used to charge a waterfall in the landscaped courtyard.
- Electronically controlled plumbing fixtures are in public restrooms with low-flow fixtures.
- Environmentally sensitive flooring products included linoleum with low-VOC adhesives, and low-VOC paints and coatings were used where possible.
- Maple flooring came from sources with certified sustainable forest-management practices.
- Native Northwest landscaping, with a high-efficiency subsurface irrigation system, reduced water consumption.
- Seventy-six percent of the previous buildings' demolition debris, which had been left on the site, was deferred from landfills to recycling, reuse, or salvage. A construction-recycling program and store-operation recycling program were also used.

Building Performance, According to the Architects

Nine years after opening, REI's flagship store continues to be a top tourist attraction in Seattle, Washington, with millions of visitors per year. The sustainable elements are as valid and effective as the day it opened.

Lessons Learned by the Architects

- The advancement and availability of sustainable materials would open us to further possibilities. Daylight and thermodynamic modeling has become more commonplace, and therefore we would have been able to design an even more efficient building.
- It is imperative that the designer and the client share the same values and goals. That way, the struggle to push the construction industry is a shared burden but also a shared reward. Successful projects take a highly committed,

integrated design and client team all working toward common goals with a shared set of values.

■ Our specifications are now structured in a performance-based methodology to meet baseline sustainable criteria established for all the firm's projects. When projects are designated to be part of a formalized sustainability metrics system, such as LEED, we incorporate those specific standards into our specifications to ensure that those key metrics are achieved.

2000 AIA/COTE Top Ten Green Projects

Bainbridge Island City Hall, Bainbridge Island, Washington

C. K. Choi Building, Institute of Asian Research, University of British Columbia, Vancouver, British Columbia, Canada

Department of Environmental Protection, Ebensburg, Pennsylvania

Emeryville Resourceful Building, Emeryville, California

The Green Institute's Phillips Eco-Enterprise Center, Minneapolis, Minnesota

Hanover House, Hanover, New Hampshire

Lady Bird Johnson Wildflower Center, Austin, Texas

McLean Environmental Living and Learning Center, Northland College, Ashland, Wisconsin

New South Jamaica Branch Library, New York, New York

World Resources Institute, Washington, D.C.

The Department of Environmental Protection (DEP) in Ebensburg was designed by Kulp Boecker Architects, P.C., to address site sustainability, improve energy efficiency, promote sustainable materials and resource conservation, enhance air quality, provide copious natural daylighting, and reduce water consumption.

At the Department of Environmental Protection, power DOE modeling indicates annual energy consumption at less than 25,000 Btu per square foot, or 60 percent better performance than ASHRAE 90.1.

Sustainable-design elements on the 3.4-acre inner-city brownfield site redevelopment of The Green Institute's Phillips Eco-Enterprise Center include geo-exchange heating and cooling, sun-tracking daylighting, air-to-air energy recovery, salvaged steel joists, wood, and brick.

Sirny Architects, Workplace Designers, LHB, and Applied Ecology collaborated to design the Eco-Enterprise Center that protects and nurtures the natural and urban environment through education and sustainable economic development.

2000 AIA/COTE Top Ten Winner
BAINBRIDGE ISLAND CITY HALL
LOCATION: Bainbridge Island, Washington
ARCHITECT: The Miller|Hull Partnership and Kathleen O'Brien (consultant)

The new Bainbridge Island City Hall (see color insert) will bring five departments together under one roof, resulting in a more efficient operation for this newly incorporated city. The project features nontoxic or non-ozone-depleting materials, including the region's first major installation of certified wood. Recycled content or reused materials have been applied, and the city's stormwater management system was significantly upgraded as part of site preparation. Daylighting, optimized natural ventilation, and nontoxic finishes will provide a healthier and safer indoor environment for City Hall employees and others using the building.

2000 AIA/COTE Top Ten Winner
C. K. CHOI BUILDING, INSTITUTE OF ASIAN RESEARCH,
UNIVERSITY OF BRITISH COLUMBIA
LOCATION: Vancouver, British Columbia, Canada
ARCHITECT: Matsuzaki Wright Architects

Primary features include the following:

- Daylight and natural ventilation are optimized.
- Design achieves 57 percent below ASHRAE 90.1 energy consumption levels.
- Occupancy and daylight sensors control lighting.

*The design of C. K. Choi
Building is virtually
unplugged.*

- Atrium designs facilitate natural ventilation by inducing a stack effect.
- Ventilation strips under windows ensure continuous air exchange.
- Double-glazed insulated frame windows have low conductivity.

Other features include the following:

- Exterior bricks are recycled from Vancouver city streets.
- Sixty percent of timber beams are salvaged from a demolished building from the 1930s.
- All doors and frames are reused from demolished buildings.
- Drywall contains 17 to 26 percent recycled gypsum and 100 percent recycled paper for the face boards.
- The carpet is laid without adhesives. The underlay is a felt made from 100 percent recycled fibers.
- There is no sewer connection: Composting toilets and urinals require no water.
- Gray water from all sinks is recycled and used for irrigation.
- Rainwater is collected from the roof and used for summer irrigation.

Building Performance, According to the Architects

The building is performing well, mostly because many items are low-maintenance or natural systems that take care of themselves (e.g., waterless composting toilets and wetlands, natural ventilation via stack effect, daylighting and lighting sensors, well-insulated building, and a high-percentage of reused materials).

Lessons Learned by the Architects

If the firm were to design the building again, we would do the following:

- Ensure that an energy-monitoring system is installed. This was contemplated, but due to budget, not implemented.
- Make sure an ongoing education process is established for users, especially new users in a university context, to help them better understand the toilets, the ventilation, the lighting, and the acoustics.
- Change some construction materials that we selected as a result of a tight budget or time frame. For example, we would use exterior stucco (only compromise to longevity) and new heavy timber (compromise to achieving 100 percent reused structural members).
- The major, invaluable lesson is the need for a commitment to sustainability. On every project we try to convince new clients to explore many of these options. Generally, there is partial success, not total. The greatest resistance has been to waterless composting toilets.

2000 AIA/COTE Top Ten Winner
EMERYVILLE RESOURCEFUL BUILDING
LOCATION: Emeryville, California
ARCHITECT: Siegel & Strain Architects

This three-unit affordable project, which won a 1999 Progressive Architecture Research Award, "proved that affordable housing and environmental sustainability are not mutually exclusive goals," according to the award jury.

The project focused on increasing energy efficiency, lowering operating costs, reducing resource consumption, and creating healthy indoor environments using only conventional means of construction common to builders of affordable housing projects.

Building Performance, According to the Architects

Approximately one year after occupancy, we reviewed utility bills. These showed that performance was meeting expectations, about 33 percent over California's Title 24. The exteriors of the buildings are maintaining their appearance, so we believe that the materials that were selected are performing as we intended. Some residents have replaced the planting materials with plants that require more water, so the water conservation is not as great as planned.

The Emeryville Resourceful Building won the 1999 Progressive Architecture Research Award, proving that affordable housing and environmental sustainability are not mutually exclusive goals.

The Emeryville Resourceful Building is an example of affordable housing built sustainably with conventional construction methods.

Lessons Learned by the Architects

- This was the first project in which we implemented an optimized-wood framing system. We have since used the system on several other projects, and each time have improved our approach and documentation. To make improvements to the building envelope, we might look into a different construction type, such as modular construction or structural insulated panels (SIPs).

- We might push harder in the planning-approvals phase to reduce the number of required parking spaces. This would allow us more flexibility in siting the buildings in relation to solar access and perhaps increase the amount of open space.

- The project would benefit from having an owner's manual that describes the goals of the project, how the units operate, and how they should be maintained.

- This was the first publicly bid green building for our firm. We implemented a number of things in the specifications that we have since refined and used again.

- Through our grant for this project, we were able to have a complete environmental life-cycle analysis for the material assemblies used in the project. This helped us to select the roof, wall, and floor systems for the best overall environmental performance. This would be ideal to incorporate into all our practice work, but the cost is prohibitive, and we have not used the method since.

- Where possible, we now do detailed resource mapping of materials to identify local and regional resources.

■ We have several LEED-certified professionals on staff, which we find is most important from a marketing point of view. We practiced sustainable design before LEED existed. We are always mindful of the primary importance of bio-climatic design; this is mostly ignored by LEED, except in energy measurement.

2000 AIA/COTE Top Ten Winner
HANOVER HOUSE
LOCATION: Hanover, New Hampshire
DESIGN ENGINEER (CONSULTANT): Energysmiths / Marc Rosenbaum, PE

The project was a solar-heated, superinsulated home. Indoor environmental quality, durability, and material-resource efficiency were as important as low energy consumption. Key features include superinsulation, superglass, heat-recovery ventilation, airtight construction, and passive-solar design. Durable and healthy materials include certified cedar shingles, linoleum, tile, and local hardwood floors. The house is extremely comfortable, with even temperatures and proper humidity, and features a very low-maintenance design as well as low water usage.

Building Performance, According to the Architect

The building's performance over the past decade has matched the detailed modeling that was done during the design process remarkably well. It continues to be one of the lowest energy-use homes anywhere, despite its cold climate location. One of the clients is a professional engineer, and as such the client was interested in pushing the envelope technically. Also, the clients were quite pleased to not have any combustion sources or fuel storage in the building.

Lessons Learned by the Architect

■ Given the drop in prices of solar electric systems, I would likely use photovoltaics and a ground-source heat pump rather than the solar thermal approach, and then I would use radiant floors as the heat-delivery method.

■ High-quality forced-air systems (airtight and fully insulated, with a return in every closable room) are expensive. Air systems are regarded as low cost only because they are being built badly.

■ I was a very early LEED-accredited professional and worked on the first certified project in New England. I find LEED to be helpful for large projects where the architects and engineers are just paying lip service to green design, because the program imposes a structure with some metrics. On more advanced projects, where the design team and the owner committed to do a great job, LEED—with its bureaucracy and minutiae—is an expensive impediment. I've been fairly successful in convincing my clients to bypass LEED, which costs between $50,000 and $75,000 to implement on a small project, if the time is really accounted for.

2000 AIA/COTE Top Ten Winner
LADY BIRD JOHNSON WILDFLOWER CENTER
LOCATION: Austin, Texas
ARCHITECT: Overland Partners

This facility accommodates research, education, and visitor needs on a 40-acre site. The center is designed as a series of outdoor spaces and facilities, including visitors' galleries, a 250-seat auditorium, and classrooms. Features include a gift shop and tearoom, botanical library, and research labs that focus on the education of visitors about the use of native plants and demonstrate an ecologically sensitive approach to the development of a site with fragile environmental conditions. The facilities and the program they support are a model of "total resource conservation" while showing the beauty of native landscape.

Elements integrated in the design include passive-solar heating, pragmatic building orientation, recycled and reclaimed materials, and excavated material. Uniting the entire complex is a rainwater capture and reuse system.

2000 AIA/COTE Top Ten Winner
MCLEAN ENVIRONMENTAL LIVING AND LEARNING CENTER (ELLC), NORTHLAND COLLEGE
LOCATION: Ashland, Wisconsin
ARCHITECTS: LHB; Hammel, Green and Abrahamson (HGA); The Weidt Group, energy analysis

This 40,000-square-foot student-housing complex is used in the curriculum for 114 residents learning about energy performance, materials, building life cycles, and

The McLean Environmental Living and Learning Center at Northland College, designed by LHB, Hammel, Green and Abrahamson (HGA), and The Weidt Group, is a student-housing complex that is used in the curriculum for 114 residents learning about energy performance, materials, building life cycles, and sustainability.

McLean Environmental Living & Learning Center, a residence hall, is Northland College's most energy-efficient building.

sustainability. Computers monitor the building's renewable systems: a 20-kilowatt Jacobs Wind Turbine, a solar domestic hot-water system, and three photovoltaic panels. LHB designed and specified systems and materials and involved students throughout the design process.

Operable windows allow natural ventilation for this building, designed without air conditioning. Products such as linoleum and low-VOC finishes ensured exceptional indoor air quality, which is being monitored. Low-flow showers and toilet fixtures, composting toilets, and high-efficiency gas boilers and light fixtures were installed, reducing resource consumption.

Resource efficiency was addressed with recycled-content materials, biocomposite counter surfaces, low-maintenance masonry, and regionally harvested wood.

2000 AIA/COTE Top Ten Winner
NEW SOUTH JAMAICA BRANCH LIBRARY
LOCATION: New York, New York
ARCHITECT: Stein White Nelligan Architects

The energy performance of the library is integral to the basic architectural design, supported by a sophisticated mechanical and electrical control system. The building's relationship to the sun drives the architectural form, and the changing effects of natural light are significant to the quality of the interior space.

The relationship to the sun drives the architectural form of the New South Jamaica Branch Library by Stein White Nelligan Architects, and the changing effects of natural light are significant to the quality of the interior space.

Automated controls regulate shades, lights, and ventilation dampers, depending on the time of day and year. In the summer, daylight levels are limited to those required for library operation. In the winter, the building captures maximum daylight with the excess heat introduced into the building mass for storage. The building uses construction materials efficiently, including recycled products.

2000 AIA/COTE Top Ten Winner
WORLD RESOURCES INSTITUTE
LOCATION: Washington, DC
ARCHITECT: Hellmuth Obata + Kassabaum (HOK)

The goal of the project was to express World Resources Institute (WRI) values in physical terms. Every material was chosen because it uses natural resources efficiently; many were chosen because they are alternatives to conventional but less environmentally friendly products. The design also focused on recognizing the manufacturers of materials and systems that are moving toward sustainable-business practices.

All wood is sustainably harvested or salvaged, and many alternatives have been used, such as bamboo flooring and biocomposites made from wheat straw, soy, and sunflower seeds for doors, cabinetry, and substrates.

The result of these and other sustainable materials is elegantly minimal, with a soft curvilinear form and eased edge. Lighting fixtures save 70 percent of the electrical energy that is typically used by energy-efficient, recessed fluorescent fixtures.

All wood in the World Resources Institute is sustainably harvested or salvaged, and many alternatives have been used, such as bamboo flooring and biocomposites made from wheat straw, soy, and sunflower seeds for doors, cabinetry, and substrates.

The design also focused on recognizing the manufacturers of materials and systems that are moving toward sustainable-business practices.

2001 AIA/COTE Top Ten Green Projects

ABN-AMRO Bank World Headquarters, Amsterdam, Netherlands

Adeline Street Urban Salvage Project, Berkeley, California

BigHorn Home Improvement Center, Silverthorne, Colorado

Chesapeake Bay Foundation Headquarters, Annapolis, Maryland

REI Denver, Denver, Colorado

Montgomery Campus, California College of Arts and Crafts, San Francisco, California

Nidus Center for Scientific Enterprise, Creve Coeur, Missouri

PNC Firstside Center, Pittsburgh, Pennsylvania

Sleeping Lady Conference and Retreat Center, Leavenworth, Washington

Zion National Park Visitor Center, Springdale, Utah

The Nidus Center for Scientific Enterprise by Hellmuth Obata + Kassabaum (HOK) is a 41,000-square-foot plant and life sciences business incubator sponsored by Monsanto and located on its Creve Coeur research campus.

The Nidus Center's aggressive energy efficiency exceeds ASHRAE/IES requirements by 33 percent.

2001 AIA/COTE Top Ten Winner
CHESAPEAKE BAY FOUNDATION HEADQUARTERS
LOCATION: Annapolis, Maryland
ARCHITECT: Smith Group

The Chesapeake Bay Foundation is dedicated to protecting and preserving the environment. Its mission and dedication to that mission drove the design and inspired the design team. The client was a major participant in all design decisions and encouraged the design team to constantly "push the envelope."

The Chesapeake Bay Foundation is dedicated to protecting and preserving the environment. That mission drove the design and inspired the design team.

Building Performance, According to the Architects

In general, the project is performing extremely well and as good if not better than expected. Some aspects of the energy usage are not exactly as anticipated (e.g., there is a slightly higher plug draw of electricity); but the systems have performed very well. Extensive and ongoing studies of the building energy profile have been done by the National Renewable Energy Laboratory (www.nrel.gov/) and are publicly available.

Lessons Learned by the Architects

- Better care must be taken in fully understanding (and detailing) the exterior components (sun screens, structure, building skin). The effectiveness of some systems is heavily affected by occupant use (heavier plug loads than previous). The integrated-design approach worked extremely well, and this needs to be utilized on other such projects for maximum effectiveness and efficiency.
- We don't necessarily utilize the LEED system on every project, but the education and experience gained by LEED-accredited professionals and LEED-registered projects is invaluable to their other work.

2001 AIA/COTE Top Ten Winner
REI DENVER
LOCATION: Denver, Colorado
ARCHITECT: Mithun

As part of the design process, REI consulted its members to help define key priorities to use in developing the Denver flagship store. The top priorities identified by the members were energy efficiency, alternative-transit options, water conservation, and sustainable building and operating principles, such as recycling.

The top priorities identified by REI members were energy efficiency, alternative-transit options, water conservation, and sustainable building and operating principles, such as recycling.

At REI Denver, reclaimed wood timbers, salvaged from an abandoned mine, were used for stair supports, and reclaimed wood decking was used for a new second-floor structure.

Energy Features

- Mechanical system uses direct and indirect, evaporative water-cooling system to reduce energy consumption during summer months.
- Energy savings are due to greater temperature spread performance requirements and variable-speed HVAC fans, resulting in temperature variances of up to 5 degrees Fahrenheit off optimum within the store.
- Natural daylighting is used extensively throughout the building.
- Large skylights within the great room allow ambient lighting to shut off when natural daylight reaches required levels.
- Carbon monoxide sensors activate garage exhaust fans only when needed.
- Motion sensors detect occupancy for lighting usage after hours.
- There are no escalators.
- High-efficiency metal halide and fluorescent lighting is used within the building.
- Computer-controlled energy-management system is used.
- There are extensive bike racks for customers and employees, with employee showers to encourage bike use.
- Transportation plan encourages employee use of alternative transportation sources.

Materials

- Reclaimed wood timbers, salvaged from an abandoned mine, were used for stair supports. Reclaimed wood decking was used for new second-floor structure.
- New stone was employed that involved no active quarrying. It was instead selected from a washed-out earthen dam.
- Large sandstone foundations discovered during site excavations were used for new landscaping and fireplace.
- Limited use of internal coatings, and the steel and wood structure inside the building was left raw with no stain or coating on structural wood and much of the wood paneling.
- Wood structure used engineered lumber available from small-diameter trees.
- Engineered-wood panel products from postindustrial waste (medium-density fiberboard, or MDF, and OSB, oriented-strand board) were used for wall elements, cabinets, and merchandise fixtures.
- Wood flooring came from certified sustainable forest sources.
- Native Colorado landscaping, with a high-efficiency subsurface irrigation system, reduces water consumption.

Keeping Items from Waste Stream

By using and recycling an existing structure, an overwhelming quantity of new material was not used; material that ordinarily would be sent to a landfill was reused. Other methods used to keep items from entering the waste stream included the use of the following methods and practices:

- A construction recycling program and store operation recycling program were established.
- Exterior-treated timbers and shoring lagging utilized environmentally friendly, low-VOC preservatives.
- Countertops used recycled newspaper and soybean composite (Phoenix Bio Composite).
- Concrete had a high fly-ash content, a waste byproduct of coal-generated power plants.
- Landscape uses composted urban green waste.
- Steel, which typically consists of more than 65 percent recycled content in the United States, was used throughout the building.
- The art program anticipates using recycled glass and salvaged steel panels.
- Salvaged timbers and decking were used within the retail space.

Lessons Learned by the Architects

- The advancement and availability of sustainable materials would have opened us to new possibilities. We are more in tune today with sustainable issues having to do with water than when we started the design of the Seattle flagship store in 1993.
- We learned the value of reusing an existing structure, and that designing a sustainable project while renovating a historic landmark is not only possible but also extremely rewarding.
- We do much of our materials and methods research on our own, with the assistance of contractors, materials suppliers, and peers within the design profession. Ideally, better information would be available to design professionals in the critical area of life-cycle analysis.

2001 AIA/COTE Top Ten Winner
MONTGOMERY CAMPUS, CALIFORNIA COLLEGE OF ARTS AND CRAFTS
LOCATION: San Francisco, California
ARCHITECT: Leddy Maytum Stacy Architects

After analyzing several different adaptive-reuse approaches for the existing structure, we convinced the client that incorporating sustainable strategies was not only consistent with its institutional and pedagogical missions but would also save hun-

Incorporating sustainable strategies was consistent with the CCAC's institutional and pedagogical mission, and also saved hundreds of thousands of dollars in both capital and operating expenses.

dreds of thousands of dollars in both capital and operating expenses. Making the new project a "solar-heated art school" added fund-raising appeal and helped jump-start the capital campaign as well.

Building Performance, According to the Architects

The project continues to perform well for two reasons. First, the systems were designed to be very simple, requiring minimal maintenance. Second, the user is a school of architecture, art, and design, so the building is used as a teaching tool and is therefore well maintained.

Lessons Learned by the Architects

- Because this was a very low-budget project, there were very few elements in play. The design benefited from the discipline of a limited budget.

The Montgomery Campus California College of Arts and Crafts building is used as a teaching tool and is therefore well maintained.

- We would require more sustainable-construction practices and documentation from the contractor.

- We would place more emphasis on natural-ventilation cooling strategies.

- We would push harder for proper skylight sun- and glare-control devices.

- Our basic approach to this project—that sustainable design fundamentally means making the most with the least—has not changed over the years. We strive for simplicity and elegance.

- In our office, *sustainable design* is simply another way of saying *good design*. We don't segregate sustainable issues. We use LEED as a guide for every project. It helps both the design team and the client understand options and trade-offs, even if certification is not being sought. We currently have 7 LEED-accredited professionals in a firm of 18. We feel it adds to our knowledge base and communicates our commitment to our clients.

2001 AIA/COTE Top Ten Winner
PNC FIRSTSIDE CENTER
LOCATION: Pittsburgh, Pennsylvania
ARCHITECT: Astorino

The client is a very forward-thinking company and was the prime motivator for sustainable design and LEED certification. The project team was together from

During peak-load periods, such as the summer, energy costs at PNC Firstside Center by Astorino are 50 percent lower than those of a conventional building.

the beginning, including the owner, architect, engineer, and construction manager, so when the client decided to go for LEED certification, the team was already working together and could adjust plans accordingly. Major decisions were consensus-built.

Building Performance, According to the Architects

PNC Firstside is performing and operating better than originally expected. Studies have compared this facility with a virtually identical facility of the same size and function that was built with conventional systems and products. During peak-load periods, such as the summer, energy costs at PNC Firstside are 50 percent lower than the conventional building's. In addition, employee retention has improved 60 percent.

Lessons Learned by the Architects

- If our firm were to design the project today, we would put more effort into sustainable-construction practices, use more efficient lamps in light fixtures, install more lighting controls, and incorporate more daylighting techniques.

- Sustainability can be applied to every project to some degree. Product and system research must be ongoing. We did not need to modify our standard professional practices to accommodate sustainable design. Our design philosophy is already based both directly and indirectly on sustainable principles.

- Materials research and an understanding of their use are important in the completion of any facility. When making hiring decisions, we review an individual's educational and project experience relative to this issue.

- We use LEED as their sustainability metrics systems, but PNC Firstside occasionally uses other systems as well. The company believes it is very important to have an LEED-accredited professional on staff to serve as both a guide on a project as well as a source of reference for the entire staff.

2001 AIA/COTE Top Ten Winner
SLEEPING LADY CONFERENCE AND RETREAT CENTER
LOCATION: Leavenworth, Washington
ARCHITECT: Jones & Jones Architects and Landscape Architects, Ltd.

The client is a champion of various environmental causes and an advocate of simple living in concert with natural systems. Rigorous dialogue and high standards for

Rigorous dialogue and high standards for environmental and financial sustainability produced the Sleeping Lady Conference and Retreat Center, a project that was distilled by research and debate.

environmental and financial sustainability produced a project that was distilled by research and debate. Consequently, it was pretested both in concept and on paper before it was built. The attitude of continually making the facility and operations more sustainable has prevailed since the project was completed.

Building Performance, According to the Architects

The building is operating well because of the following:

- Low-tech to no-tech solutions
- Natural infrastructure (i.e., infiltration, shade or trees, cooling breezes, user control)
- Durable construction systems
- Climate-responsive design
- Easily maintainable systems

Lessons Learned by the Architects

- The project endorsed our firm's beliefs about integrated design, simplicity, placeness, climate-responsive design, and enhancing the relationships of social and natural systems.
- We would have liked to add more renewable, local energy systems; but with the low cost of abundant hydroelectric power, it was difficult to justify the added cost. It is a similar case with rainwater collection and storage (costly, compared to the low water rates). As it is, rainwater infiltrates into the ground, closely matching the natural regime. Plantings are primarily natives.
- The Center was a project that relied on a background in deep ecology, resource and energy efficiency, and common sense about good design. We use GreenSpec and other sources already mentioned. We take care in cost-estimating and value analysis that considers environmental costs as well as price and that is accurate and fair to the project budget and to the construction team. We include specific LEED criteria and required documentation when applicable.
- Sometimes. LEED is helpful to a project for third-party verification and/or public relations. Having a tool for client, user, subconsultant, and contractor education is always useful. LEED-accredited professionals are an advantage in that they are not only knowledgeable in green design but conversant in LEED protocol. In nearly all of our projects, we have found it incumbent on us to be the visionaries, teachers, and keepers of the integrated and holistic design idea.

2001 AIA/COTE Top Ten Winner
ZION NATIONAL PARK VISITOR CENTER
LOCATION: Springdale, Utah
ARCHITECT: National Park Service and Denver Service Center

As a primary component of the Zion Canyon Transportation System, this low-energy, sustainable facility is the entry to a transit- and pedestrian-centered visitor experience, providing park information, interpretation, and trip-planning assistance within a resource environment. The new visitor center is part of a transportation system that seeks to reduce resource impacts and enhance the visitor experience. Consisting of indoor and outdoor spaces for visitor services, this facility creates a setting to promote and interpret park resources and agency conservation values. In creating the Zion National Park Visitor Center, the National Park Service (NPS), working with DOE's National Renewable Energy Lab (NREL), has complemented Zion's natural beauty.

Environmental Aspects

Several effective energy features were included: daylighting, Trombe walls for passive solar heating, downdraft cool-towers for natural ventilation cooling, energy-efficient lighting, and advanced building controls. A roof-mounted photovoltaic (PV) system provides electric power. This project will save roughly $14,000 and about 10 kW of electric demand per year through these energy-saving measures.

Several effective energy features were included in the Zion National Park Visitor Center: daylighting, Trombe walls for passive solar heating, downdraft cool-towers for natural ventilation cooling, energy-efficient lighting, and advanced building controls.

Lessons Learned by the Architects

Designing the electrical system and installing the conduit for future PV was ideal. When PV was added, it was installed in a few hours. The photovoltaic system and inverter are used for an uninterruptible power supply (UPS) system. A better definition of what loads were to be UPS-powered would have been useful, however. The UPS system is not guaranteed to provide continuous power. About 5 percent of the outgates have left the building with a brief (less than 1 second) outage—enough to reset computers. Some small UPS computer backups have been installed for the brief outages.

Cool-towers have worked as well as direct evaporative coolers except in the enclosed offices, where additional small fans were added. The recommendation is that cool-towers be used only in large open spaces.

Daylighting levels have been lower than anticipated. This was due to the large number of dark beams in the space and the white stained ceilings (instead of white paint, as modeled). In addition, bug screens on the operable windows have affected the daylighting level. The result has been additional operation of artificial lighting.

Trombe walls have exceeded operational expectations. However, a design change resulted in two enclosed offices against Trombe walls, and these offices tend to overheat. In large open zones, the Trombe walls are very effective.

2002 AIA/COTE Top Ten Green Projects

Adam Joseph Lewis Center for Environmental Studies, Oberlin, Ohio

Bank of Astoria, Manzanita, Oregon

Navy Building 850, Port Hueneme, California

Camp Arroyo, Livermore, California

Edificio Malecon, Buenos Aires, Argentina

Iowa Association of Municipal Utilities, Ankeny, Iowa

National Wildlife Federation Headquarters, Reston, Virginia

Pier 1, San Francisco, California

Puget Sound Environmental Learning Center, Bainbridge Island, Washington

Tofte Cabin, Tofte, Minnesota

2002 AIA/COTE Top Ten Winner
ADAM JOSEPH LEWIS CENTER FOR ENVIRONMENTAL STUDIES
LOCATION: Oberlin, Ohio
ARCHITECT: William McDonough + Partners

Designed to be a model of restorative design, in terms inspired by the late John Lyle, the center celebrates the interaction of human and natural environments. With a goal to be a net energy exporter, the teaching and public space integrates natural

The Adam Joseph Lewis Center for Environmental Studies celebrates the interaction of human and natural environments.

The fundamental mover behind this project was David Orr, the head of the Environmental Studies Program at Oberlin and client representative.

energy flows while blurring the distinction between indoors and out. The light-drenched, two-story atrium serves as the primary organizing feature and the southern campus's town hall. Daylighting and natural ventilation enhance the atrium's feeling of an outdoor room. The center project demonstrates how state-of-the-art thinking applies to readily available state-of-the-shelf materials and building systems. Throughout, the design team remained mindful of how even the most advanced systems still must serve the needs of the building's occupants.

Building Performance, According to the Architects

In many ways the project is exceeding expectations, particularly in regard to how the building has been used as a learning tool for students and faculty. The project has garnered a tremendous amount of interest and attention, leading to levels of systems monitoring beyond initial hopes. The project has also benefited by continuous commissioning efforts that have helped optimize performance.

Lessons Learned by the Architects

- The fundamental mover behind this project was David Orr, the head of the Environmental Studies Program at Oberlin and client representative. David worked for a number of years before engaging an architect to develop the project's aspirations and story. This allowed for the firm's design team to begin the project with a clear set of objectives, perhaps the most ambitious environmental agenda for an academic building that had ever been established. The project's design phases preceded LEED.

- The firm learned that design momentum and continuity is one of the most important aspects of design success. Fund-raising and campus politics led to the project going on hiatus a number of times, disrupting design flow and causing turnover for key members of the design team, particularly at the project manager level.

- Actually, for this project, the design might have benefited from slightly lower expectations! The design team was tasked with designing a building that went effectively "beyond LEED Platinum" before LEED existed. Today, our firm would try to give a greater level of hierarchy to the project goals, allowing the team to focus on the most important items.

2002 AIA/COTE Top Ten Winner
BANK OF ASTORIA
LOCATION: Manzanita, Oregon
ARCHITECT: Tom Bender

This 7,500-square-foot bank building blends energy performance, local ecological fitness, community benefit, and economic success. The design process focused on community, cultural, spiritual, and energetic dimensions of sustainability, as well as

The design process of Bank of Astoria by Tom Bender focused on community, cultural, spiritual, and energetic dimensions of sustainability, as well as the more conventional energy and material aspects.

The facility benefits from significant daylight, on-site stormwater retention, and natural ventilation and cooling.

the more conventional energy and material aspects. The facility benefits from significant daylight, on-site stormwater retention, and natural ventilation and cooling. Zoned high-efficiency fluorescent lighting is used during just a quarter of the building's occupied time. Local materials were used where possible, and landscaping is local native coastal plants. The energy-efficient bank opened just before the 2000–2001 West Coast energy shortages, which led to a strong sense of local pride in the facility.

2002 AIA/COTE Top Ten Winner
NAVY BUILDING 850
LOCATION: Port Hueneme, California
ARCHITECT: CTG Energetics

The project is home to the Naval Base Ventura County Public Works Department and consists of 10,000 square feet of renovated space and 7,000 square feet of new construction. Concepts and systems that have been incorporated into the design include daylighting, shading, and innovative glazing elements; maximum use of natural ventilation; photovoltaic (PV) power generation; solar space and domestic water-heating systems; lighting with continuously dimming electronic ballasts and occupancy- and photo-sensor controls; real-time energy monitoring; HVAC systems demonstrating several new technologies including prototype natural-gas heat-pump air conditioning, variable air volume underfloor air distribution, and high-efficiency pulse boilers; gray-water system for capture and reuse of rain water and lavatory discharge; self-sustaining landscaping and water-conserving irrigation system;

Home to the Naval Base Ventura County Public Works Department, consisting of 10,000 square feet of renovated space and 7,000 square feet of new construction.

At this Naval Base Building, project designers used physical and computerized modeling to optimize the interaction of daylighting with building envelope, interiors, and systems.

indoor air-quality monitoring; and extensive use of recycled building materials. Project designers used physical and computerized modeling to optimize the interaction of daylighting with building envelope, interiors, and systems.

The client was committed to building a project that was a showcase of sustainability and energy efficiency features. There was an extremely strong sense of collaboration and joint commitment to the project goals between client and the design team. Even with this, funding challenges meant that only through the extreme perseverance of the client was the project successfully completed.

Building Performance, According to the Architects

The building is performing as expected, although some features are not. Features that have worked well are daylighting, high-efficiency lighting, photovoltaic solar electric power, natural ventilation and operable windows, solar thermal heating, water-efficient landscape, underfloor air distribution, digital controls, water-efficient plumbing fixtures, and green materials. Features that have not worked as well as expected are the gray-water system and the recycled roofing material.

Lessons Learned by the Architects

- The project was the firm's first to use a gray-water system or a PV solar system, and it was one of their first truly green buildings, incorporating all sustainability issues (i.e., site, water, energy, indoor environmental quality, or IEQ, and materials) into a single project. That was in 1995–1997, and the firm has since done this on more than 100 projects. All subsequent projects reflected lessons learned from this first demonstration.

- The collaborative and integrated design process that we used served us very well, and we would use a very similar process today. Many of the green materials and systems used in this project were prototypes or early products that have since been significantly changed and improved by the evolution of the market.

- CTG Energetics uses LEED as a way of focusing the client and project team on sustainability and interdisciplinary issues affecting integrated design. For this reason, we find it essential to have LEED-accredited professionals on staff.

- Our entire practice has always been built around leading-edge technologies and design concepts, so accommodating sustainability was the next logical extension of the practice. The impact of sustainability has been to significantly expand the purview and professional backgrounds of the staff to now include ecologists, landscape planners, and materials science and indoor air quality professionals. These staff are part of the "Green group" that is dedicated to sustainability, while part of the larger "Energetics group," which also incorporates energy efficiency.

2002 AIA/COTE Top Ten Winner
CAMP ARROYO
LOCATION: Livermore, California
ARCHITECT: Siegel & Strain Architects

This environmental education camp, which serves middle-school students as well as critically ill children and other guests, was designed to demonstrate a series of ecological design principles as part of the curriculum. Bathhouses are made of stabilized earth, the cabins are efficient wood structures, and the dining hall is a straw-bale building. Low-tech solutions to heating, cooling, and water treatment were favored over more complex mechanical technologies for energy efficiency, lower cost, and simplicity. The bathhouses are open-air, seasonal structures with natural ventilation and no mechanical system. The cabins and dining hall depend on shading strategies and operable clerestory windows to keep them cool. The cabins have south-facing sunrooms for winter heat gain and solar panels for water heating and backup radiant heat. The biological wastewater-treatment system treats water with minimal energy input, demonstrating that there is no waste in nature.

Building Performance, According to the Architects

A postoccupancy study conducted by University of California, Berkeley architecture students one year after the project was built found that the buildings are performing

At Camp Arroyo, low-tech solutions to heating, cooling, and water treatment were favored over more complex mechanical technologies for energy efficiency, lower cost, and simplicity.

well despite some neglect in maintenance of mechanical systems. Passive design measures proved to be working as anticipated to decrease building heating and cooling loads. The exteriors of the buildings are maintaining their appearance, so it seems that the materials selected are performing as intended.

Lessons Learned by the Architects

There were two clients for the project, a public agency and a private foundation, each with somewhat different goals. In addition, three separate construction contracts were let for this project—two public and one private. This greatly complicated the design and delivery process. Nonetheless, there was strong support for a very green project. The public agency, a regional park district and the owner of the property, had strong input into the site design.

The project remains a very green project within the constraints of the program requirements and budget. In retrospect, we would probably have completed earlier and more in-depth temperature modeling on the dining hall; it might have allowed for the elimination of the evaporative-cooling unit for the dining room. Given the testing on straw-bale systems that is now available, we might also consider lime or even earthen plaster for the walls. We would certainly push much harder for a single contract for all of the buildings.

These were our first straw-bale and stabilized-earth buildings, and the largest project that incorporates Forest Stewardship Council (FSC)–certified wood. We have continued to design straw-bale buildings and have continued to refine our details and construction methods, including simplifying window details and structural interfaces. One of the contractors had difficulty obtaining FSC-certified wood for parts of the project, and we continue to look for ways to deal with supply issues on large, publicly bid projects. We have learned more about finishing and curing high-fly-ash concrete and would instigate tighter controls on water content and curing. Most importantly, we have developed a stronger integrated design process, involving our consultants even earlier in the design process.

The project would have benefited from having an owner's manual that described the goals of the project, how the passive-design systems work, how the mechanical systems operate, and how they should be maintained.

2002 AIA/COTE Top Ten Winner
EDIFICIO MALECON
LOCATION: Buenos Aires, Argentina
ARCHITECT: Hellmuth Obata + Kassabaum (HOK), Ripley Rasmus

This 125,000-square-foot office building was built on a reclaimed brownfield site (its garage was built within the foundations of a nineteenth-century warehouse) at Puerto Madero, a redevelopment area in Buenos Aires. The building was developed

The broad northern face of Edificio Malecon, the primary solar exposure, is shaped to track the sun and is fully screened with deep sunshades that virtually eliminate direct solar radiation during peak cooling months.

as a long, narrow slab to minimize solar gain on the structure, the east and west ends of which are "pinched." The broad northern face, the primary solar exposure, is shaped to track the sun and is fully screened with deep sunshades that virtually eliminate direct solar radiation during peak cooling months. The south face, which reflects the geometry of the northern facade, is equipped with the same high-performance curtain-wall system as the other facades, minimizing solar gain. A green roof helps insulate the 40,000-square-foot podium from solar radiation and manages stormwater runoff. Open floor plates and raised floors provide flexibility for multitenant office or alternative future uses.

2002 AIA/COTE Top Ten Winner
IOWA ASSOCIATION OF MUNICIPAL UTILITIES
LOCATION: Ankeny, Iowa
ARCHITECT: RDG Bussard Dikis

The 13,000-square-foot facility, the Iowa Association of Municipal Utilities (IAMU) Office and Training Headquarters, was conceived as a teaching tool. Designed and

The Iowa Association of Municipal Utilities project has also restored a suburban farm field, destined for commercial development, into a native Iowa tall-grass prairie.

At the Iowa Association of Municipal Utilities Building, the reconstructed prairie, wetlands, and filtration ponds have recreated habitat for flora and fauna.

built within a modest budget, its energy consumption is 48 percent less than a conventional design, and it is 98 percent daylit. The building uses a geothermal heat-pump system for heating and cooling. Building occupants enjoy multiple views of the landscape and sky from any point inside the building. The project has also restored a suburban farm field, destined for commercial development, into a native Iowa tall-grass prairie. Soil erosion had been plaguing the site, harming nearby Carney Marsh, a 40-acre protected wetland. The reconstructed prairie, wetlands, and filtration ponds have recreated habitat for flora and fauna.

The client is passionate about sustainable design and demonstrated that to its membership within the IAMU organization. The client mandated a high level of sustainability and measurable performance. Also, the client brought together multiple organizations in the design process as stakeholders, including the energy provider for the project. These collaborators on the project were invaluable in making the site restoration to native prairie viable, as well as providing invaluable rebates for energy-efficiency upgrades.

Building Performance, According to the Architects

The building has been using less energy than what was modeled during design: actual metered energy is 55 percent less than a code-compliant building in Iowa. The ground-source heat-pump system is working well. The daylighting systems and controls are performing as designed. The building has a very considerate owner that is diligent about operating the building effectively.

2002 AIA/COTE Top Ten Winner
NATIONAL WILDLIFE FEDERATION HEADQUARTERS
LOCATION: Reston, Virginia
ARCHITECT: Hellmuth Obata + Kassabaum (HOK), William Hellmuth

The new 85,000-square-foot headquarters serves 300 employees and guests. The National Wildlife Federation made a commitment to build a headquarters facility

The south facade of the National Wildlife Federation Headquarters has a vertical trellis planted with deciduous vines that leaf out in summer to provide shade and fall off in winter to allow sunlight to help heat the facility.

The National Wildlife Federation Headquarters' orientation capitalizes on solar energy sources to reduce energy expenditure and increase natural light.

that would demonstrate sensible stewardship of its financial resources. It accomplished this through a rigorous payback analysis to select state-of-the-shelf construction technologies and materials. Native plantings support local wildlife and reduce the need for irrigation and frequent mowing. The building's orientation capitalizes on solar energy sources to reduce energy expenditure and increase natural light. The facility's north side, which overlooks the park, is a curtain wall of glass that offers vistas and floods the interior spaces with light to create a welcoming atmosphere. The south facade has a vertical trellis planted with deciduous vines that leaf out in summer to provide shade and fall off in winter to allow sunlight to help heat the facility. The plantings provide a vertical habitat for indigenous wildlife.

2002 AIA/COTE Top Ten Winner
PIER 1
LOCATION: San Francisco, California
ARCHITECT: SMWM, Dan Cheetham

This adaptive-reuse project transformed a dilapidated warehouse on San Francisco's waterfront to 140,000 square feet of class A office space and an acre of new public open space. The design reflects the history and nature of the site, uses green materials garnered from green sources, and provides clean air and natural light for occu-

The design of Pier 1 reflects the history and nature of the site, uses green materials garnered from green sources, and provides clean air and natural light for occupants.

pants. Pier 1 is surrounded by water, which flows through radiant tubes in floor slabs for heating and cooling. This system moderates the interior climate according to each zone's location and orientation. Generated heat is rejected into a submerged condenser water loop under the building, dissipating energy into the bay within a tightly prescribed temperature range.

2002 AIA/COTE Top Ten Winner
PUGET SOUND ENVIRONMENTAL LEARNING CENTER
LOCATION: Bainbridge Island, Washington
ARCHITECT: Mithun

The 70,000-square-foot facility includes an interpretive center, a great hall, offices, learning studios, dining hall, art studio, maintenance building, and visitor accommodations. Wastewater is treated on site and reused. Rainwater is collected for irrigation and other uses. Photovoltaic installations provide more than half of the power for the learning-studio building. Rooftop solar hot-water panels reduce hot water demand at lodges and dining hall by 50 percent. Ventilation replaces air conditioning, with operable skylights providing maximum through-ventilation. High-efficiency fluorescent lighting with photocells reduces energy use. High-quality metal roofs and metal-clad windows will provide long life in the heavily wooded Northwest environment.

At the Puget Sound Environmental Learning Center, wastewater is treated on site and reused, and rainwater is collected for irrigation and other uses.

Photovoltaic installations provide more than half of the power for the learning-studio building.

Building Performance, According to the Architects

Initial feedback indicates that the natural ventilation is working well, even in the warm summer months, and that the sustainable-building systems focused on daylight harvesting, water conservation, photovoltaic electricity, and solar hot water have been performing as expected.

The IslandWood design process was highly collaborative and involved an integrated design team working toward sustainable goals from the earliest days of programming through construction. We approached the design of this project in a highly immersive fashion. During the programming process, we camped out on site, undertook extensive materials and systems research, and engaged a sustainable-design peer-review team for ongoing feedback.

Lessons Learned by the Architects

Since the beginning of this project, the sustainable-design industry has evolved significantly. If starting the project anew today, we would be armed with much more scientific information about materials, systems, and the integrated components that comprise a sustainable-design project. As a result, we would be able to refocus some of our energies from basic research to the analysis and incorporation of integrated systems.

2002 AIA/COTE Top Ten Winner
TOFTE CABIN
LOCATION: Tofte, Minnesota
ARCHITECT: Sarah Nettleton Architects

The renovation of this 1947 cabin resulted in a 950-square-foot, soul-satisfying retreat that is a model of sustainable design. The cabin's original site and adjacent trees were retained to shelter the cabin from winter winds and open it to sun and wind from the east and south. The locally quarried granite's color echoes the colors of the spruce and the lake, as it references the granite bedrock beneath the house. Natural stack ventilation through low and high windows cools the cabin. An air-to-air heat exchanger provides ventilation. A super-insulated thermal envelope minimized the load on the geothermal heat-pump, in-floor heating system. The heat pump provides domestic hot water as well. Built with long-lasting materials and careful details, the cabin is a beautiful retreat that will serve for generations.

Project Goal as Expressed by the Client

The goal of this project was to explore as consciously as possible what the idea of sustainable design means in the context of this particular project. In general, sustainable design requires paying attention to the short- and long-term consequences of any transformation of the environment. We are concerned about consequences to the natural environment, the human and nonhuman neighbors to the site, the com-

The renovation of this 1947 cabin resulted in a 950-square-foot, soul-satisfying retreat that is a model of sustainable design.

munity in which the project is located, and the communities that supply the materials for and receive the waste that manufacturing and construction produces and the resulting dwelling.

Because we understand this project to be an exploration of what is unknown rather than an application of what is known, we invite everyone involved in the project in any way to contribute their knowledge and expertise to our understanding of the ways in which we can best meet the project goal.

Natural stack ventilation through low and high windows cools the cabin. An air-to-air heat exchanger provides ventilation.

2003 AIA/COTE Top Ten Green Projects

Argonne Child Development Center, San Francisco, California

Chicago Center for Green Technology, Chicago, Illinois

Colorado Court Affordable Housing, Santa Monica, California

Cusano Center at Tinicum, Philadelphia, Pennsylvania

The Fisher Pavilion, Seattle, Washington

Herman Miller Marketplace, Zeeland, Michigan

Hidden Villa Hostel and Summer Camp, Los Altos Hills, California

San Mateo County Sheriff's Forensic Laboratory, San Mateo, California

Steinhude Sea Recreation Facility, Steinhude, Germany

Wine Creek Road Home, Healdsburg, California

2003 AIA/COTE Top Ten Winner
ARGONNE CHILD DEVELOPMENT CENTER
LOCATION: San Francisco, California
ARCHITECT: 450 Architects

Strong community advocacy pushed for the Argonne Child Development Center to be a green building in its solar performance and materials selections but, even more, to be a sheltering and celebratory spot for their community garden and their children. The building has no mechanical cooling and a minimal heating system; it makes simple but effective use of San Francisco's mild climate. Its single-room, deeply shaded, east-west solar orientation allows for plenty of shade and ventilation in summer and passive gains in winter. Its classrooms can be used almost year-round without artificial lighting, and the building's solar-electric system generates 25 percent of the remaining energy load. As San Francisco's first solar-powered school, it serves as a model and research tool for the whole school district.

The center fits into a dense yet low-rise residential neighborhood with an efficient site plan that creates a wide array of useful outdoor spaces. The street-facing administrative wing and perpendicular classroom wing enclose a sheltered but open play area that takes in the southern sun. Sloping down to the west, the building keeps its shadows off the community's planting beds but extends reading nooks so students can absorb the sights and smells of the garden.

Jury Comments: "The Argonne Child Development Center is a simple, straightforward, elemental building that responds to the community's request for a green building. The coupling of the skylights and the photovoltaic panels, as well as the building and site water-conservation strategies, are indicative of an economy of means throughout the project."

The Argonne Child Development Center was the firm's first from-the-ground-up building. Thus, it did not require modifying its practice. The firm used this project to define the goals and aspirations of the practice. The office has always hired the most sustainable, progressive-thinking individuals possible. Everyone on staff and both principals are LEED accredited, and this will remain the business model as it moves forward.

Building Performance, According to the Architects

The Argonne Child Development Center still functions well as an educational facility and source of inspiration for other schools and municipal agencies. The first goal was to design a sustainable school appropriate to San Francisco's mild climate as well as demonstrate that solar power was possible in the foggy Richmond District of San Francisco. In those respects, the project is a huge success.

Some performance shortcomings include the following:

- The school is designed to have natural daylight in the classroom spaces. However, the teachers and staff tend to turn all the lights on all the time, sunny or not (this is how the children have been trained that nap time is over). If only the staff would raise and lower the blinds—also, perhaps getting the children to help by making a game out of this daily activity—the school's electrical demand would decrease and the percentage of power generated by the solar collectors versus consumed would greatly increase!

- The goal was for 30 percent of the facility's power to be generated by the solar collectors (photovoltaics). Currently, the school is averaging 10 percent. Our firm has measured the required natural illumination of daylight within each classroom, which exceed the amounts required for prekindergarten spaces.

Lessons Learned by the Architects

- We learned that achieving sustainable results in the public sector requires enormous time commitments working with city officials, district representatives, janitors, teachers, parents, children, and neighbors. All these important people will either help or hurt the progress of sustainable building. Everyone needs to be a part of a progressive and forward-thinking team with common goals.

- Since this project was designed, the USGBC's LEED program has been implemented, the city of San Francisco has signed a Sustainable Development Plan, the city has signed legislation requiring new publicly funded projects to achieve LEED Silver rating, and the state of California has implemented legislation requiring all schools to exceed the state's minimum energy-efficiency regulations, commonly referred to as Title 24. If our office were to design this project now, everything we were fighting so hard for (ten years ago) would be required by state or local ordinances, and we would have been able to deliver a far more sustainable building.

2003 AIA/COTE Top Ten Winner
CHICAGO CENTER FOR GREEN TECHNOLOGY
LOCATION: Chicago, Illinois
ARCHITECT: Farr Associates

Through collaboration between a variety of public and private entities, a blighted and unsafe industrial site has become an example of how one project can help rebuild a community. This center does just that by instigating an overhaul for a part of Chicago that has seen neglect and disinvestment for decades. The once-decrepit building had been extensively vandalized. Everything of value had been removed. The building now houses a high-tech factory, educates the public on sustainability, and houses a community gardening–training facility that helps people find good jobs in the industry.

The Chicago Center for Green Technology is an example of how one building can help to transform a blighted and unsafe industrial site and have an impact on the neighboring community.

Farr Associates strove to use every design feature and technology in multiple ways.

This project represents the city of Chicago's commitment to sustainable design. It is an ambitious LEED Platinum design that uses almost 50 percent less energy than comparable construction, gets over 17 percent of its energy from photovoltaic (PV) cells, and utilizes more than 36 percent recycled materials in the construction. Additionally, the building manages all stormwater on site, including collecting rainwater for irrigation. The architects strove to use every design feature and technology in multiple ways. Photovoltaic panels also serve as sunshades. A public bench is also a major heating duct. Entrances combine as project gateways and sun protection.

Chicago Center's tenants are involved in environmental-related pursuits and include companies such as Spire Solar Chicago, a manufacturer of solar panels; Green Corps, a landscape training arm of the city government; and WRD Environmental, a firm focused on sustainable landscape practice.

Jury Comments: "Chicago Center for Green Technology transforms an existing, abandoned, industrial building in a brownfield into an environmental showcase of both high- and low-tech systems and components. It now is home to an unusual mix of uses and tenants, including office, warehouse, interpretative center, assembly, and community garden, all in an urban context that manages 100 percent of precipitation on site."

2003 AIA/COTE Top Ten Winner
COLORADO COURT AFFORDABLE HOUSING
LOCATION: Santa Monica, California
ARCHITECT: Pugh + Scarpa

The 44-unit, five-story building is the first affordable housing project in the United States to be 100 percent energy neutral. It won various national awards in 2003, including an Honor Award for Architecture and Housing PIA Award. This project provides an excellent model of sustainable development in an urban environment and promotes diversity through strategically placed affordable housing.

Innovative sustainable-energy technologies developed for Colorado Court include a natural gas–powered turbine heat-recovery system that generates the base electrical load and services the building's hot-water needs as well. A solar electric-

Colorado Court Affordable Housing provides an excellent model of sustainable development in an urban environment and promotes diversity through strategically placed affordable housing.

panel system integrated into the facade and roof supplies most of the peak-load energy demand. This unique cogeneration system converts utility natural gas to electricity to meet the building's power needs. This same system also captures and uses waste heat to produce hot water and space heating for the residents throughout the year. The unused energy from these passive solar panels is returned to the grid during daytime hours and retrieved from the grid at night as needed. The *green electricity* produced at the building site releases no pollutants into the environment. Colorado Court's energy-conservation systems have been designed to pay for themselves in less than ten years. Annual savings in electricity and natural gas exceed $6,000. The building also collects rainwater runoff from the entire city block behind the property and funnels it into a series of underground chambers. The water slowly percolates back into the soil, which filters the pollutants from the water while preventing contaminated water from spilling into Santa Monica Bay. Prevailing breezes cool the building, which has no air conditioning.

Jury Comments: "Colorado Court incorporates a comprehensive array of offensive and defensive energy and environmental strategies in a relatively high-density project in an urban setting. The PV panels were seamlessly integrated into the architecture, which demonstrated extraordinary design sophistication, especially for an affordable housing project."

Description of Process

Every year, Colorado Court Santa Monica (CCSM) does an outreach to all the faith-based organizations, schools, and social service agencies in Santa Monica. The purpose is to let them know that we have affordable housing available for their low-income students, clients, and parishioners. Each year, we get about 3,000 households asking for housing, and we have about 100 vacancies. CCSM has a list of about 120 organizations and works with them as a group and as individuals to tailor their projects to meet the needs of their tenant population and potential future residents. Because Santa Monica is very rich in social services, we try to connect our tenants with other organizations for non-housing-related needs, like senior assistance, counseling, gang diversion, after-school programs, etc. Colorado Court is located in the downtown core of Santa Monica, and it is surrounded largely by commercial and institutional buildings with few residential structures in the area. The participatory design process was open to all residents of Santa Monica. The workshops focused on the social service organizations located in the downtown core that would likely serve this tenant population.

2003 AIA/COTE Top Ten Winner
CUSANO CENTER AT TINICUM
LOCATION: Philadelphia, Pennsylvania
ARCHITECT: Susan Maxman & Partners, Architects

The Cusano Environmental Education Center at the 1,200-acre John Heinz National Wildlife Refuge is the U.S. Fish and Wildlife system's most urban refuge. This largest

The whole Cusano Center building becomes an exhibit as signage is placed throughout to describe sustainable initiatives used in the project.

tidal marsh in Pennsylvania is the only remaining piece of what was a 5,700-acre marsh. The site claims Philadelphia International Airport and Sun Oil Company Tank Farm for neighbors; yet, it is an extraordinary place where one can gaze upon a great blue heron as a plane takes off in flight.

The marsh has undergone intense pressure from development companies, and it has taken extensive efforts by environmentalists to preserve it. Along with creating a safe habitat for migrating birds, the preservation of the marsh demonstrates the importance of preserving wetlands for their role in maintaining the health of our ecological systems. There is an exhibit on site called the *marsh machine*. This working exhibit treats the facility's wastewater in a greenhouse attached to the classroom wing, allowing for observation by visitors. The treated water is used to flush toilets. In addition to responsible water use, the marsh machine demonstrates the critical purification characteristics of the marsh.

This working exhibit treats the facility's wastewater in a greenhouse attached to the classroom wing, allowing for observation by visitors.

Sustainable-design strategies include energy efficiency, use of recycled materials, and restorative treatment of the site. Energy conservation is achieved through a building form that maximizes daylighting, natural ventilation, and passive solar heating. Materials were chosen for recycled content and environmental impact, including 60-year-old salvaged timbers, certified Pennsylvania hardwood, and recycled and rapidly renewable materials. The whole building becomes an exhibit as signage is placed throughout to describe sustainable initiatives used in the project.

Jury Comments: "Cusano Environmental Education Center incorporates a wetland while restoring natural habitat, recycling wastewater, and utilizing multiple strategies for recharging groundwater. A simple architectural vocabulary fits the modesty of the project and effectively communicates its interpretive mission."

Building Performance, According to the Architects

The project is performing even better than anticipated from an energy standpoint. It also makes a very positive impression on its visitors and raises their awareness of the fact that they can make choices in their lives that positively affect our ecological systems. It was one great aim of the building to be didactic, and that is working. Architect Susan Maxman, FAIA, conveys this with an anecdote: "Several years ago, my granddaughter visited the Center with her school class, and when I asked her how she liked it, her response was, 'Now I know where my soda bottles go!'"

Our client for this project was U.S. Fish and Wildlife Foundation, so the project began with the client knowing that it wanted to do the "right thing." One of the criteria in selecting the architect was the firm's commitment to sustainable design. That said, there were still times when we had to convince our client of certain strategies, such as the living machine, which we felt was the perfect means of illustrating the purification capabilities of a marsh or wetland and the need to preserve them.

2003 AIA/COTE Top Ten Winner
THE FISHER PAVILION
LOCATION: Seattle, Washington
ARCHITECT: The Miller|Hull Partnership, LLP

The Fisher Pavilion at Seattle Center (see color insert) is a multipurpose exhibition hall nestled into the heart of the 74-acre Seattle Center campus. It replaces the old Flag Pavilion on the same site that was constructed 40 years ago as a temporary building for the Seattle World's Fair. The primary function of Fisher Pavilion is to promote community and sense of place. Seattle Center has been described as the "front yard" of Seattle.

The four major spaces of this 2.6-acre project—the Exhibition Hall, Upper Plaza, Lower Plaza, and Civic Green—create a wide variety of opportunities for public gatherings and events within walking distance from downtown. Rather than dominate the site, the earth-sheltered building becomes a backdrop for the various activities that unfold there, from cat shows to concerts, and AIDS walks to the September 11, 2001, Memorial Garden, which has been established along the main entry to the building. The terminus of the existing monorail line between Seattle Center and downtown is one block away, and it will be an important hub in the future citywide monorail now in design. Fisher Pavilion is one of the first buildings in Seattle to be designed and constructed under the city policy requiring all public facilities over $5 million to achieve an LEED Silver rating. Burying the building and using the high-mass thermal capacity of a concrete roof decreases envelope loads on the building.

Jury Comments: "Fisher Pavilion, an underground civic building, is carefully sited within Seattle Center, serving more than a quarter million people for events and cultural festivals throughout the year, while retrieving valuable urban land for a public plaza. Fisher Pavilion exhibits careful attention to lighting efficiency and quality while providing significant daylight for exhibitions."

2003 AIA/COTE Top Ten Winner
HERMAN MILLER MARKETPLACE
LOCATION: Zeeland, Michigan
ARCHITECT: Integrated Architecture

Located in a commercial development next to a McDonald's restaurant, the project demonstrates that green buildings can be woven successfully into our commercial landscape. The expectation of this office space began as nothing less than the creation of a great place to work. The challenge was to deliver, without compromise, a balanced solution to all of the following requirements: rapid deployment, a green building, improvement of organizational effectiveness, adaptability, effective space use, and (last but not least) *great design*. The resulting Herman Miller Marketplace

Herman Miller Marketplace demonstrates that green buildings can be woven successfully into commercial landscape.

is among the nation's first design/build Gold LEED-certified buildings, and the U.S. Green Building Council features this building in its "Making the Business Case." Additionally, the building's documented operational costs are becoming a national benchmark for sustainable and energy-efficient design solutions. The design team worked to create an efficient building filled with the luxuries of natural light, fresh air, and space, carefully crafted for maximum human comfort, without losing track of cost issues. Project goals included increasing the efficiency of the heating and cooling systems to reduce energy costs by 40 percent and minimizing lighting-system energy demands by using a combination of natural daylight and direct task light. Sustainable materials utilized throughout the building include recycled carpet and walls covered with composite board made from agricultural fiber waste.

The goal of the project—to develop an environmentally sensitive, economically viable office project—began before soil was moved with the development of a site-sediment and erosion-control plan that conforms to the EPA standard. Prior to the start of this project the land had been used for a place to store fill materials; it was void of trees and consisted only of sparse vegetation. The county agency requires that a 25-year storm event be detained. The project was designed to detain a 100-year storm event.

Jury Comments: "Herman Miller Marketplace, a prefabricated-system building, exhibits unusual interior flexibility while providing a significantly high level of amenity and indoor environmental quality including water and light, and the ability of the site to detain a 100-year storm event. This is a promising prototype for an

The challenge for Herman Miller Marketplace was to deliver a balanced solution to the following requirements: rapid deployment, a green building, improvement of organizational effectiveness, adaptability, effective space use, and great design.

economically viable, environmentally sensitive, and sustainable solution in the spec-ulative office market."

2003 AIA/COTE Top Ten Winner
HIDDEN VILLA YOUTH HOSTEL AND SUMMER CAMP
LOCATION: Los Altos Hills, California
ARCHITECT: Arkin Tilt Architects

Hidden Villa is an environmental education foundation sited on a bucolic farm and wilderness preserve in the coastal hills between San Francisco and San Jose. For the past 75 years, the foundation has engaged visitors in innovative, hands-on outdoor education programs, including a demonstration organic farm, a summer camp, and a youth hostel since 1937 (the oldest hostel west of the Mississippi).

The new hostel facility brings the playful, educative, community-oriented spirit of Hidden Villa to structures that harmonize with the site's agrarian past. Constrained in a narrow canyon by the sacred climbing tree to the west and by existing cabins to the east, the new structures hug the northern slope, maximizing winter sun and reestab-lishing the visual connection up-canyon through a series of courtyards. The dining hall, the literal and figurative heart of both programs, can expand into the screen porch via large bifold doors that incorporate windows and doors reused from the original hostel. A large dormer captures low winter sun while permitting natural ven-tilation. Concrete floors and a rammed-earth wall along the north mediate extreme temperatures as well as heat from the kitchen. A ground-source geothermal heat pump supplies the radiant-floor system as well as preheating for hot water.

The design represents a delicate balance between the simplicity of a barn, the sophistication of careful energy modeling, and a tumble of ad-hoc shacks that typ-

The new Hidden Villa Youth Hostel and Summer Camp brings the playful, educative, community-oriented spirit of Hidden Villa to structures that harmonize with the site's agrarian past.

At this youth hostel and summer camp, concrete floors and a rammed-earth wall along the north mediate extreme temperatures as well as heat from the kitchen.

ify summer camp. A threshold between the natural and built environment, the facility demonstrates how one's living affects nature: the buildings have become part of the educational experience at Hidden Villa.

Jury Comments: "This dining hall, kitchen, and staff quarters serves as the new center for an existing assemblage of small camp buildings in a secluded, Bay area wilderness farm. The modest syntax of recycled and sustainably harvested wood incorporates a number of low-tech strategies that provide rustic comforts while moderating summer heat; the site water strategies reduce consumption and runoff."

Building Performance, According to the Architects

In terms of its meeting the needs of the camp and hostel programs and being a place that the staff and users have grown to love, it is performing and operating well. Actual performance is difficult to gauge, as the entire environmental education center and site—containing dozens of buildings—is served by a single utility meter. Liquid propane is used only for cooking; all other space and water heating needs are met with a ground-source heat pump, which by all accounts is performing as anticipated. The daylight in the restrooms could be better, but the clients requested obscure glass, even in the clerestory windows, which has lower-light transmittance.

Lessons Learned by the Architects

- Careful communication of the priorities of the project to both the clients and the contractors is important, and while all went smoothly, it could have been stronger here. The contractor shared the commitment to sustainable building, but not to every detail. We ended up performing the retrofit of some of the doors and windows salvaged from the previous building and seeing these built into the custom bifold doors. It was only our commitment to seeing this detail through that made it happen. We still go further than we should to see certain details make their way into our projects, but often these are what make them special.

- When we started our practice, we made the conscious decision to incorporate some level of solar and green design into every project. Some of our early projects were recognized for this, and we now serve a clientele looking specifically for the marriage of design and ecology.

- For every CSI section of our specifications, we have some degree of green building incorporated. We indicate materials specifications as thoroughly as possible, but with flexibility where appropriate. We try to include the manufacturer and supplier contact information, and alternates when there are any.

- As for LEED, our approach to ecological design is on a much more intuitive, holistic level than that captured by any of the rating systems. We have our own systems, which are not targeted so much at "points" as they are at achieving higher levels of integration, and balancing these with the overall design goals and relationship to the greater landscape.

2003 AIA/COTE Top Ten Winner
SAN MATEO COUNTY SHERIFF'S FORENSIC LABORATORY
LOCATION: San Mateo, California
ARCHITECT: Hellmuth Obata + Kassabaum (HOK)

The San Mateo County Sheriff's Forensic Laboratory and Coroner's Office is a highly secure and technologically innovative laboratory facility designed to provide a superior workplace, flexibility to accommodate changing needs over time, and advanced

The orientation of the San Mateo County Sheriff's Forensic Laboratory building, large roof overhangs, north-facing clerestory windows, and canted windows on the southwest reduce glare while maximizing daylight.

approaches to resource efficiency. The facility houses several key public safety and essential public service functions, including 911 dispatch, emergency-operations center, sheriff's training facility, forensics laboratory, and the coroner's office. The facility combines the various agencies into one essential structure that must remain functional after a major earthquake, thereby minimizing the risk of disruption of services. The orientation of the building, large roof overhangs, north-facing clerestory windows, and canted windows on the southwest reduce glare while maximizing daylight. Energy usage has been reduced by more than 50 percent relative to the stringent California Title 24 energy requirements, and renewable energy systems supply all non-HVAC energy requirements.

Twenty-six thousand square feet of rooftop-mounted photovoltaic panels will produce enough power to accommodate all of the building's non-HVAC electrical requirements.

Twenty-six thousand square feet of rooftop-mounted photovoltaic panels will produce enough power to accommodate all of the building's non-HVAC electrical requirements. The photovoltaic roof generates more than 180 kilowatts of electricity, over half of the summertime peak load. During off-peak daylight hours this facility exports energy to other buildings in San Mateo County. Assuming energy cost savings estimated at about $70,000 per year, the installation has a simple payback period of about ten years.

Jury Comments: "The San Mateo County Forensics Laboratory is a *tour de force* in photovoltaic power generation that meets more than half of the peak summer electrical load, while water conservation strategies for site and building reduce water use by over 40 percent. This building devotes its entire 26,000-square-foot roof area to the harvesting of sunlight, meeting more than 28 percent of total energy demands."

2003 AIA/COTE Top Ten Winner
STEINHUDE SEA RECREATION FACILITY
LOCATION: Steinhude, Germany
ARCHITECT: Randall Stout Architects

This project was conceived as an amenity to EXPO 2000 visitors to the rural region of the Steinhude Sea, north of Hannover, Germany. The theme for EXPO 2000, "Man, Nature, Environment," led to the goal of an artistically intriguing structure that was fully self-sustaining with minimal impact on the surrounding ecosystem. This small recreation facility is located on an island at the south shore of the Steinhude Sea. The island ecosystem consists of a beach area, green fields, nature walk, children's play area, and a bird sanctuary. The new 3,057-square-foot facility accommodates, with minimal ecological impact, a café, lifeguard facilities, boathouse, storage, public toilets and showers, and an exhibition area and observation deck. Prefabrication of the building in a nearby factory resulted in waste minimization and ecosystem protection. The ecologically sensitive island would have been damaged by heavy construction equipment, so building components were panelized off-site, test-assembled, delivered to the sea dock, loaded onto barges, and floated to the island's edge, where a barge-mounted crane placed the panels.

Energy self-sufficiency is achieved via photovoltaic panels, solar hot-water collectors, seed-oil-fueled cogeneration microturbine, daylighting, natural ventilation, passive solar, building automation, and high-performance materials. These systems provide complete lighting and power needs for the building, recharge for a fleet of eight photovoltaic-powered boats, and also produce excess electricity to sell back to the utility grid. Other sustainability practices are incorporated, such as gray-water and harvested-water systems, green materials, and waste reduction. Integration of solar and renewable ideas, from conceptual design to partnering with the local utility company and a technically savvy contractor, has led to a building that is a joy to its users.

Randall Stout designed Steinhude Sea Recreation Facility, an artistically intriguing structure that is fully self-sustaining with minimal impact on the surrounding ecosystem.

Jury Comments: "The Steinhude Sea Recreation Facility on an island on the northern German coast is a visually powerful and compelling expression of sustainability. With photovoltaic, solar hot water, daylighting, renewable-source power generation, and a gray-water system utilizing rainwater collected from the roof and landscaped terraces, this prefabricated building uses no fossil fuels, eliminating all greenhouse gas emissions."

2003 AIA/COTE Top Ten Winner
WINE CREEK ROAD HOME
LOCATION: Healdsburg, California
ARCHITECT: Siegel & Strain Architects

This modest family retreat in northern California was conceived of as a single gable that spans enclosed living and sleeping areas separated by an open breezeway, or *dogtrot*. The form and construction of the house reflects the spirit of local vernacular buildings, taking maximum advantage of the site and climate to make the house comfortable while minimizing energy use and environmental impacts. The chief strategy for saving energy was to keep the building cool during the long, hot summers without mechanical cooling, which was accomplished by employing natural ventilation, thermal mass, and superior insulation. The thin building section, the dogtrot, and the placement of windows optimize opportunities for natural ventilation. The interior plaster walls and concrete floor provide enough thermal mass to minimize temperature swings and integrate well with the radiant-heating system. Opening the windows at night cools the house enough that it remains cool through the hottest part of the day. A high-efficiency water heater provides radiant floor heating. These measures resulted in a design that exceeds California's strict energy-efficiency standards by 29 percent and keeps the building cool except for the hottest hours of the hottest days. The owners chose high-efficiency, low-water-use appliances.

Jury Comments: "This modest home in northern California is a basic, high-performance, low-tech building in the spirit of traditional Japanese residential architecture. This simple retreat uses natural ventilation rather than mechanical cooling, thermal mass, radiant floor heating, straw-bale construction, and on-site management of almost all stormwater."

At the Wine Creek Road Home, the design of the Wine Creek Road Home reflects the spirit of local vernacular buildings, taking maximum advantage of the site and climate to make the house comfortable while minimizing energy use and environmental impacts.

Summer comfort without mechanical cooling was accomplished by employing natural ventilation, thermal mass, and superior insulation.

2004 AIA/COTE Top Ten Green Projects

20 River Terrace–The Solaire, New York, New York

City of White Rock Operations Building, White Rock, British Columbia, Canada

F10 House, Chicago, Illinois

Genzyme Center, Cambridge, Massachusetts

Greyston Bakery, Yonkers, New York

Herman Miller Building C1, Zeeland, Michigan

Lake View Terrace Branch Library, Lake View Terrace, California

Pierce County Environmental Services Building, University Place, Washington

The Plaza at PPL Center, Allentown, Pennsylvania

Woods Hole Research Center, Falmouth, Massachusetts

2004 AIA/COTE Top Ten Winner
20 RIVER TERRACE—THE SOLAIRE
LOCATION: New York, New York
ARCHITECT: Cesar Pelli & Associates Architects

The Solaire is a 27-story, glass-and-brick residential tower in Battery Park City, Manhattan, directly adjacent to the site of the former World Trade Center (see color insert). The design meets both the recently enacted New York State Green Building Tax Credit and Gold LEED Certification. The 357,000-square-foot, 293-unit building is estimated to require 35 percent less energy than conventional code-complying design; reduce peak demand for electricity by 65 percent; require 50 percent less potable water; and provide a healthy indoor environment. An integrated array of photovoltaic panels generates 5 percent of the building's energy at peak loading. The building incorporates an advanced HVAC system, fueled by natural gas and free of ozone-depleting refrigerants. Daylighting has been optimized, and high-performance casement windows are used throughout. All residential units include programmable digital thermostats, ENERGY STAR fixtures and a master shutoff switch.

Jury Comments: "The architect set a high agenda in terms of bringing sustainability and social responsibility to a mainstream project in a competitive market."

2004 AIA/COTE Top Ten Winner
CITY OF WHITE ROCK OPERATIONS BUILDING
LOCATION: White Rock, British Columbia, Canada
ARCHITECT: Busby & Associates Architects

The mandate of the city of White Rock was to make its new operations building as environmentally sustainable as reasonably possible, in accordance with the city's own policy (see color insert). The 6,545-square-foot building earned an LEED Gold Certification through a great variety of strategies that include photovoltaic panels for electricity and solar tubes to provide base radiant heating for the building. Daylight light shelves provide balanced daylight and reduce electric lighting needs. A green-sod roof reduces runoff from impermeable surfaces, while a pervious parking lot allows infiltration of water into the ground. The facility also uses stormwater rather than potable water to wash city vehicles and for toilets, and waterless urinals and low-flow faucets throughout the facility further reduce water consumption. Extensive use of materials produced within a 500-mile radius of the site also reduced transportation effects on the environment.

Jury Comments: "A truly sustainable building that humans will use, cherish, and maintain over time, this collaborative achievement succeeds at all levels: massing, use of daylight, orientation, the way the water works on the site, and the use of materials."

2004 AIA/COTE Top Ten Winner
F10 HOUSE
LOCATION: Chicago, Illinois
ARCHITECT: Esherick Homsey Dodge and Davis

In 2000, the city of Chicago's departments of environment and housing sponsored a national competition to identify creative modifications to the existing New Homes

F10's modular design responds to a narrow city site with adjacent buildings, with an open 1,834-square-foot floor plan that incorporates a solar chimney in the stairwell.

Window placement at F10 maximizes reflected light; the solar chimney includes a south-facing clerestory window that brings natural light to the house's core.

for Chicago program. F10 House's cutting-edge design was one of five affordable case-study designs to be built. F10's modular design responds to a narrow city site with adjacent buildings, with an open 1,834-square-foot floor plan that incorporates a solar chimney in the stairwell. The open plan enhances cross-ventilation. Window placement maximizes reflected light; the solar chimney includes a south-facing clerestory window that brings natural light to the house's core. A high-efficiency, gas-fired boiler and perimeter fin-tube baseboard provide heating, while natural ventilation delivers the cooling. A wall of water bottles acts as a heat sink in winter.

Jury Comments: "In a grassroots movement toward sustainability, the Chicago Housing Authority has built its first affordable housing cooled passively without central air conditioning, helping to lead the building community, including the major retail stores, to these concepts."

2004 AIA/COTE Top Ten Winner
GENZYME CENTER
LOCATION: Cambridge, Massachusetts
ARCHITECT: Behnisch Architects

This building, headquarters for a biotechnology company, sits on a former brownfield site in Cambridge at Kendall Square, a dense, massive 1970s urban renewal devel-

The Genzyme Center's central atrium space acts as a huge return-air duct and light shaft, and steam from a nearby power plant supplies central heating and cooling.

opment project built on wetlands fill. All of the environmental-design strategies—energy efficiency, water conservation, material selection, urban-site selection, and indoor environmental quality—not only contribute to the Platinum LEED rating the building is expected to achieve from the U.S. Green Building Council but also establish an open spatial atmosphere for the building occupants. The high-performance curtain-wall system boasts operable windows on all 12 floors. These windows, linked to the building-management system, allow for automated control and night cooling. Also, a third of the exterior envelope is a ventilated double facade with a four-foot buffer that tempers solar gains year-round. The building's central atrium space acts as a huge return-air duct and light shaft, and steam from a nearby power plant supplies central heating and cooling. The building will also use 32 percent less water than a comparable office building by having waterless urinals, dual-flush toilets, automatic faucets, and low-flow fixtures.

Genzyme as client for the interiors and a big part of the sustainable elements was a rare example of how an ideal client-architect relationship and decision-making process can happen. The CEO of Genzyme and Stefan Behnisch took the lead to establish the major sustainable-design criteria, but there was also a huge international design-team effort and a broad response from the entire Genzyme Company. The sustainable design in this building is fully integrated into architecture, space, and light. Sustainability in this sense is not an extra you could add or not. It is interwoven with the vital parts of architecture. Genzyme as a client fully understood and supported this issue.

Jury Comments: "The corporation invested heavily to make this great piece of architecture a model for corporate offices in the coming decade, with its sophisticated glazing, lighting, and mechanical systems that create a growing, active place supportive of its occupants."

Building Performance, According to the Architects

It takes time to adjust, correct, and tune the systems. Today, the building performs reasonably close to what was planned and expected, in spite of items that had to be corrected during the first year of operation. The facade, for instance, was leaking the first winter. This magnitude of air infiltration was not expected. The facade was repaired, and now it performs well.

However, how people use the building, what temperature range they want to accept, has a big impact on the performance of the building. If you ask: Can the building perform better over time? The answer is yes, over time with the help of habit changing and acceptance of a wider range of ideas on what constitutes comfort.

2004 AIA/COTE Top Ten Winner
GREYSTON BAKERY
LOCATION: Yonkers, New York
ARCHITECT: Cybul & Cybul

The Greyston Bakery offers a 23,000-square-foot, state-of-the-art production bakery on a 1.6-acre former brownfield site in an old industrial area near downtown Yonkers. Intended as a revitalization catalyst to this blighted neighborhood, the new bakery functions as a continuous automated machine to produce brownies and other baked products. The building is bisected by a three-level light shaft with translucent floors and then bisected again in the opposite direction by a two-story

The light shaft and atrium in Greyston Bakery allow natural airflow throughout the bakery.

atrium, which separates the office areas from the production bakery and introduces light and air into the offices. The light shaft and atrium also allow natural airflow throughout the bakery. Outside ambient air cools the baked products as they travel down a continuous spiral conveyor.

Jury Comments: "This is a cultural ecology where the design team understood that a workplace is not just a box you work in, but a quality environment to maintain workers; one in which the fundamental processes reveal the greatest potential for energy savings."

2004 AIA/COTE Top Ten Winner
HERMAN MILLER BUILDING C1
LOCATION: Zeeland, Michigan
ARCHITECT: Krueck & Sexton

Reuse of a building is one of the most sustainable strategies available. This project restored, revitalized, and transformed a classic but aging modern building into an environmentally responsive, high-quality workplace, exemplifying Herman Miller's core values of human-centered, spirited, and purposeful design. Located on the company's main campus, this two-story 1974 office building housed Herman Miller executives until 1997. The architects stripped the building to its structure and rebuilt it with minimal finishes, using more than 50 percent recycled content. The floor plates are organized to provide maximum daylight penetration and 100 percent line of sight to the landscape. With 69 percent of its total energy produced on site, the redesign achieves a 29 percent reduction in energy consumption, mainly through envelope improvements and high-efficiency mechanical equipment and lighting. The project also supports the regional economy, with 57 percent of construction materials sourced within 500 miles.

Jury Comments: "As if Saarinen had returned with more tools and an additional 30 years of experience in sustainable use, good light, and air, this sweet little exposed-structure box shows that the Top 10 is also about extending the life of existing buildings in clever ways."

Herman Miller Building C1 is an example of smart reuse of a building, which is one of the most sustainable strategies available.

At the Herman Miller Building C1, spaces are organized to provide maximum daylight penetration and 100 percent line of sight to the landscape.

2004 AIA/COTE Top Ten Winner
LAKE VIEW TERRACE BRANCH LIBRARY
LOCATION: Lake View Terrace, California
ARCHITECTS: Fields Devereaux and GreenWorks

Lake View Terrace Branch of the city of Los Angeles's public library system enjoys a spacious main reading room that stretches along the east-west axis, providing dra-

Of the public spaces in Lake View Terrace Branch Library, 80 percent are naturally ventilated via mechanically interlocked windows controlled by an energy-management system.

The design provides nearly 100 percent shading of glazing for solar control and daylight.

matic views of the park to the south. The site's stormwater runoff was reduced by 25 percent with landscaping features that include a series of radial bioswales for efficient rainwater infiltration. More than 75 percent of construction waste was diverted from landfills to local recycling facilities. The library's energy performance is more than 40 percent more efficient than California standards. Night venting takes advantage of its exterior insulated, high-mass concrete block shell. Approximately 80 percent of the public spaces are naturally ventilated via mechanically interlocked windows controlled by a sophisticated energy-management system. A building-integrated photovoltaic system shades the entry and roofs the community room while providing 15 percent of the building's energy. The design provides nearly 100 percent shading of glazing for solar control and daylight. The program called for an LEED Platinum building; it is the first project of the city to attempt this level.

Jury Comments: "Ample daylight without glare, the distinguished evaporative cooling tower that greets you at the entryway, natural ventilation, inventive use of color, careful material selection, and outstanding views make this library wonderful."

2004 AIA/COTE Top Ten Winner
PIERCE COUNTY ENVIRONMENTAL SERVICES BUILDING
LOCATION: University Place, Washington
ARCHITECT: The Miller|Hull Partnership

This building sits on a 900-plus-acre site, much of which has been extensively mined for gravel for over 100 years, resulting in a barren landscape. As the first major build-

The Pierce County Environmental Services Building is built on a brownfield site once mined for gravel.

ing constructed under "Reclaiming Our Resources," the county's 50-year master plan for the site, it sets the tone for future development. Its driving concepts call for a more humane work environment, natural light, interior vegetation, and views to the exterior. The project attempts to make people aware of being part of a greater regional context by developing a Mount Rainier axis through the site. Space planning follows a European office model: no desk is more than 30 feet from a window. Extensive daylighting studies led to the use of baffles in the skylights, a large western overhang, and exterior sunscreens on the east facade. A raised-floor air-distribution system reduces the size and energy consumption of the mechanical system, improves indoor air quality, provides for future flexibility, and gives individuals direct control of their immediate environment. Nighttime flushing lowers the temperature of the concrete structure by several degrees, resulting in "free" cooling at the beginning of the day.

Jury Comments: "A brownfield site becomes a benchmark for future buildings as the design team applies nontraditional daylighting strategies to create interior spaces that are very humane and sophisticated."

2004 AIA/COTE Top Ten Winner
THE PLAZA AT PPL CENTER
LOCATION: Allentown, Pennsylvania
ARCHITECT: Robert A.M. Stern Architects; Kendall/Heaton Associates; Atelier Ten

This LEED Gold high-performance urban office building was designed and built in 18 months on a suburban real-estate budget (see color insert). The eight-story building offers Allentown's downtown its first new office development in over 25 years. A dramatic eight-story glass atrium brings natural light deep into the core of the building, while extensive perimeter glazing provides panoramic views and abundant daylight, filtered through *brises-soleil,* directly to all building spaces. Carbon dioxide (CO_2) sensors ensure that fresh air is supplied directly to each building area as needed. A pair of two-story, plant-filled winter gardens along the south facade of the building provide unique workspaces for occupants, bring daylight deeper into the floor plates, control glare, and improve indoor air quality. Other features include efficient building systems, use of zero-emitting or very-low-VOC-emitting paint, adhesives, sealants, carpet, and composite wood. Estimated energy demand is 30 percent less compared to code requirements. Water use is 45 percent below code requirements. Construction materials contained more than 20 percent recycled content.

Jury Comments: "With a clean aesthetic in a conventional building block, this project makes a number of nice moves with double envelopes, daylight, and a winter garden to frame a public space and contribute it to the city."

2004 AIA/COTE Top Ten Winner
WOODS HOLE RESEARCH CENTER
LOCATION: Falmouth, Massachusetts
ARCHITECT: William McDonough + Partners

Placed within a challenging and constrained site, the design preserves the cultural landscape represented by an existing nineteenth-century summer home, respectfully and adaptively reusing the original house and adding contemporary office, laboratory, and common spaces. The all-electric building relies on renewable energy sources, including a grid-connected and net-metered 26.4-kilowatt photovoltaic array that powers the building's closed-loop, ground-source heat-pump system. A planned on-site wind turbine will likely make the building a net-energy exporter. Icynene spray foam insulates all exterior walls and roof assemblies, creating a technically and ecologically effective air barrier and optimized R-values. Other components reinforce the performance benefits of this extremely secure envelope, including offset-stud framing; double- and triple-glazed argon-insulated low-E windows; enthalpy wheels that recapture heat and moisture from exhaust air and precondition incoming fresh air; and high-efficiency lighting controls and occupancy monitors.

Jury Comments: "By testing and understanding how to achieve the highest level of performance in environmentally sensitive elements, such as water recovery and sole-source wind-turbine energy, this building raises the bar very high for the next generation of buildings."

Building Performance, According to the Architects

The client had very high ambitions, as did the designers. The building not only performs extraordinarily well, but it is full of light and air, generous common space, and safe materials, all of which were goals that competed in the design process with the quantitative goal of the lowest possible energy use. The owner was very knowledgeable, appreciative, and very involved. A commissioning process helped ensure optimal performance. The client's entire organization is delighted with the building.

2005 AIA/COTE Top Ten Green Projects

Only nine projects received this award in 2005:

> Austin Resource Center for the Homeless, Austin, Texas
>
> The Barn at Fallingwater, Mill Run, Pennsylvania
>
> Eastern Sierra House, Gardnerville, Nevada
>
> Evergreen State College Seminar II, Olympia, Washington
>
> Heimbold Visual Arts Center, Sarah Lawrence College, Bronxville, New York
>
> Leslie Shao-ming Sun Field Station, Woodside, California
>
> Lloyd Crossing Sustainable Urban Design Plan, Portland, Oregon

Pittsburgh Glass Center, Pittsburgh, Pennsylvania

Rinker Hall, University of Florida, Gainesville, Florida

2005 AIA/COTE Top Ten Winner
AUSTIN RESOURCE CENTER FOR THE HOMELESS
LOCATION: Austin, Texas
ARCHITECT: LZT Architects

The Resource Center is on a former brownfield in downtown Austin, within easy access of several bus lines. Much more than an emergency shelter, the center serves as a meeting place and support center, helping people make the transition out of homelessness through its many programs. A 13,000-gallon rainwater-collection system supplements the building's water supply. A passive-solar hot-water system preheats water for the showers, and a photovoltaic array supplements electricity usage. Many of the materials used in the project contain rapidly renewable or recycled content.

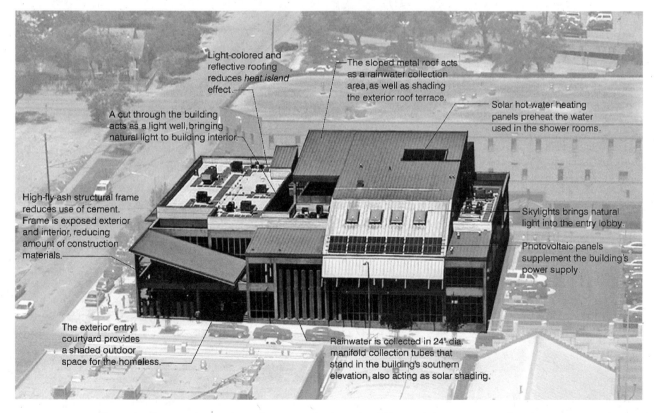

Light-colored and reflective roofing reduces *heat island* effect.

The sloped metal roof acts as a rainwater collection area, as well as shading the exterior roof terrace.

A cut through the building acts as a light well, bringing natural light to building interior.

Solar hot-water heating panels preheat the water used in the shower rooms.

High-fly-ash structural frame reduces use of cement. Frame is exposed exterior and interior, reducing amount of construction materials.

Skylights brings natural light into the entry lobby.

Photovoltaic panels supplement the building's power supply.

The exterior entry courtyard provides a shaded outdoor space for the homeless.

Rainwater is collected in 24"-dia. manifold collection tubes that stand in the building's southern elevation, also acting as solar shading.

Austin Resource Center for the Homeless is the reclamation of a former infill-brownfield in downtown Austin.

At the Austin Resource Center for the Homeless, a passive-solar hot-water system preheats water for the showers, and a photovoltaic array supplements electricity usage.

Building Performance, According to the Architects

- We have had problems with the mechanical systems functioning properly, but this is more a subcontractor performance problem than a design issue.

- The complex rainwater-collection system needs periodic maintenance, and we have had some issues with pumps going out intermittently.

- Occupants have little interest in or education with regard to use and functionality of these systems and devices. Much of what we did pushes occupants into unfamiliar modes of use in the building.

Lessons Learned by the Architects

- The client was essential in supporting the building design and ideas and required that the building be LEED rated. There is a strong green community in Austin, always very supportive and helpful in seeing the building design and construction through. Groups like the Center of Maximum Potential Building Systems (our sustainability consultant) and Austin Energy Green building program help to make Austin fertile ground for new and experimental green building.

- We would spend more time and money in design with energy modeling and look at alternative mechanical systems. We chose to be conservative with the mechanical system. The building uses high-efficiency DX units with ceiling-mounted air handlers. The forced-air equipment throughout the building has caused use a lot of postoccupancy grief. If we were to do it again, we would look at a central water-based system and study the energy use through modeling during the design phase.

- Building use is critical to maintaining and implementing sustainable features and systems. If a building is to be used for 50 years, its performance to a large degree often relies on a user who understands its functionality and maintains the systems and sustainable use. This often clashes with the normative behavior rather than meshing with it.

- Our firm seeks ways to create experimental projects that enrich the world in some way. Sustainability is one of those criteria. The mandate to create a sustainable building (LEED-rated) gave us a kind of bureaucratic leverage to introduce ideas and methods we have always been exploring.

2005 AIA/COTE Top Ten Winner
THE BARN AT FALLINGWATER
LOCATION: Mill Run, Pennsylvania
ARCHITECT: Bohlin Cywinski Jackson

The Barn at Fallingwater is an adaptive reuse of a nineteenth-century heavy-timber bank barn and its twentieth-century addition, framed in dimension lumber. The existing glazed dairy-block walls, glass-block windows, and site-built roof trusses were exposed. Salvaged fir, new sunflower-seed composite panels, and sound-absorptive straw panels complement the palette of original materials while underscoring the structure's connection to farming. A zero-discharge wastewater-reclamation system, gray-water flushing, and low-flow fixtures reduce potable water use. A ground-source heat-pump system, daylighting, and electric light sensors minimize energy use.

Building Performance, According to the Architects

The building is occupied and performing in accordance with projections. The mechanical controls systems are unusually sophisticated for a project of this scale. Further operating economies can be achieved as the owner's personnel learn to take full advantage of the energy-conserving features of the HVAC systems.

Lessons Learned by the Architects

- The Western Pennsylvania Conservancy is one of the oldest conservation organizations in the country. Its commitment to the frugal use of natural resources and environmental stewardship is deep and fundamental. The Conservancy came to us seeking advice about the best strategies to accomplish these broader goals in the context of this project. The Conservancy's belief in

Salvaged fir, new sunflower-seed composite panels, and sound-absorptive straw panels complement the palette of original materials while underscoring The Barn at Fallingwater's connection to farming.

the values of sustainability made it more willing to invest in sustainable design than other owners might be. The Conservancy looked at design decisions from a standpoint of ethical payback, in addition to economic payback.

- Today we are aware of new technologies for controlling and modulating light from skylights. We might have made more extensive use of skylights with these controls to provide daylight to interior spaces. We would try to achieve a greater use of natural ventilation, in addition to efficient HVAC systems with economizer cycles. Such strategies depend on the availability of controls systems developed for this purpose.

- This project utilizes a field of drilled wells for a geothermal heat sink in the heat-pump system. Like all aspects of construction that take place below the ground surface, there is a greater risk of encountering unexpected circumstances in drilling these wells. When we use this strategy in the future, we will budget a greater contingency and build time into the schedule to better manage these uncertainties.

- Another lesson learned is how important it is to stay current with the ongoing construction record keeping needed to support LEED certification. Even with a capable and well-intentioned builder, it is a good idea for the architect to monitor the progress of documentation as part of the regular job-meeting agenda.

- We didn't alter our professional practice to design this or other projects that feature sustainable strategies. We did more research to uncover some unusual materials that were both green and highly appropriate to a building that is an agricultural artifact. But as for thinking about energy conservation, natural light, and a healthy environment for building occupants, these we bring to every design assignment. Our early projects also illustrate our preference for the use of simple, "real" materials, often of local origin, to help create architecture with a sense of being grounded in its setting. We have always desired to create architecture that will last, and improve, with the effects of natural aging.

■ We are deeply interested in the potential for using innovative approaches to energy conservation and sustainable practices to generate fresh, expressive architectural forms. We pursued these interests in our work long before the terms *sustainable* and *green* were popularized.

■ There is some humor in the fact that we find that the best information on sustainable materials and techniques comes from both the newest and, in some cases, much older sources. The Internet contains a wealth of information from manufacturers who have embraced the green agenda as a way to promote their products. On the other end of the time line, it is often informative to see how earlier generations created buildings we still see around us, without the use of petrochemicals, treated lumber, and energy-intensive climate-control systems. A favorite source is *Architectural Details: Classic Pages from Architectural Graphic Standards 1940–1980* (Charles George Ramsey, Harold Reeve Sleeper, and Donald Watson [eds.], New York: John Wiley, 2001). Lots of these details still work. They have certainly passed the test of time.

■ We are now evaluating nearly all our projects against the LEED metrics. This has emerged because many of our institutional clients come to us requesting an LEED-certified building. It has become very widely accepted by colleges and universities. We find it important to have LEED-accredited professionals on staff, because they know the ropes. This said, we think that there is plenty of room for improvement in the LEED standard. Energy consumption is the dominant component of a building's environmental footprint over its useful life. It should be weighted more heavily than it currently is in the standard. We also believe that there are tremendously important issues of sustainability that just don't fit into any system of quantitative metrics. Call them traditional or humane values of good design.

■ Peter Bohlin, FAIA, concludes with this reflection:

> Technology is evolving very rapidly, and at the same time, human beings as a species are evolving very, very slowly. The things that make us happy, calm, productive, and comfortable don't really change very much from one generation to the next. Really well designed buildings have always recognized these fundamental human values, and it's one of the reasons that we preserve well-liked older buildings and adapt them to new uses. So, how do we build a facility to adapt to the demands of technology 10, 20, or 30 years from now? We don't think anyone who is honest can offer a simple,

sound-bite solution. Surely part of the answer is to design buildings that are really good places for people by recognizing the fundamental physical and psychological needs of human beings. If we get that right, it is less likely that what we build will wind up on the scrap heap a generation from now.

2005 AIA/COTE Top Ten Winner
EASTERN SIERRA HOUSE
LOCATION: Gardnerville, Nevada
ARCHITECT: Arkin Tilt Architects

This sustainable demonstration home is designed to take advantage of the rugged beauty of its site on the eastern slope of the Sierra Nevada Mountains, overlooking the Carson Valley. The house is virtually energy independent: shading, high insulation values, and thermal mass, aided by flushing with cool night air, prevent overheating in the summer. Solar hot-water panels at the edge of the terrace feed a heating system and provide domestic hot water. A photovoltaic system meets the home's electricity needs. Using a variety of natural, efficient, and durable materials, including straw bale with an earthen finish, metal roofing, and slatted cement-board siding, the home's finishes harmonize with the landscape.

The Eastern Sierra House is virtually energy independent. Comfort is attained by shading, high insulation values, and thermal mass, aided by flushing with cool night air.

Building Performance, According to the Architects

The owner was aware that there would be a fine-tuning period, where we'd need to optimize the systems. For example, last year the flow of heat to the sand beds wasn't turned on until late October. That, coupled with the worst winter in 80 years, meant that the house required additional heat (although the energy bills were still less than 10 percent of the neighbors'). This year the thermal mass is being charged in early September, and we expect better performance. Generally, it is performing as anticipated, thermally speaking. The renewable energy system has also been optimized, but there are still phantom loads (a landscape pump, septic blower, night-flush blower) that have not allowed us to fully achieve the zero-energy goal. Options are being explored to run these systems less and power the house with 100 percent solar energy.

Lessons Learned by the Architects

- The owner established the goal of demonstrating solar living. The relationship was and is built on respect and trust, as is most often the case. The fact that our goals were in complete sync was the key to the success and multiple levels of integration that this project achieved.

- Other than the increasing efficiency of the inverters of the renewable energy systems, we don't know that we would change too many aspects of the project. We are using more sophisticated tools to predict passive heating and cooling performance, but these wouldn't have affected this design.

- We employed a variety of building construction systems, and many renewable energy and mechanical systems in this house, probably too many. We don't advise using so many systems, and we certainly will try not to again. As a demonstration project for a willing client with specific needs, particularly in the area of indoor air quality and filtration, this made some sense for this project, but generally we aim to simplify all aspects of our designs.

2005 AIA/COTE Top Ten Winner
EVERGREEN STATE COLLEGE SEMINAR II
LOCATION: Olympia, Washington
ARCHITECT: Mahlum Architects

The design for this 168,000-square-foot academic facility reflects Evergreen State College's commitment to rigorous interdisciplinary teaching and to environmental advocacy. A central open volume allows daylighting, natural stack ventilation, and visual connections between the academic programs. To safeguard the site's forest ecology, Seminar II is fingered into the landscape. Planting features a mix of native species organized according to their natural setting and replaces the forest disturbed by construction. To reduce the impact of the project on Thornton Creek and its native salmon, a 20,443-square-foot vegetated roof was installed.

A central, open volume allows daylighting, natural stack ventilation, and visual connections between the academic programs in this Evergreen State College building.

2005 AIA/COTE Top Ten Winner
HEIMBOLD VISUAL ARTS CENTER, SARAH LAWRENCE COLLEGE
LOCATION: Bronxville, New York
ARCHITECT: Polshek Partnership

The Monika A. and Charles A. Heimbold, Jr. Visual Arts Center at Sarah Lawrence College is integrated into the topography of the existing hilltop. To fulfill the pro-

Ten Measures of Sustainable Design

The following ten measures of sustainable design have been developed to provide guidelines and evaluation criteria for submissions to the AIA/COTE Top Ten Green Projects awards program. The list of measures, with summarized descriptions here, includes both qualitative and quantitative elements.

Measure 1: Sustainable Design Intent and Innovation

Describe the most important sustainable design ideas and innovations for your project as well as the specific circumstances or constraints that generated those ideas. How does the architectural expression demonstrate the sustainable design intent? How did the sustainable design effort lead to a better overall project design?

Measure 2: Regional/Community Design and Connectivity

Describe how the design promotes regional and community identity and an appropriate sense of place. Describe how the project contributes to public space and community interaction. Does the project make use of any alternative local or regional transportation strategies as well as successful efforts to reduce locally mandated parking requirements?

Measure 3: Land Use and Site Ecology

Describe how the development of the project's site responds to its ecological context. How does the site selection and design relate to ecosystems at different scales, from local to regional? Describe the landscape design and the creation, re-creation, or preservation of open space, permeable groundscape, and/or on-site ecosystems.

Measure 4: Bioclimatic Design

Describe how the building responds to bioclimatic conditions through passive design strategies. Describe how the building footprint, section, orientation, and massing respond to the site, climate conditions, the sun path, prevailing breezes, and seasonal and daily cycles.

Measure 5: Light and Air

Outline design strategies that create a healthful and productive indoor environment through daylighting, lighting design, ventilation, indoor air quality, view corridors, and personal control systems.

Measure 6: Water Cycle

Describe how building and site design strategies conserve water supplies, manage site water and drainage, and capitalize on renewable sources on the immediate site. Outline water-conserving landscape and building design strategies, as well as any water-conserving fixtures, appliances, and HVAC equipment.

Measure 7: Energy Flows and Energy Future

Describe how the design of building systems contributes to energy conservation, reduces pollution, and improves building performance and comfort. Describe effective use of controls and technologies, efficient lighting strategies, and any on-site renewable energy systems.

Measure 8: Materials and Construction

Describe the most important selection criteria, considerations, and constraints for materials or building assemblies for your project. Describe construction waste reduction and any strategies to promote recycling during occupancy.

Measure 9: Long Life, Loose Fit

Describe how the project's design creates enduring value through long-term flexibility and adaptability. Identify the anticipated service life of the project, and describe materials, systems, and design solutions developed to enhance versatility, durability, and adaptive reuse potential.

Measure 10: Lessons Learned: Evaluation and Collective Wisdom

Describe how your design process enhanced the ultimate performance and success of the building. How did collaborative efforts between the design team, consultants, client, and community contribute to success? What lessons were learned during the design, construction, and occupation of the building?

The Heimbold Visual Arts Center has a green roof.

grammatic needs, given the constraints of the site, more than one-third of the total building area is embedded in the ground. Photography labs and other studios that do not lend themselves to daylight are below grade. A stepped, grass-covered green roof reduces the building's overall impact on the natural environment and controls stormwater runoff.

2005 AIA/COTE Top Ten Winner
LESLIE SHAO-MING SUN FIELD STATION
LOCATION: Woodside, California
ARCHITECT: Rob Wellington Quigley

This is Stanford University's first green building, and it is designed to make a statement about the importance of conserving natural resources. Site selection considered solar access and impact on natural habitats and archaeological resources. Construction-site management included fencing to prevent work under the drip line of mature oaks. Ninety-five percent of the construction waste was diverted from landfill. Water-free urinals, dual-flush toilets, tankless water heaters, and native landscaping reduce water use, and rainwater collected from the roof is reused. Passive-cooling and solar-heating systems combine with good insulation and extensive daylighting to minimize energy use.

Building Performance, According to the Architects

- A complete energy-monitoring system was installed to collect data on building energy efficiency and to see if the goal of annual net-zero carbon emissions was achieved. Right now it has met 85 percent of its goal. The reasons this goal is not yet fully met are as follows:

1. Pacific Gas & Electric (PG&E) used numbers based on the original PG&E meter. Stanford's monitoring system is more sensitive and detects about 8 percent more consumption than the PG&E meter.

2. PG&E now has three electric vehicles that were not part of original calculations.

3. The building itself has been such an attraction for housing events that more intensive event programming and energy is used than had been planned. The single largest consumption of electricity since the project was completed was when the university hosted the International Sustainability Conference and used floodlights for outdoor dining!

■ The energy-monitoring system, with 14 sensors, has been collecting data on energy production and consumption since March 2003. Real-time data, data summaries, and a complete description of the system are available on the Web (http://jr-solar.stanford.edu). The system collects data five times per second, summarized in one-minute intervals and recorded in a data logger. One of the major benefits of this system has been the identification of inefficiencies that we have been able to adjust at little cost in order to maximize performance. For instance, we discovered a mismatch between photovoltaic (PV) voltage output and the inverter as the PV panels got warmer, resulting in significant system degradation. With this information, we devised a strategy that was implemented at the end of May 2004, which has resulted in more than a 30 percent improvement in PV system output.

■ For the client, one of the unexpected benefits of the design was the very comfortable and ergonomically superior indoor environment. Building users and visitors often comment on the natural daylighting and lack of noise from the mechanical system.

Lessons Learned by the Architects

■ The client was willing to put in the time required to realize sustainable goals. The preserve's director was willing to *walk the talk*. In addition, the staff at Jasper Ridge Biological Preserve was committed to designing a building that would minimize its environmental footprint and serve as an educational tool and role model.

■ We would change the process—not the design of the building. The design/build process didn't always work, especially for the mechanical system.

■ The client would change numbers for calculating energy loads so that systems could be more reflective of actual needs (see previous comment about PG&E meter). The university would also use a different PV panel that was more efficient in producing energy. In addition, it would put in a switch for the transformer between PV system and grid to make it active only when PV panels are working.

- The client would also put in motion-activated light sensors in a couple of rooms (library, classrooms, bathrooms).
- We would conduct a peer review of the design goals and plans during schematic design.
- We would hire only those subcontractors who are already predisposed to or interested in green- or sustainable-design strategies, rather than try to educate traditional elements of the construction industry. We would require all subcontractors to have a representative who will work on the project attend a preconstruction meeting to learn in detail the building's integrated sustainability goals and systems and how they are designed to function.

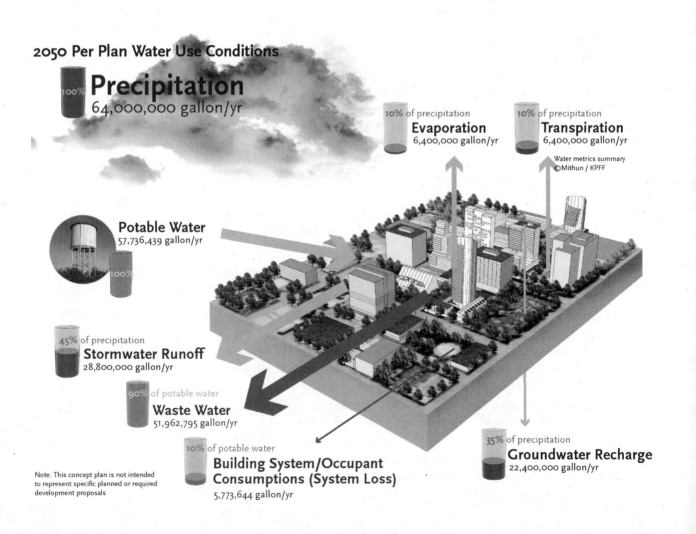

2050 Per Plan Water Use Conditions

100% **Precipitation**
64,000,000 gallon/yr

10% of precipitation
Evaporation
6,400,000 gallon/yr

10% of precipitation
Transpiration
6,400,000 gallon/yr

Water metrics summary
©Mithun / KPFF

Potable Water
57,736,439 gallon/yr
100%

45% of precipitation
Stormwater Runoff
28,800,000 gallon/yr

90% of potable water
Waste Water
51,962,795 gallon/yr

10% of potable water
Building System/Occupant Consumptions (System Loss)
5,773,644 gallon/yr

35% of precipitation
Groundwater Recharge
22,400,000 gallon/yr

Note: This concept plan is not intended to represent specific planned or required development proposals

2005 AIA/COTE Top Ten Winner
LLOYD CROSSING SUSTAINABLE URBAN DESIGN PLAN
LOCATION: Portland, Oregon
ARCHITECT: Mithun

The Lloyd Crossing Sustainable Urban Design Plan integrates multiple sustainable strategies for energy, water, and habitat to transform and create a new identity for a 35-block, inner-city commercial Portland neighborhood (see color insert). The plan creates a new analytical design and economic framework for adding eight million square feet of development over 45 years while dramatically improving the district's environmental performance. A four-block, mixed-used project, the Catalyst Project, will serve as the testing ground for key elements of the design.

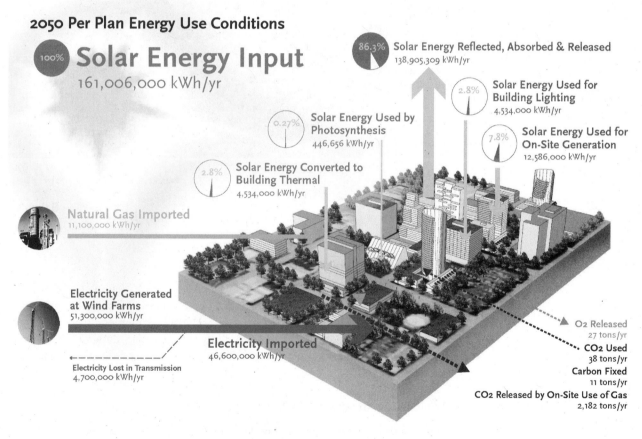

2050 Per Plan Energy Use Conditions

100% **Solar Energy Input**
161,006,000 kWh/yr

86.3% Solar Energy Reflected, Absorbed & Released
138,905,309 kWh/yr

2.8% Solar Energy Used for Building Lighting
4,534,000 kWh/yr

0.27% Solar Energy Used by Photosynthesis
446,656 kWh/yr

7.8% Solar Energy Used for On-Site Generation
12,586,000 kWh/yr

2.8% Solar Energy Converted to Building Thermal
4,534,000 kWh/yr

Natural Gas Imported
11,100,000 kWh/yr

Electricity Generated at Wind Farms
51,300,000 kWh/yr

Electricity Imported
46,600,000 kWh/yr

Electricity Lost in Transmission
4,700,000 kWh/yr

O2 Released
27 tons/yr

CO2 Used
38 tons/yr

Carbon Fixed
11 tons/yr

CO2 Released by On-Site Use of Gas
2,182 tons/yr

Note: This concept plan is not intended to represent specific planned or required development proposals

Carbon Balance
Net add to atmosphere: 2,144 tons/yr

2004 Existing Energy Use Conditions

Note: This concept plan is not intended to represent specific planned or required development proposals

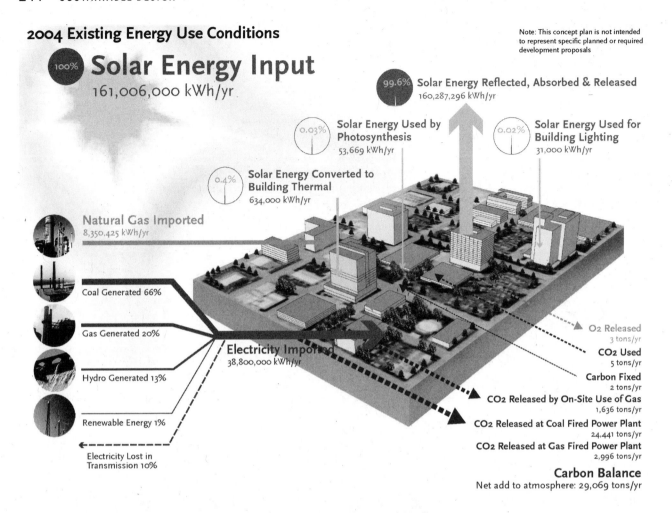

100% Solar Energy Input
161,006,000 kWh/yr

99.6% Solar Energy Reflected, Absorbed & Released
160,287,296 kWh/yr

0.03% Solar Energy Used by Photosynthesis
53,669 kWh/yr

0.02% Solar Energy Used for Building Lighting
31,000 kWh/yr

0.4% Solar Energy Converted to Building Thermal
634,000 kWh/yr

Natural Gas Imported
8,350,425 kWh/yr

Coal Generated 66%

Gas Generated 20%

Hydro Generated 13%

Renewable Energy 1%

Electricity Imported
38,800,000 kWh/yr

Electricity Lost in Transmission 10%

O2 Released
3 tons/yr

CO2 Used
5 tons/yr

Carbon Fixed
2 tons/yr

CO2 Released by On-Site Use of Gas
1,636 tons/yr

CO2 Released at Coal Fired Power Plant
24,441 tons/yr

CO2 Released at Gas Fired Power Plant
2,996 tons/yr

Carbon Balance
Net add to atmosphere: 29,069 tons/yr

Building Performance, According to the Architects

Lloyd Crossing is a neighborhood sustainability study, and a unique COTE Top Ten entry, rather than the typical building or building complex. The study has generated extensive discussion internationally and has created a new methodology for expanding the scope and criteria for urban and city infrastructure design. The Portland Development Commission (PDC) is reviewing the next steps required to implement the project.

Lessons Learned by the Architects

The client and stakeholder groups both brought a strong interest in sustainable design to the process. A major private landholder and team stakeholder within the district had worked with Natural Step and had a sustainability advisor as a staff member. The PDC developed a Technical Advisory Group (TAG) that brought

2004 Existing Habitat Conditions
Tree cover **14.5%**
Tree species include: red maple, scarlet oaks, sweet gum, tulip tree

Existing On-Site Conditions

Lack of tree canopy and middle story provide little habitat for birds or arboreal mammals.

Virtually no habitat for terrestrial mammals such as beaver, deer and raccoon.

Virtually no habitat is left for invertebrates because of the large percentage of impervious surfaces in the study area.

No aquatic habitat such as streams, creeks or wetlands remain from pre-development condition.

Natural predator/prey relationships have been replaced by urban adapted species such as starling, raven pigeon, seagull, squirrels, rats and feral cats.

Existing Off-Site Conditions

Increased water temperatures from stormwater harms aquatic and amphibious species

Sediments and pollution carried in stormwater runoff harm aquatic and amphibious species

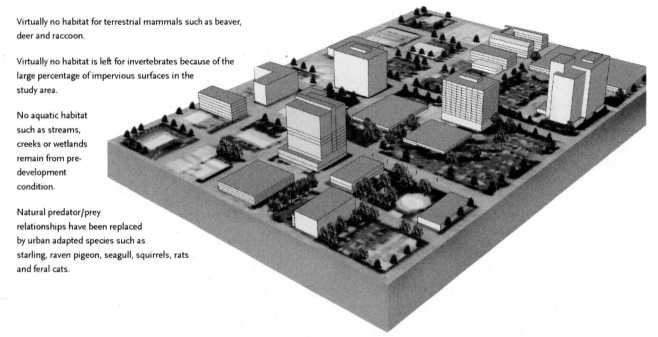

together diverse city agencies to coordinate water, stormwater, energy, streetscape, and other infrastructure elements within the public right-of-way. PDC and the design team also worked with a core design group that included neighborhood groups, key landowners, businesses, and utilities to create early buy-in to the complex process of resource-integrated urban design.

- We learned about the complex issues of designing within the urban right-of-way. In most American cities, the sidewalks, streets, and infrastructure areas can take up 30 to 45 percent of the cityscape. Extensive governmental agency interaction and cooperation is required to bridge the departmental silos that prevent truly integrated design of water, energy, transportation, and habitat strategies. We would continue to seek "top-of-the-pipe solutions" that can reduce the burden on centralized municipal infrastructure and seek to recoup the large-scale capital funds to reinvest in localized neighborhood solutions.

- With additional time and funding resources, we could fully model the design of a three-dimensional zoning envelope that optimized solar and wind response.

- Creative design of financial and governmental mechanisms is as important as the creative integration of renewable energy strategies, expressive stormwater design, and other conventional sustainable-design concepts.

- We needed to create a new set of metrics for this urban-design project. We chose to use metrics from the ecological performance of the predevelopment mixed conifer forest that existed 200 years ago on the site. The question asked was: "Can we add more than eight million square feet of development to the neighborhood and reduce the environmental footprint from its current level?" And can we go further? Could we approach some of the key environmental metrics of the predevelopment forest? Could we match its solar efficiency, create comparable habitat, and mimic the forest hydrology? The study details the metrics of what is proposed, the costs, and the actions required to implement the following strategies and key metrics:

1. Achieving carbon neutrality

2. Living within the solar budget

3. Living within the water budget of rainfall within the site boundaries

2005 AIA/COTE Top Ten Winner
PITTSBURGH GLASS CENTER
LOCATION: Pittsburgh, Pennsylvania
ARCHITECT: dggp Architecture and Bruce Lindsey

The Pittsburgh Glass Center is an art studio and nonprofit organization dedicated to teaching, creating, and promoting glass art. The building includes daylighting and control of the quality of the light. It also includes extensive natural ventilation, as air conditioning is prohibitively expensive as well as prohibitive for a glassmaking environment. Heat from the glassmaking equipment is recovered. Thermal mass inside the building moderates temperature swings. A reflective and emissive roof system reduces both internal heat loads and the building's contribution to the urban heat-island effect. The parking lot uses pervious limestone and is landscaped with indigenous plants; it doubles as an event courtyard and reduces heat build-up in summer months.

Building Performance, According to the Architects

The diversification of building and equipment used is not yet maximizing the energy efficiency of the heat-recovery system capabilities. Other user decisions with regard to space utilization have lessened the efficiencies and user comfort for some of the spaces. The firm can only hope that with the still ongoing first-year commissioning process and extensive discussions about the building operation, the design intent

and the agreed-upon functional/spatial arrangements will help guide adjustments and modifications over time.

Lessons Learned by the Architects

The client-architect relationship was such that an openness existed in investigating possibilities, and the Pittsburgh Glass Center was already on board with the basic intentions of sustainable design. This clearly comes from the culture of glassmaking. Almost everyone in the glass art community seems to be part artist, part engineer, out of necessity and to be able to make glass art and run a glass studio. Therefore, the client and the architect had different words but a similar approach to things and once the vocabulary began to mesh, we had a very good dialogue.

2005 AIA/COTE Top Ten Winner
RINKER HALL, UNIVERSITY OF FLORIDA
LOCATION: Gainesville, Florida
ARCHITECTS: Croxton Collaborative Architects and Gould Evans

This LEED Gold building is oriented on a pure north-south axis, demonstrating the ability to use low-angle light for daylighting. Egress paths from all classrooms at all levels are continuously lit, allowing for emergency exit during a daytime power failure. Large-scale open, linear accessibility was "mapped" through major classroom spaces to provide nondisruptive servicing and flexibility for future retrofit. Two major areas, the assembly room on the north and the construction shop on the east, were fully or partially incorporated in the design as indoor and outdoor spaces.

Daylight in Rinker Hall classrooms allows for minimal use of lights in daytime.

Rinker Hall relies on low-angle daylight.

2006 AIA/COTE Top Ten Green Projects

Alberici Corporation Headquarters, Overland, Missouri

The Animal Foundation Dog Adoption Park, Las Vegas, Nevada

Ballard Library and Neighborhood Service Center, Seattle, Washington

Ben Franklin Elementary School, Kirkland, Washington

Philadelphia Forensic Science Center, Philadelphia, Pennsylvania

Renovation of the Immaculate Heart of Mary Motherhouse, Monroe, Michigan

The University of Texas Health Science Center at Houston School of Nursing and Student Community Center, Houston, Texas

Solar Umbrella House, Venice, California

Warren Skaaren Environmental Learning Center at Westcave Preserve, Round Mountain, Texas

World Birding Center Headquarters, Mission, Texas

The following summaries of the 2006 AIA/COTE Top Ten Green Projects are adapted with permission from the AIA's project descriptions.

2006 AIA/COTE Top Ten Winner
ALBERICI CORPORATION HEADQUARTERS
LOCATION: Overland, Missouri
ARCHITECT: Mackey Mitchell Associates

The adaptive reuse of a 1950s office building and a former metal manufacturing facility created a new headquarters for one of St. Louis's oldest and largest construction companies. The newly designed facility provides an open office environment, structured parking, training rooms, exercise facilities, and dining facilities. The interiors open onto three large atriums that provide natural light and air while also serving as thermal flues to induce ventilation. The company sought to lead the industry by example with this building, which earned 60 out of a possible 69 points for a LEED Platinum Certification.

2006 AIA/COTE Top Ten Winner
THE ANIMAL FOUNDATION DOG ADOPTION PARK
LOCATION: Las Vegas, Nevada
ARCHITECT: Tate Snyder Kimsey Architects

This dog adoption facility is organized into *dog bungalows* containing 12 kennels each, outdoor runs, and a visitation room on a three-acre, parklike campus, shaded

The space between kennels at the Animal Foundation Dog Adoption Park is shaded by canopies of photovoltaic panels.

by canopies of photovoltaic panels. This is phase one of the Animal Foundation's expansion plan, designed to serve the animal adoption needs of the larger Las Vegas area. Providing a dignified way to introduce the dogs to potential adopters, the complex also incorporates abundant natural air and light—an ideal setting for dogs. Because a large amount of water is needed for waste removal, a wastewater treatment plant is incorporated on the site. The facility has been designed to potentially receive LEED Platinum Certification.

2006 AIA/COTE Top Ten Winner
BALLARD LIBRARY AND NEIGHBORHOOD SERVICE CENTER
LOCATION: Seattle, Washington
ARCHITECT: Bohlin Cywinski Jackson

At the crossroads of an emerging neighborhood center, this site is accessible to foot and bicycle traffic, as well as by public transit. A gently sloping roof and generous setback provide a wide front porch and entrances to the 15,000-square-foot library and 3,600-square-foot neighborhood service center. The roof is planted with sedums and grasses, with which patrons can interact via a periscope and observation deck. The building lets in varying intensities of natural light while also employing photovoltaic glass panels to provide cover in the lobby.

2006 AIA/COTE Top Ten Winner
BEN FRANKLIN ELEMENTARY SCHOOL
LOCATION: Kirkland, Washington
ARCHITECT: Mahlum Architects

This new 55,000-square-foot elementary school preserves its wooded setting and allows a visual and physical connection between the students and their surroundings. The school's naturally ventilated and daylighted classrooms are organized in clusters of four around shared multipurpose activity areas. These classrooms, organized in two-story wings, reflect the school's commitment to small learning communities to educate the 450 students in grades K–6. As designed, the school anticipates that it will need only 16,405 Btu per square foot annually.

2006 AIA/COTE Top Ten Winner
PHILADELPHIA FORENSIC SCIENCE CENTER
LOCATION: Philadelphia, Pennsylvania
ARCHITECT: Croxton Collaborative Architects with associate architect Cecil Baker & Associates

Housed in a 1929 brick-and-concrete school building that had laid abandoned for many years, this forensic science center for the city of Philadelphia now includes a firearms unit, a crime-scene unit for gathering evidence, and laboratories for chemistry, criminalistics, and DNA analysis. Due to the highly specialized program require-

Philadelphia Forensic Science Center is an example of an extensive reuse and reconfiguration of a building with new, specialized program requirements.

ments, the architects provided many tools for sustainable building functions. These include precise mapping and load separation of areas requiring 100 percent outside air to minimize mechanical loads; envelope and insulation upgrades; clean products and finishes for improved indoor air quality; deep daylighting; photovoltaic power; and primary access to all mechanical and infrastructure systems outside of lab areas.

2006 AIA/COTE Top Ten Winner
RENOVATION OF THE IMMACULATE HEART OF MARY MOTHERHOUSE
LOCATION: Monroe, Michigan
ARCHITECT: Susan Maxman & Partners, Architects

The architects updated historically significant 1930s convent buildings to an ecologically sustainable twenty-first century community at the request of the sisters of the Servants of the Immaculate Heart of Mary. They made changes to housing to better accommodate aging residents, while keeping the complex adaptable for future uses.

Wastewater from lavatories and showers is routed to a nearby constructed wetland and reused for toilets. Ground-source heating and cooling systems are implemented. The buildings, situated on a 280-acre site, now better integrate daylighting, natural ventilation, and outdoor views, drastically reducing the energy load and improving the residents' quality of life.

2006 AIA/COTE Top Ten Winner
THE UNIVERSITY OF TEXAS HEALTH SCIENCE CENTER AT HOUSTON SCHOOL OF NURSING AND STUDENT COMMUNITY CENTER
LOCATION: Houston, Texas
ARCHITECT: BNIM Architects

This new academic building offers spatial flexibility, such as raised floor and demountable partitions, to accommodate a nursing program that experiences fluctuations of student population. As part of an overall university effort to improve its indoor environments and reduce energy loads, this building employs operable windows, views to the outside, three atriums, and ambient daylighting. The building is designed to use about 41 percent less energy than a conventionally designed higher education facility, and a 48 percent reduction in potable water use is expected through rainwater harvesting, water-free urinals, and efficient fixtures.

2006 AIA/COTE Top Ten Winner
SOLAR UMBRELLA HOUSE
LOCATION: Venice, California
ARCHITECT: Pugh + Scarpa

For the addition to and renovation of a 1923 bungalow set in a neighborhood of similar houses, the architects took inspiration from Paul Rudolph's 1953 Umbrella House. They erected a canopy made up of 89 amorphous silicon solar panels, to shield the house from thermal heat gain and provide 95 percent of the home's electricity. Home to the architects and their young son, the house was reoriented 180 degrees on the block-through lot to take advantage of the energy-rich southern California sunlight. The solar-heating system supplies heat through the new addition's concrete floors. Three solar panels preheat the home's hot water, and another panel heats the swimming pool.

2006 AIA/COTE Top Ten Winner
WARREN SKAAREN ENVIRONMENTAL LEARNING CENTER AT WESTCAVE PRESERVE
LOCATION: Round Mountain, Texas
ARCHITECT: Jackson & McElhaney Architects

The architects aimed to create a "three-dimensional textbook" for this educational center, set on a 30-acre nature preserve 28 miles northwest of Austin, Texas. As part of the educational demonstration, the building's water quality and recycling functions mimic naturally occurring cycles, including a rainwater-collection and filtration system, as well as a wastewater recycling system. The 3,030-square-foot building obtains energy in part from natural sources including a photovoltaic array and ground-source heat pumps.

2006 AIA/COTE Top Ten Winner
WORLD BIRDING CENTER HEADQUARTERS
LOCATION: Mission, Texas
ARCHITECT: Lake|Flato Architects

To combat the rapid suburban and agricultural development of one of the richest bird habitats in the world, the Texas Parks & Wildlife Department worked with the

Structural arched panels enclose the World Birding Center Headquarters with the least material and use less steel than traditional steel framing.

local communities to found the World Birding Center. Adjacent to more than 1,700 acres of native wildlife habitat, which is home to indigenous plants that are quickly disappearing, the center's landscaping uses only native plants and contains a 47,000-gallon rainwater system of rainwater guzzlers, natural pools, and water seeps. The architects were also able to reduce the proposed building program from 20,000 square feet to 13,000 square feet.

afterword

When I started writing this book in early 2005, regular gasoline was $1.47 per gallon; as 2006 was wrapping up, gasoline was around $2.68. There is an informed acceptance in the United States that this is the way it will be, this is the new limit to growth, the new state of the union. Good—it is important that we get the challenge correct. We are learning that life of any sort on a constant growth curve is unachievable, unsustainable, and quite possibly undesirable.

Earlier I mentioned the considerable impact Dr. Howard T. Odum had on me—creating an interest in the general systems problem-solving approach. It is interesting to note that one of his last books is titled *A Prosperous Way Down* (Odum and Odum, 2001). Their book gives us considerable pause, bearing in mind that—as with all systems—growth cycles come and go. Growth is a function of the available energy, the storage of that energy, and the available materials that when put to use create structure. Any systems ability to put the available energy to use—efficiently or inefficiently—is a function of its structure, its form and pattern. Why can't the next phase of human-centric development be more prosperous than before? Of course, the answer is, it can.

The only constant is change. Reduced supplies and storages of fossil fuel and virtually all resources already characterize the new millennium. Tons of resources chased by tons of consumers cannot be sustained, and using materials and energy at a rate faster than they regenerate, reduces the carrying capacity of the region and place. Therefore, the new forms and patterns in architecture and urbanism must evolve to capturing available energies and designing the built environment to use less and do more with it. "Less is more" takes on a whole new meaning. This change in designing and design programming will help to increase prosperity and reduce consumption—getting better using less and then getting better using none—no deleterious materials or processes.

The need is more apparent today than when I started writing this book; but the opportunities are not only greater now but more compelling, more essential. Changing the initial questions we ask ourselves at the beginning of a project can reduce our carbon output by 50 percent, an interim goal of the American Institute of Architects' 2010 *50 to 50* initiative on the way to carbon-neutral design by 2030.

The current global and local challenges present an opportunity and a responsibility to inform our practices with the issues of sustainability. As generalists, architects are well suited for this leadership role, helping to facilitate multidisciplinary teams that work toward rethinking how things are done and challenging standard practice. The joining of science and design, a mutually beneficial collaboration, offers a new conversation, one that is holistic and inclusive. Bringing environmental fields together with government and the public and illustrating the power of design as a tool in helping to achieve a sustainable future is a compelling challenge and a call to bold action. This challenge requires that our profession expand its reach both in knowledge and scope, and to not only require multiple disciplines at the table but to learn these disciplines well enough to understand and address the challenges facing us.

The case studies presented in this book illustrate the scales of sustainable design from the region to architecture as simple, affordable examples that accomplish huge changes while they improve the quality of life for less cost—less taxes. These solutions have been informed by the natural sciences; they capture and optimize the use of the free energy of the place. They illustrate that through sustainable thinking, architects and planners can help communities, clients, and public officials create a better future—one that is more desirable, more affordable, and essential for all of the communities of the planet.

Daniel E. Williams, FAIA
Summer Solstice, 2006

sustainability terms

Appropriate technology. A technology that provides services, such as heating, cooling, water heating, and lighting, by efficiently using the available energy that most closely provides the service. An example of an appropriate technology is a solar water heating that provides hot water from solar radiation. The performance for hot water is in the 110–120 degree Fahrenheit range. A rooftop can provide up to 140 degrees Fahrenheit; collecting that surface heat is an appropriate technology. An example of inappropriate technology for water heating is electricity, which requires 2,000-degrees-Fahrenheit steam production to turn a turbine to create electricity and to make the resistance coil-rod heat the water to the required 110 degrees.

Biodegradable. A material or substance that, when left exposed to soil, air, and water (not in landfills), will decompose over time without harmful effects to the environment. *Note:* Most biodegradable materials do *not* degrade in landfills, because these sites are usually devoid of the natural processes.

Bioregionalism. The study of a region's biology and climate and the incorporation of that knowledge into the design process and the choice of construction methods. It implies the use of local materials and information derived from historically successful case studies.

Biourbanism. Urban systems designed to work as biology, combining economic, community, and environmental elements all powered by renewable energy and place-based resources.

Brownfield. The U.S. Environmental Protection Agency's (EPA) designation for existing facilities or sites that have been abandoned, demolished, or underused because of real or perceived environmental contamination. The EPA sponsors an initiative to help mitigate these health risks and return the facility or land to renewed use. Use of brownfields for mixed use improves the community; infills development near existing utilities, transit, and infrastructure; and heals polluted land.

Building envelope. The entire perimeter of a building enclosed by its roof, walls, and foundation.

Carrying capacity. The population within an area that can be sustained by a set flow of energy and materials that are resident to that area over time.

Cradle-to-cradle (C2C). A phrase in biology that describes the continuous usefulness of most elements in nature. *Cradle-to-cradle* is a concept introduced by architect William McDonough, FAIA, in his book of the same name. It prescribes that at the end of a product's useful life it should be used as a postconsumer resource and given new life in the form of new products and materials or recycled into new products and materials or alternative uses.

Embodied energy. The sum total of energy used to grow, extract, and manufacture a product, including the amount of energy needed to transport it to the job site and complete the installation.

Fossil fuels. Fuels, such as coal, oil, and natural gas, extracted from beneath the Earth's surface, often with significant environmental and capital cost. These fuels are a finite resource; are nonrenewable; and create extreme environmental, economic, and health impacts with use.

Free energy / Free work. The power and work that are accomplished without cost to the human economy. Examples include water distribution by gravity; water filtration in soil and by bioremediation; heating and lighting with sunlight; and cooling by ventilation and evaporation.

Green design. The process of designing anything with materials that before, during, and after use positively impact users and nonusers, have no toxic impact, and can be safely returned to natural-systems cycles or reused.

Green infrastructure. The utility that natural systems provide when preserved and protected and allowed to function. Examples include water purification and distribution, air purification, carbon sequestering, microclimate cooling and heating, etc. Communities and regions that maximize this *free work* tend to have a competitive advantage, lower taxes, and a higher quality of life.

LEED™. The Leadership in Energy and Environmental Design (LEED) Building Rating System (BRS) sets industry standards for green building design. Developed by the United States Green Building Council, it has become the international standard for the measurement of green design.

Natural systems. A system that works without the interaction of humans.

Net energy. The available useful energy left over after the energy needed for its extraction is subtracted. This value, in fossil-fuel extraction, has created powerful economic growth engines in the developed countries.

Nonrenewable. A finite resource. Resources such as fossil fuels are, due to the extreme time period of their production, considered nonrenewable.

Off-the-grid. Systems and structures that run effectively without the regional or national fossil-fuel-driven electric grid.

Place-based design and planning. Design and planning based on the incorporation of green and sustainable principles, powered by local energies, built with local labor and local materials, and respectful of region and culture.

Resident energies. Renewable energies—such as solar, wind, soil, gravity, and others—specific to a region, its ecology, and its climate. The energy "resides" in the place.

Sustainability. Continuing, evolving, and adapting to renewables.

Sustainable design. The creation and construction of projects that contribute to the improving and continuing of community, economy, and environment.

Thermal comfort. The effective combination of temperature, warm or cool, combined with air movement and humidity, which is comfortable to the average user within the confines of a space. Comfort can be achieved through careful design and planning, including the strategic orientation and location of windows, light shelves, color, texture, and building mass that captures and puts to use the resident energies and resources.

With regard to physiology and psychology of comfort, the answer is complex. The long-established science of thermal comfort was very rigorous. The late P. Ole Fanger's work is the international reference standard; he and many others established the parameters of the comfort zone, which have been found to be principally physiological but with both cultural and personal differences (e.g., determined by age, sex, predisposition based on culture). This work shows a slightly larger comfort zone than adopted by ASHRAE—that is, a range of perceived comfort, itself a psychological response. Fanger showed that, while there is agreement among people on the approximate comfort zone, there is very wide disagreement about "when I am uncomfortable"; this is explained partly by literal differences in physical body type but also by perception and anticipated anxiety of discomfort (Watson, 1983).

Waste stream. The total flow of waste from homes, businesses, institutions, and manufacturing that is treated, recycled, burned, or disposed of in landfills. The waste stream has tremendous potential for energy production and reuse (see *cradle-to-cradle*).

Wastewater. Water that has been used and degraded (from drinking water standards) and must be processed before it can be used again. Since water supply is a limiting factor in development, wastewater has become a valuable resource. Thinking of wastewater as a resource will lead to solutions that help reduce water shortages while they improve regional and urban patterns (see *watershed design and planning*).

Watershed. An area defined by the gravity distribution of precipitation. Watersheds are metaphorically a "bowl," described by contours of the land, soils, slope, and geology.

Watershed design and planning. A practical vision and plan that is informed by the system sciences and urban and regional design principles. Water, used as the common denominator, helps establish areas for recharge and water storage as well as transportation corridors, agricultural preservation zones, smart growth, and natural-system protection and conservation zones.

bibliography

Addington, Michelle, and Daniel Schodek. 2005. *Smart Materials and New Technologies for the Architecture and Design Professions*. Burlington, MA, and Oxford: Elsevier, Architectural Press.

ASHRAE, 2004. *Advanced Energy Design Guide for Small Office Buildings*. Atlanta: W. Stephen Comstock.

Bonan, Gordon B. 2002. *Ecological Climatology: Concepts and Applications*. Cambridge: Cambridge University Press.

Bryson, Bill. 2003. *A Short History of Nearly Everything*. New York: Broadway Books.

Caldwell, Lynton K. 1970. "The Ecosystem as a Criterion for Public Land Policy." *Natural Resources Journal* 10 (2): 203–221.

Carter, Luther J. 1974. *The Florida Experience: Land and Water Policy in a Growth State*. Baltimore, MD: Johns Hopkins University Press.

Crowe, Norman. 1995. *Nature and the Idea of a Man-Made World: An Investigation into the Evolutionary Roots of Form and Order in the Built Environment*. Cambridge, MA: MIT Press.

Davis, S. M., and J. C. Ogden, eds. 1994. *Everglades: The Ecosystem and Its Restoration*. Delray Beach, FL: St. Lucie Press.

DeGrove, John M. 1984. *Land, Growth, and Politics*. Washington, DC: American Planning Association.

———. 1992. *Planning and Growth Management in the States*. Cambridge, MA: Lincoln Institute of Land Policy.

Fanger, P. O. 1970. *Thermal Comfort: Analysis and Applications in Environmental Engineering*. Malabar, FL: R. E. Krieger.

Fischer, Adelheid. 1994. "Coming Full Circle: The Restoration of the Urban Landscape." *Orion* 13 (4): 29.

Fuad-Luke, Alastair. 2002. *The Eco-Design Handbook: A Complete Sourcebook for the Home and Office*. San Francisco: Chronicle Books.

Gissen, David. 2003. *Big and Green: Toward Sustainable Architecture in the Twenty-First Century*. New York: Princeton Architectural Press.

Golany, Gideon S. 1995. *Ethics and Urban Design: Culture, Form, and Environment*. New York: John Wiley and Sons, Inc.

Grumbine, R. Edward. 1994. "What Is Ecosystem Management?" *Conservation Biology* 8 (1): 27–38.

Hardin, Garrett. 1968. "The Tragedy of the Commons." *Science* 162 (3859): 1243–1248.

Hawken, Paul. 1993. *The Ecology of Commerce: A Declaration of Sustainability.* New York: HarperBusiness.

Hough, Michael. 1995. *Cities and Natural Process.* New York: Routledge.

Hunter Interests, Inc. 2001. *Rio Nuevo Master Plan.* Tucson, AZ.

Jennings, Lucinda, Victoria Schomer, and Daniel Williams. 2003. Presentation: *Green Terms*, The Summit of the Professionals, Atlanta, Georgia (American Institute of Architects, American Society of Interior Designers, Construction Specification Institute, International Facility Management Association, Urban Land Institute, United States Green Council, and ASHRAE).

Knowles, Ralph L. 1974. *An Ecological Approach to Urban Growth.* Cambridge, MA: MIT Press.

Kolbert, Elizabeth. 2006. *Field Notes from a Catastrophe: Man, Nature, and Climate Change.* New York: Bloomsbury Publishing.

Lechner, Norbert. 2001. *Heating, Cooling, Lighting: Design Methods for Architects.* 2nd ed. New York: John Wiley and Sons, Inc.

Lincoln Institute of Land Policy. 1994. *Managing Growth on Cape Cod: The Use of Transferable Development Rights in Local Comprehensive Plans.* New York: Lincoln Institute Press.

MacDonnell, Lawrence J., and Sarah Bates, eds. 1993. *Natural Resources Policy and Law: Trends and Directions.* Denver: Natural Resources Law Center, University of Colorado School of Law.

MacKay, B. April 27, 1994. Speech giving the charge to the Governor's Commission for a Sustainable South Florida, West Palm Beach, FL.

———. September 26, 1994. "Water Limits May Halt Growth." In *Lakeland (FL) Ledger*.

Marsh, William M. 2005. *Landscape Planning: Environmental Applications.* Hoboken, NJ: John Wiley and Sons, Inc.

McDonough, William, and Michael Braungart. 2002. *Cradle to Cradle: Remaking the Way We Make Things.* New York: North Point Press.

McHarg, Ian L. 1967. *Design with Nature.* New York: John Wiley and Sons, Inc.

Mendler, Sandra, William Odell, and Mary Ann Lazarus. 2006. *The HOK Guidebook to Sustainable Design.* 2nd ed. Hoboken, NJ: John Wiley and Sons, Inc.

Morrish, William R. 2000. *Farmington Minnesota Study, Design Center for the American Urban Landscape.* Minneapolis: University of Minnesota.

Odum, Eugene. 1971. *Fundamentals of Ecology.* 3rd ed. Philadelphia: W. B. Saunders Company.

Odum, Howard T. 1971. *Power, Environment and Society.* New York: John Wiley and Sons, Inc.

Odum, Howard T., and Elisabeth C. Odum. 1976. *Energy Basis for Man and Nature.* New York: McGraw-Hill.

————. 2001. *A Prosperous Way Down: Principles and Policies*. Boulder: University Press of Colorado.

Olgyay, Victor. 1992. *Design with Climate: Bioclimatic Approach to Architectural Regionalism*. New York: John Wiley and Sons, Inc.

Orr, David W. 2002. *The Nature of Design*. New York: Oxford University Press.

Pimm, Stuart L., Gary E. Davis, Lloyd Loope, Charles T. Roman, Thomas J. Smith III, and James T. Tilmant. 1994. "Hurricane Andrew." *Bioscience* 44 (4): 224–229.

Postel, Sandra. 1996. *The Last Oasis*. Washington, DC: Island Press.

Strahler, Arthur, and Alan Strahler. 1989. *Elements of Physical Geography*, 4th ed. New York: John Wiley and Sons, Inc.

Suzuki, David. 1994. *Time to Change*. Toronto, ON: Stoddart.

Vale, Brenda, and Robert Vale. 1991. *Green Architecture: Design for an Energy-Conscious Future*. Boston: Little, Brown.

van Hinte, Ed, et al. 2003. *Smart Architecture*. Rotterdam, Netherlands: 010 Publishers.

Veri, Albert R., William W. Jenna Jr., and Dorothy Eden Bergamaschi. 1975. *Environmental Quality by Design: South Florida*. Miami: University of Miami.

Wackernagel, Mathis, and William Rees. 1996. *Our Ecological Footprint*. Gabriola Island, BC: New Society Publishers.

Watson, Donald, and Kenneth Labs. 1983. *Climatic Design: Energy-Efficient Building Principles and Practices*. New York: McGraw-Hill.

Williams, Daniel. 1992. *The WIN Plan—Watershed Interactive Network: Towards a Sustainable Watershed Design Methodology*. Miami: Center for Urban and Community Design, University of Miami.

————. 1993. *Regional Studies—Introduction. The New South Dade Planning Charrette: From Adversity to Opportunity*. Miami: University of Miami.

————. 1994. *South Dade Watershed Project Workshop Report*. Miami: Center for Urban and Community Design, University of Miami.

————. 1995. *The South Dade Watershed Project*. West Palm Beach: South Florida Water Management District.

————. 1996. *The Belle Glade Regional Design Charrette*. Miami: Center for Urban and Community Design, University of Miami.

————. 1998a. *The Eastward Ho Vision. Florida Department of Community Affairs*. Miami Beach: Miami Education and Research Center, University of Florida.

————. 1998b. Sustainability Panel. American Planning Association Conference: Florida Conference. Naples, Florida.

————. 2002. "The Design of Regions." In *Handbook of Water Sensitive Planning and Design*, ed. Robert L. France. Boca Raton, FL: Lewis Publishing.

Wines, James. 2000. *Green Architecture: The Art of Architecture in the Age of Ecology*. New York: Taschen.

World Wildlife Fund. 1992. *Statewide Wetlands Strategies: A Guide to Protecting and Managing the Resource*. Washington, DC: Island Press.

Zerubavel, Eviatar. 1991. *The Fine Line: Making Distinctions in Everyday Life*. New York: Free Press.

index

A

ABN-AMRO Bank World Headquarters (Amsterdam, Netherlands), 170
Adam Joseph Lewis Center for Environmental Studies (Oberlin, Ohio), 182–184
Adeline Street Urban Salvage Project (Berkeley, California), 170
Adversity-to-opportunity approach, 66
Aerodynamics, 108, 109
Affordable Housing Development Corp., 148
AIA, see American Institute of Architects
AIA Committee on the Environment (COTE), 121, 129
AIA/COTE Top Ten Green Projects, 129–130
AIA/COTE Top Ten Green Projects (1997), 130–140
Center for Regenerative Studies, 132–133
Durant Road Middle School, 133–135
New Canaan Nature Center Horticultural Education Center, 135–137
Prince Street Technologies, 137–139
Women's Humane Society Animal Shelter, 139–140
AIA/COTE Top Ten Green Projects (1998), 140–147
Florida House Learning Center, 140, 143, 144
Ridgehaven Green Demonstration Project, 144–145

Thoreau Center for Sustainability, 145–147
AIA/COTE Top Ten Green Projects (1999), 147–159
CCI Center, 147
Denver Drygoods, 148–150
Duracell Headquarters, 150–151
Kansas City Zoo Deramus Pavilion, 152–153
Real Goods Solar Living Center, 153–156
REI Seattle, 156–159
AIA/COTE Top Ten Green Projects (2000), 159–169
Bainbridge Island City Hall, 160
C. K. Choi Building, Institute of Asian Research, University of British Columbia, 161–162
Emeryville Resourceful Building, 163–165
Hanover House, 165
Lady Bird Johnson Wildflower Center, 166–167
New South Jamaica Branch Library, 167–168
World Resources Institute, 168–169
AIA/COTE Top Ten Green Projects (2001), 170–182
Chesapeake Bay Foundation Headquarters, 171–172
Montgomery Campus, California College of Arts and Crafts, 175–177
PNC Firstside Center, 177–179
REI Denver, 172–175

Sleeping Lady Conference and Retreat Center, 179–180
Zion National Park Visitor Center, 181–182
AIA/COTE Top Ten Green Projects (2002), 182–199
Adam Joseph Lewis Center for Environmental Studies, 182–184
Bank of Astoria, 184–186
Camp Arroyo, 188–190
Edificio Malecon, 190–191
Iowa Association of Municipal Utilities, 191–193
National Wildlife Federation Headquarters, 193–194
Navy Building 850, 186–188
Pier 1, 194–195
Puget Sound Environmental Learning Center, 195–197
Tofte Cabin, 197–199
AIA/COTE Top Ten Green Projects (2003), 200–218
Argonne Child Development Center, 200–201
Chicago Center for Green Technology, 202–203
Colorado Court Affordable Housing, 204–205
Cusano Center at Tinicum, 205–208
The Fisher Pavilion, 208
Herman Miller Marketplace, 208–211
Hidden Villa Youth Hostel and Summer Camp, 211–213
San Mateo County Forensic Laboratory, 213–215

AIA/COTE Top Ten Green Projects
(2003) (Continued)
Steinhude Sea Recreation Facility,
215–216
Wine Creek Road Home, 217–218
AIA/COTE Top Ten Green Projects
(2004), 218–230
City of White Rock Operations
Building, 219–220
F10 House, 220–221
Genzyme Center, 221–223
Greystone Bakery, 223–224
Herman Miller Building C1, 224–225
Lake View Terrace Branch Library,
226–228
Pierce County Environmental Services
Building, 228–229
The Plaza at PPL Center, 229
20 River Terrace—The Solaire, 219
Woods Hole Research Center, 230
AIA/COTE Top Ten Green Projects
(2005), 230–247
Austin Resource Center for the
Homeless, 231–233
The Barn at Fallingwater, 233–236
Eastern Sierra House, 236–237
Evergreen State College Seminar II,
237–238
Heimbold Visual Arts Center, Sarah
Lawrence College, 238–240
Leslie Shao-Ming Sun Field Station,
240–242
Lloyd Crossing Sustainable Design
Plan, 243–246
Pittsburgh Glass Center, 246–247
Rinker Hall, University of Florida, 247
AIA/COTE Top Ten Green Projects
(2006), 247–254
Alberici Corporation Headquarters,
249
The Animal Foundation Dog
Adoption Park, 249–250
Ballard Library and Neighborhood
Service Center, 250
Ben Franklin Elementary School, 250
Immaculate Heart of Mary
Motherhouse renovation, 251–252
Philadelphia Forensic Science Center,
250–251

Solar Umbrella House, 252
The University of Texas Health
Science Center at Houston School
of Nursing and Student
Community Center, 252
Warren Skaaren Environmental
Learning Center at Westcare
Preserve, 252–253
World Birding Center Headquarters,
253–254
Air movement, in regional design, 32.
See also Wind
Alberici Corporation Headquarters
(Overland, Missouri), 249
American Institute of Architects (AIA).
See also AIA/COTE Top Ten Green
Projects
Headquarters project of, 121–126
National SDAT of, 49–50
Principles for Livable Communities, 74
Sustainable Design Assessment
Teams of, 43
The Animal Foundation Dog Adoption
Park (Las Vegas, Nevada),
249–250
Applied Ecology, 160
Architects:
and climate change, xvi–xvii
as three-dimensional problem
solvers, 14–15
Architectural design, 103–128
building skin in, 116–120
environmental analysis in, 105–116
evolving sustainable design practice
in, 120–121
infrastructure in, 116
site analysis in, 103–106
and sustainable interior architecture,
126–128
and sustainable re-design of existing
buildings, 121–126
Argonne Child Development Center
(San Francisco, California),
200–201
Arkin Tilt Architects, 211, 236
Astorino, 177
Atelier Ten, 229
Austin Resource Center for the
Homeless (Austin, Texas), 231–233

B
Bainbridge Island City Hall (Bainbridge
Island, Washington), 160
Ballard Library and Neighborhood
Service Center (Seattle,
Washington), 250
Bank of Astoria (Manzanita, Oregon),
184–186
"Barcelona Declaration on Sustainable
Design," 70–72
The Barn at Fallingwater (Mill Run,
Pennsylvania), 233–236
Basics, 2
Behnisch, Stefan, 223
Behnisch Architects, 221
Belle Glade, Florida case study, 81–83
Bender, Tom, 184
Ben Franklin Elementary School
(Kirkland, Washington), 250
Berkebile, Bob, 103, 130
Bernstein, Scott, 20
BigHorn Home Improvement Center
(Silverthorne, Colorado), 170
Bioclimates:
in architectural design, 105
as character of regions, 70
ecological adaptation to, 5
regional, 33
in urban and community design, 70
Biomes, 2
defined, 2
desert, 70
evergreen, 70
knowledge of, in regional design, 36
study of, 12
world-wide, 30
Bioregionalism, 10, 23
process for, 42–43
in southeastern Florida case study, 66
Biosphere, 2
Biourbanism, 11, 24
natural systems and green
processes in, 70
process for, 43
in regional design process, 36
and regional ecology, 72–73
in southeastern Florida case study, 66
Blackouts, xxiii–xxiv
BNIM Architects, 152, 252

Body Shop U.S. Headquarters (Wake Forest, North Carolina), 130, 131
Bohlin, Peter, 235–236
Bohlin Cywinski Jackson, 233, 250
Bonsignore, Regina C., 59
Boundaries:
    human vs. natural, 4
    of natural systems/biomes, 12
    on urban systems maps, 35
Bowers, Ken, 49, 101
Breedlove, Ben, 2
Brinkley, James, 130
Brown, Catherine R., 59
Brownfields, 6
Buchanan Associates Architects, 135
Buildings:
    emissions from, xvi
    envelopes of, 117
    green, 16
    microclimates affected by, 105
    nonsustainable, xxiv
    as organisms vs. objects, 16
    orientation of, 75
    renovation of, 116
    skin of, 116–120
    sustainable, xxv
Building codes:
    regional, 33
    urban, 35
Busby & Associates Architects, 219

C
C. K. Choi Building, Institute of Asian Research, University of British Columbia (Vancouver, British Columbia, Canada), 161–162
Cache Valley, Utah case study, 6, 43–50
    action summary for, 47–49
    principles and guidelines for, 46, 47
    SDAT discoveries, 43–45
    Sustainable Design Assessment Team for, 43
    Valley as group of communities, 45, 47
Cambridge Cohousing (Cambridge, Massachusetts), 140, 141
Camp Arroyo (Livermore, California), 188–190
Carrying capacity:
    of land, 28–29
    regional, 33
CCI Center (Pittsburgh, Pennsylvania), 147
Cecil Baker & Associates, 250
Cedar River Watershed (Seattle, Washington), 29
Center for Community and Neighborhood Design, University of Miami, 83
Center for Regenerative Studies (Pomona, California), 132–133
Cesar Pelli & Associates Architects, 219
Charrettes, 27, 121, 122
Cheetham, Dan, 194
Chesapeake Bay Foundation Headquarters (Annapolis, Maryland), 171–172
Chicago Center for Green Technology (Chicago, Illinois), 202–203
Choices, 74
City of White Rock Operations Building (White Rock, British Columbia, Canada), 219–220
Clark, E. Ann, 49
Climates. See also Bioclimates
    microclimates, 105
    in regional design, 32
Climate change:
    architects' role in, xvi–xvii
    global, xv
Climax state, 2
Colorado Court Affordable Housing (Santa Monica, California), 204–205
"Coming Full Circle" (Adelheid Fischer), 9, 67
Commons, development of, 7–8
Commoner, Barry, 1
Community(-ies). See also Urban and community design
    as central to ecology, 69
    defined, 69
    environmental context as, 1
    green, 16
    in Jeffersonian grid, 7
    liveable, AIA principles for, 74
    sustainable, 72
Community-based vision:
    in regional design, 27, 29
    teaching process for describing, 26
Community-design principles, 55–57
Congress for New Urbanism, 69
Connectivity in design, 18
Conservation areas, regional, 36, 37
Constraints, 4
Contaminated sites, 6
Le Corbusier, xxii, 69
Cornish School of the Arts (Seattle, Washington), 126–128
Correra, Jamie, 83
COTE, see AIA Committee on the Environment
Courtyards, 109, 111–112
Croxton Collaborative Architects, 131, 247, 250
Crystal River Power Plant (Florida), 9
CTG Energetics, 186
Cusano Center at Tinicum (Philadelphia, Pennsylvania), 205–208
Cybul & Cybul, 223

D
Dade County, Florida, regional development, 36–42. See also Southeast Florida coastal communities case study
Darwin, Charles, 2
Database for sustainable design, 120–121
Deep sustainability, xv
Denver Drygoods (Denver, Colorado), 148–150
Department of Environmental Protection (Ebensburg, Pennsylvania), 159
Desert biomes, 70
Design:
    as dynamic/living process, 17
    green, 15–16
    importance of, 13–14
    for livable communities, 74
    post-disaster, 106, 108
    power and potential of, 15
    as systems problem, 17
Design Center for American Urban Landscape, 57

Design codes, regional, 33
Design Harmony, 131
Design with Nature (Ian McHarg), xv
Development:
　growth vs., 4, 5
　sustainable, xxii
DeWitt, Charlotte, 101
dggp Architecture, 246
Dougherty + Dougherty, 132
Duracell Headquarters (Bethel,
　　Connecticut), 150–151
Durant Road Middle School (Raleigh,
　　North Carolina), 133–135

E

Eastern Sierra House (Gardnerville,
　　Nevada), 236–237
EBN (Environmental Building News),
　121
Ecological capital, 45
Ecological model, 3–5
Ecologic/economic model, 6
Ecology, 2–12
　and bioregionalism, 10
　and biourbanism, 11
　defined, 1
　50 percent benchmark in, xxii
　idea of community in, 69
　as model, 3–5
　regional, 23
　seasonal changes in, 106
　as sustainable design, 1
　value of land in, 7–8
　waste debts in, 5–7
The Ecology of Commerce (Paul
　　Hawkin), 16, 27
Economy:
　dependence on nonrenewables
　　in, 25
　urban, 36
Ecosystems, 2
　regional, 33
　restoration of, 9
Edge condition, 67
Edificio Malecon (Buenos Aires,
　　Argentina), 190–191
Electric power grids, 25–26
Emeryville Resourceful Building
　　(Emeryville, California), 163–165

Emissions:
　from buildings, xvi
　curbing, xvii
Energy:
　in ecological model, 3
　from fossil fuels, xxii–xxiii
　natural, *see* Natural energy
　nonrenewable, 1–2, 16
　nuclear, 5, 6
　on-site, xix–xx, xxi
　regional, 33
　renewable, 2. *See also* Natural
　　energy
　resident (local), xxi–xxii
　solar, 3, 4
　within vs. outside site, 5
Energy and Form (Ralph Knowles),
　108
Energy efficiency, sustainability vs.,
　17–18
Energy Resource Center (Downey,
　　California), 140, 141
Energysmiths/Marc Rosenbaum, PE,
　165
ENSAR Group, Inc., 131
Envelope, building, 117
Environmental analysis, 105–116
　to inform design, 116
　and post-disaster design and
　　planning, 106–113
　site relationships in, 113–114
Environmental Building News (EBN),
　121
Environmental Defense Fund, 6
Environmental protection, impact of
　　regional design on, 23
Environmental Showcase Home
　　(Phoenix, Arizona), 140, 141
EPA (United States Environmental
　　Protection Agency), 26
Esherick Homsey Dodge and Davis,
　220
Evergreen biomes, 70
Evergreen State College Seminar II
　　(Olympia, Washington),
　237–238
Existing buildings, sustainable re-design
　　of, 121–125
Exponential growth, xxii

F

Farmington, Minnesota case study,
　50–59
　community-design principles, 55–57
　dependence on waterways in, 50–52
　objectives of, 51
　prairie waterway design principles,
　　52–55
　study team for, 59
Farr Associates, 202, 203
Fields Devereaux, 226
Fischer, Adelheid, 9, 67
The Fisher Pavilion (Seattle,
　　Washington), 208
Fitzsimons, M. Elizabeth, 59
Florida House Learning Center
　　(Sarasota, Florida), 140, 143, 144
F10 House (Chicago, Illinois), 220–221
Fossil fuels, xxii–xxiii, 18
450 Architects, 200
Fraker, Harrison S., Jr., 59
Franta, Greg, 130
Free work of the natural system, 16,
　23–25
　in regional design, 43
　systems-design approach to
　　capturing, 38, 39
Fuller, Buckminster, xxi

G

Gandhi, Mahatma, 125
Gannett Center Journal, 5
Gastinger, Kirk, 130
Genzyme Center (Cambridge,
　　Massachusetts), 221–223
Geohydrology, 34
Georgia Institute of Technology
　　Olympic Aquatic Center (Atlanta,
　　Georgia), 147
The Glades Community Development
　　Corporation, 83
Glenn, John, 33
Global climate change, xv
Gordon, Harry, 130
Gould, Kira, 130
Gould Evans, 247
Gravity, topography and, 32
Gravity-based water distribution
　　systems, 26

Great River Park (St. Paul, Minnesota)
case study, 91–101
concept of Park, 92
connections
development/improvement in, 100
developing Park program, 99
development potential in, 97–99
economic development in, 92–93
neighborhoods in, 93–95
sustainable practices in, 95–97
Greenberg, Ken, 101
Green design, sustainable design vs.,
15–16
Green infrastructure, 24, 35, 74–77
The Green Institute's Phillips Eco-
Enterprise Center (Minneapolis,
Minnesota), 159, 160
The Green Village Co., 41
Greenways, 55
GreenWorks, 226
Greystone Bakery (Yonkers, New York),
223–224
Groundwater contamination, 6
Growth:
defined, 5
development vs., 4, 5
exponential, xxii
regional patterns of, 27
relying on nonrenewables, xxiii–xxiv

H
Habitats:
Farmington, Minnesota case study,
52
regional, 33
Haeckel, Ernst Heinrich, 2–12
Hammel, Green and Abrahamson
(HGA), 166
Hammerberg, Thomas A., 59
Hanover House (Hanover, New
Hampshire), 165
Hardin, Garrett, 7–8
Hawkin, Paul, 16, 27
Heimbold Visual Arts Center, Sarah
Lawrence College (New York City),
238–240
Hellmuth, William, 193
Hellmuth Obata + Kassabaum (HOK):
Edificio Malecon, 190–191

Missouri Historical Society Museum,
148
National Wildlife Federation
Headquarters, 193–194
Nidus Center for Scientific Enterprise,
170
San Mateo County Forensic
Laboratory, 213
SC Johnson Wax Commercial
Products Headquarters, 142
World Resources Institute, 168–169
Herbert S. Newman and Partners, 150
Herman Miller Building C1 (Zeeland,
Michigan), 224–225
Herman Miller "Greenhouse" Factory
and Offices (Holland, Michigan),
130, 131
Herman Miller Marketplace (Zeeland,
Michigan), 208–211
HGA (Hammel, Green and
Abrahamson), 166
Hickok, Eugene A., 59
Hidden Villa Youth Hostel and Summer
Camp (Los Altos Hills, California),
211–213
Highest and best use, 4
Hill, Burt, 131
HOK, see Hellmuth Obata +
Kassabaum
Human-settlement energies, regional,
33
Humidity, 32
Hurricanes, 60, 62, 105, 106, 108, 109,
111–112
Hydrologic cycle, 28

I
Immaculate Heart of Mary
Motherhouse (Monroe, Michigan)
renovation, 251–252
Indigenous design, 19
Infill of urban grid, 116–118
Infrastructure:
in architectural design, 116
green, 24, 35, 74–77
in regional design, 24
renovating/reusing, 116
understanding costs of, 26
Innovative Design, 133

Integrated Architecture, 208
Interface Showroom and Offices
(Atlanta, Georgia), 140, 142
Interior architecture, sustainable,
126–128
Iowa Association of Municipal Utilities
(Ankeny, Iowa), 191–193

J
Jackson, Chris, 83
Jackson & McElhaney Architects, 252
Jefferson, Thomas, 4, 6–7
Jeffersonian grid, 7
John Heinz National Wildlife Refuge,
205
Jones & Jones Architects and Landscape
Architects, Ltd., 179
Jones Studio, 41
Jukuri, Mary, 101

K
Kansas City Zoo Deramus Pavilion
(Kansas City, Missouri), 152–153
Kendall/Heaton Associates, 229
Knowles, Ralph, 108
Krueck & Sexton, 224
Kulp Boecker Architects, P.C., 159

L
Lady Bird Johnson Wildflower Center
(Austin, Texas), 166–167
Lai, Elaine, 49
LakelFlato Architects, 253
Lake View Terrace Branch Library (Lake
View Terrace, California), 226–228
Land:
carrying capacity of, 28–29
contaminated, 6
ethic for dealing with, 3
value of, 7–8
Landscapes, conservation of, 74
Land use, 3
issues in, 4
Jeffersonian grid for, 7
by Native Americans, 7
unsustainable, 8
and urban sprawl, 24
in watersheds, 18
Leddy Maytum Stacy Architects, 175

The Ledger, 60
Lee, Joyce, 130
Leopold, Aldo, 3
Leslie Shao-Ming Sun Field Station
    (Woodside, California), 240–242
LHB, 160, 166, 167
Lindsey, Bruce, 246
Lindsey, Gail, 130
Living roof, 115
Living standards, urban, 35
Livingston, Ann, 50
Lloyd Crossing Sustainable Design Plan
    (Portland, Oregon), 243–246
Loftness, Vivian, 130
Long life, loose fit principle, 19, 126
Lovins, Amory, 140
Lyle, John T., 132
LZT Architects, 231

M
The MacArthur Foundation, 83
McHarg, Ian, xv, 27
"Machine for living," xxii
MacKay, Buddy, 60
Mackey Mitchell Associates, 249
McLean Environmental Living and
    Learning Center, Northland
    College (Ashland, Wisconsin),
    159
Mahlum Architects, 237, 250
Malecha, Marvin, 132
Malvern Elementary School (McKinney,
    Texas), 147, 148
Maps:
    natural systems, 30–35
    smart-growth areas, 37–39
    systems conflict, 36–38
    urban systems, 35–36
    water supply, 35
Martin, Muscoe, 130
Matsuzaki Wright Architects, 161
Maximum system value, 8
Maxman, Susan, 140, 207
Mendler, Sandra, 130
Metrics/measurements:
    for energy efficiency vs.
        sustainability, 17–18
    for urban and community design,
        78–81

Microclimates, 105, 114
The Miller|Hull Partnership, 142, 160,
    208, 228
Mississippi River, *see* Great River Park
    (St. Paul, Minnesota) case study
Missouri Historical Society Museum (St.
    Louis, Missouri), 147, 148
Mithun, 156, 172, 195, 243
Mixed-use development, 74
Model:
    defined, 3
    ecology as, 3–5
Mohr, Ray, 49
Montgomery Campus, California
    College of Arts and Crafts (San
    Francisco, California), 175–177
Morrish, William R., 59
Murcutt, Glenn, 13

N
National Park Service (NPS), 181
National Public Radio Headquarters
    (Washington, DC), 130, 131
National Renewable Energy Lab
    (NREL), 181
National Wildlife Federation
    Headquarters (Reston, Virginia),
    193–194
Native Americans, 7
Natural (renewable, sustainable)
        energy, xxi
    infrastructure powered by, 24
    resident, xxi–xxii
    solar, 3, 4
Natural forms, 1
Natural processes, 24–25
Natural resources:
    in green design, 16
    for livable communities, 74
    on-site, 106
    regional, 33
Natural Resources Defense Council
    Headquarters (New York City),
    130, 131
Natural system(s):
    climax state of, 2
    free work of, *see* Free work of the
        natural system
    and individual property rights, 8

removal of, 1–2
study of, 12
in urban and community design,
    72–73
Natural systems map, 30–35
Nature, constraints of, 4
The Nature of Design (David W. Orr),
    12
Navy Building 850 (Port Hueneme,
    California), 186–188
Neighborhoods:
    in Great River Park case study, 93–94
    identities of, 74
New Canaan Nature Center
    Horticultural Education Center
    (New Canaan, Connecticut),
    135–137
New South Jamaica Branch Library
    (New York City), 167–168
New York City, watershed purchases
    by, 28
New York Life Building (Kansas City,
    Missouri), 147
Nidus Center for Scientific Enterprise
    (Creve Coeur, Missouri), 170
Nonrenewable energy, 1–2, 16
Nonrenewable resources:
    economic dependence on, 25
    exponential growth in consumption
        of, xxii–xxiii
    fossil fuels, xxii–xxiii
    hyperextended growth patterns
        relying on, xxiii–xxiv
    systems powered by, 2
    unplugging completely from, xxi
Northeast blackout of 2003, xxiii–xxiv
NPS (National Park Service), 181
NREL (National Renewable Energy
    Lab), 181
Nuclear power, 5, 6

O
O'Brien, Kathleen, 160
Odum, Howard T., xxii, 3, 9, 27
Odum's model, 3
Office database, 120–121
Olgyay brothers, 27
On-site energy, xix–xxi
On-site resources, 106

"Organisms for living," xxii
Orr, David, 12, 183, 184
Osborn Sharp Associates, 140
Overland Partners, 166

P
Paradigm, defined, 8
Paradigm shifts, 8–9
Parks, Daniel M., 59
Patagonia Distribution Center (Reno, Nevada), 140, 142
PDC, see Portland Development Commission
Philadelphia Forensic Science Center (Philadelphia, Pennsylvania), 250–251
Photosynthesis, 3
Physical environment, 2
Pier 1 (San Francisco, California), 194–195
Pierce County Environmental Services Building (University Place, Washington), 228–229
Pittsburgh Glass Center (Pittsburgh, Pennsylvania), 246–247
Place-based design, 105
Planning:
   community vision in, 26
   post-disaster, 106, 108
   of watersheds, 28–29
Plato, 32
Platt/Whitelaw Architects, 144
The Plaza at PPL Center (Allentown, Pennsylvania), 229
PNC Firstside Center (Pittsburgh, Pennsylvania), 177–179
Pollution abatement, 17
Polshek Partnership, 238
Portland Development Commission (PDC), 244, 245
Post-disaster design and planning, 76, 106, 108
Power grid, 25–26
Prairie waterway design principles, 52–55
Precipitation, 32–35
Predevelopment pattern illustration:
   in regional design process, 36, 37
   in southeastern Florida case study, 60, 61

Presettlement patterns, on natural systems maps, 30, 32
Prince Street Technologies (Cartersville, Georgia), 137–139
Property rights, 4
Public policy, 8
Public spaces:
   for livable communities, 74
   urban, 35
Puget Sound Environmental Learning Center (Bainbridge Island, Washington), 195–197
Pugh + Scarpa, 204, 252

Q
Quality of life, 16

R
Randall Stout Architects, 215, 216
RDG Bussard Dikis, 191
Real Goods Solar Living Center (Hopland, California), 153–156
Regional design, 12, 23–68
   Cache Valley, Utah case study, 43–50
   challenges in, 33
   community-based vision informed by, 29
   evolution from nonrenewables in, 25
   evolving systems-design approach to, 38–40
   Farmington, Minnesota case study, 50–59
   knowledge of biome in, 36
   level of detail in, 26, 27
   natural processes in, 24–25
   natural systems map in, 30–35
   and power grid, 25–26
   predevelopment pattern illustration in, 36, 37
   process for, 42–43
   smart-growth areas map in, 37–39
   southeast Florida coastal communities case study, 59–68
   sustainability impact of, 23, 24
   Sustainable Development Vision in, 39–42
   systems conflict map in, 36–38
   urban systems maps in, 35–36
   utilities and infrastructure in, 24

   of water systems, 27–29
   working knowledge of regional ecology for, 23
Regional ecology, working knowledge of, 23
REI Denver (Denver, Colorado), 172–175
REI Seattle (Seattle, Washington), 156–159
Renewable energies, 2. See also Natural energy
Renovation:
   of buildings for sustainability, 121–126
   Immaculate Heart of Mary Motherhouse, 251–252
   of infrastructure, 116
Resident (local) energy, xxi–xxii
Resources. See also Natural resources
   and community sustainability, 69
   resident, xxi
Restoration, 9
Retrofitting, for sustainability, 121–126
Ricks, Karina, 49
Ridgehaven Green Demonstration Project (San Diego, California), 144–145
Rinker Hall, University of Florida (Gainesville, Florida), 247
Rio Nuevo Master Plan (Tucson, Arizona) case study, 84–91
   cultural and environmental issues in, 84, 85
   economic development in, 86
   reclamation of Santa Cruz River in, 88–91
Robert A.M. Stern Architects, 229
Rob Wellington Quigley, 240
Rocky Mountain Institute, 150
Root-bed heating, 136
Ruckelshaus, William D., xxii, 45, 94
Rue, Harrison, 83
Rylander, Mark, 130

S
St. Vincent Millay, Edna, 106
San Mateo County Forensic Laboratory (San Mateo, California), 213–215
Sarah Nettleton Architects, 197

Scales:
  bioregional, 10, 23
  biourban, 11, 24
  human, 74
  interrelationship of, 19
  regional, 10. See also Regional design
  relationships between, 70
  urban/community, 11. See also Urban and community design
Scheaffer, John, 154
Schunn, R. G., 59
Scientific American, 45, 94
SC Johnson Wax Commercial Products Headquarters (Racine, Wisconsin), 140, 142
Seattle watershed, 29
Sense of place, 74
SHW Group, Inc., 148
Siegel & Strain Architects, 163, 188, 217
Sirny Architects, 160
Site analysis, 103–106
Skin, building, 116–120
Sleeping Lady Conference and Retreat Center (Leavenworth, Washington), 179–180
Smart growth:
  infrastructure costs for, 26
  southeast Florida coastal communities case study, 59–68
  vision for, in southeastern Florida case study, 62–66
Smart-growth areas map, 37–39
Smith Group, 171
SMWM, 194
Soils:
  on predevelopment pattern illustration, 36
  in regional design, 33
Solar energy, 3
  in Cornish School of the Arts project, 126–128
  and potential for sustainability, 4
Solar Umbrella House (Venice, California), 252
Southeast Florida coastal communities case study, 59–68
Spatial connectivity, 1
Spatial relationships, 14, 15

Steinhude Sea Recreation Facility (Steinhude, Germany), 215–216
Stein White Nelligan Architects, 167
Straka, Ron, 50
Streets, orientation of, 75
Sunlight, xxi. See also Solar energy
Superfund sites, 6
Susan Maxman & Partners, Architects, 139, 205, 251
Sustainability, 14–15
  as continuum, 17
  deep, xv
  energy efficiency vs., 17–18
  impact of regional design on, 23, 24
  three spheres of, 14–15
Sustainable design, 13–21
  architects' role in, 14–15
  in architectural design, 120–121
  beginning steps in, 12
  challenges in, xix–xx
  criteria for, 20–21
  defined, 2
  ecology as, 1
  for emergency conditions, xxv
  for existing buildings, 121–126
  as functioning "unplugged," 17
  green design vs., 15–16
  of interior architecture, 126–128
  office database for, 120–121
  as paradigm shift, 8–9
  place-based energy/resources in, 18
  planning in, 2, 16–17
  principles for, 18–20
  purpose of, 13
  as response to environmental clues of site/region, 13
  as system design, xxv
  to-do list for, 20
Sustainable development, defined, xxii
Sustainable Development Vision, 39–42
Sustainable energies, see Natural energy
Sustainable site analysis, 103–106
Suzuki, David, 4
Systems:
  neighborhoods as, 94
  power sources of, 2
System(s) design:
  in regional design, 38–40
  sustainable design as, xxv

Systems conflict map:
  in regional design process, 36–38
  in southeastern Florida case study, 60, 62
Systems thinking:
  in architectural design, 103
  in regional planning, 29
  taxonomy of system layer, 140

T
Tai + Lee Architects, 147
Tanner Leddy Maytum Stacy, 145
Tate Snyder Kimsey Architects, 249
Temperature:
  building skin's relation to, 117
  in regional design, 32
The Solaire (New York City), 219
Thompson, Ventulett, Stainback & Associates, 137, 142
Thoreau Center for Sustainability (San Francisco, California), 145–147
Three-dimensional methods:
  environmental analysis as, 105–116
  interdependence of elements in, 14
  place-based, 27
Time to Change (David Suzuki), 4
Tofte Cabin (Tofte, Minnesota), 197–199
Topography, 32, 33
"The Tragedy of the Commons" (Garrett Hardin), 7–8
Transportation:
  urban, 35
  varying options for, 74
Transverse glades, 39, 40
20 River Terrace—The Solaire (New York City), 219

U
U.S. Department of Energy, 129
United States Environmental Protection Agency (EPA), 26
The University of Texas Health Science Center at Houston School of Nursing and Student Community Center (Houston, Texas), 252
Urban and community design, 69–101
  and "Barcelona Declaration on Sustainable Design," 70–72
  Belle Glade, Florida case study, 81–83

bioclimatic conditions in, 70
Great River Park case study, 91–101
metrics for, 78–81
natural system in, 72–73
resources for, 69–70
Rio Nuevo Master Plan case study, 84–91
urban system in, 74–77
Urban centers:
  infill development for, 116–118
  preservation of, 74
Urban Design Group, 148
Urban gateways, 57
Urbanism:
  and dependence on nonrenewables, 25
  and human ecology, *see* Biourbanism
  power grid for, 25–26
Urban sprawl, 24
Urban systems, in urban and community design, 74–77
Urban systems maps, 35–36
Utilities, 24

V
Valle, Eric, 83
Valle, Estella, 83
Value(s):
  of land, 7–8
  in public policy, 8
Van der Ryn Architects, 153
Vegetation patterns:
  in architectural design, 113–115
  on natural systems map, 31
Vermillion River watershed, *see* Farmington, Minnesota case study

Vision, community-based, 29
Vitruvius' Principles, xxv, 14

W
Walls, forces on, 119–120
Wal-Mart Environmental Demonstration Store (City of Industry, California), 140
Warren Skaaren Environmental Learning Center at Westcare Preserve (Round Mountain, Texas), 252–253
Wastes, 5
Waste debts, 5–7
Watershed design and planning, 28–29
  Farmington, Minnesota case study, 50–59
  southeast Florida coastal communities case study, 59–68
Water supply:
  EPA's watershed approach to, 26
  as indication of sustainability, 18
  regional conservation areas, 36, 37
Water supply map: geohydrology, 35
Water systems:
  gravity-based vs. antigravity, 26
  regional design of, 27–29
Watson, Donald, 29, 130, 135, 137
The Way Station (Frederick, Maryland), 130, 131
Web sites, information from, 120, 121
The Weidt Group, 166
Wells, H. G., 108
Western Pennsylvania Conservancy, 233, 234

William McDonough + Partners, 131, 182, 230
Williams, Daniel, 49, 83, 101, 103, 130
Wilson, Alexander, 9
Wind:
  actions of energy from, 108
  and microclimates, 105
  mitigating damage from, 108–109, 111–113
Wind-cooling effect, 32
Wind shadow, 79, 112
Wine Creek Road Home (Healdsburg, California), 217–218
WLC Architects, 41
Women's Humane Society Animal Shelter (Bensalem, Pennsylvania), 139–140
Women's Network for a Sustainable Future, 151
Woods Hole Research Center (Falmouth, Massachusetts), 230
Workplace Designers, 160
World Birding Center Headquarters (Mission, Texas), 253–254
World Commission on Environment and Development, xxii
World Resources Institute (Washington, DC), 168–169

Z
Zimmerman Design Group, 142
Zion National Park Visitor Center (Springdale, Utah), 181–182
Zoning codes/laws, 8
  regional, 33
  and urban sprawl, 24

photo credits

All photos, unless otherwise indicated, were provided by the author.

Chapter 3

page 50   Copyright William R. Morrish.
page 53   Copyright William R. Morrish.
page 56   Copyright William R. Morrish.
page 58   Copyright William R. Morrish.

Chapter 4

page 85   From Jones & Jones Architects and Landscape Architects, Ltd.
page 86   From Jones & Jones Architects and Landscape Architects, Ltd.
page 87   From Jones & Jones Architects and Landscape Architects, Ltd.
page 88   From Jones & Jones Architects and Landscape Architects, Ltd.
page 89   From Jones & Jones Architects and Landscape Architects, Ltd.
page 95   From St. Paul Riverfront Corporation, St. Paul, Minnesota.
page 96   From St. Paul Riverfront Corporation, St. Paul, Minnesota.
page 98   From St. Paul Riverfront Corporation, St. Paul, Minnesota.

Chapter 6

page 130   From Doug Van de Zande.
page 130   From Doug Van de Zande.
page 131, *top left*   Courtesy William McDonough and Partners.
page 131, *bottom right*   From Maxwell MacKenzie.
page 131, *bottom left*   From Maxwell MacKenzie.
page 131, *top right*   From Croxton Collaborative Architects, P.C.
page 132, *top*   From RMI/ENSAR Built Environment.
page 132, *bottom*   From Milroy McAleer Photographers.

page 133   From Innovative Design.
page 134   From Innovative Design.
page 135   From Donald Watson.
page 136   From Donald Watson.
page 137   From Brian Gassel/TVS.
page 138   From Brian Gassel/TVS.
page 139   From Catherine Tighe.
page 140, *left*   From Bruce M. Hampton, AIA.
page 140, *right*   From Bruce M. Hampton, AIA.
page 141, *top left*   From WLC Architects, Inc.
page 141, *top right*   From WLC Architects, Inc.
page 141, *bottom left*   From Scot Zimmerman.
page 141, *bottom right*   From Scot Zimmerman.
page 142, *top left*   Photo by Brian Gassel/TVS.
page 142, *top right*   Photo by David Wakely, www.davidwakely.com
page 142, *bottom left*   From E. J. Purcell.
page 142, *bottom right*   From E. J. Purcell.
page 143, *left*   From William Terry Osborn.
page 143, *right*   From William Terry Osborn.
page 146   Copyright Richard Barnes Photography.
page 148, *top left*   From SHW Group.
page 148, *top right*   From SHW Group.
page 148, *bottom left*   From Balthazar Korab Ltd.
page 148, *bottom right*   From Balthazar Korab Ltd.
page 152   Copyright 1998 Mike Sinclair.
page 154   Copyright Charles C. Benton, Kite Aerial Photography.
page 157   Copyright Robert Pisano.
page 160, *left*   From Don Wong Photography and LHB.
page 160, *right*   From Don Wong Photography and LHB.
page 161   From Mike Sherman Photography.
page 163   Copyright Muffy Kibbey.
page 164   Copyright Muffy Kibbey.
page 166   From Peter Bastianelli Kerze and LHB.
page 167   From Peter Bastianelli Kerze and LHB.

page 168   From Stein White Nelligan Architects.
page 169, *top*   Copyright Alan Karchmer.
page 169, *bottom*   Copyright Alan Karchmer.
page 170, *left*   Steve Hall/Hedrich Blessing.
page 170, *right*   Steve Hall/Hedrich Blessing.
page 171   Copyright 2001 Prankash Patel.
page 172   Copyright Scott Dressel-Martin.
page 173   Copyright Scott Dressel-Martin.
page 176   Copyright Richard Barnes Photography.
page 177   Copyright Richard Barnes Photography.
page 178   Photo by Ed Massery.
page 179   From Jones & Jones Architects and Landscape Architects, Ltd.
page 181   Courtesy of Lisa Ogden, Zion National Park.
page 183, *top*   Courtesy Oberlin College.
page 183, *bottom*   Copyright 2003 Judy Watts Wilson.
page 185, *top*   Copyright Tom Bender, architect.
page 185, *bottom*   Copyright Tom Bender, architect.
page 189   Copyright J. D. Peterson.
page 190   From Daniella Mac Adden.
page 191   Photo by Assassi Productions.
page 192   Photo by Assassi Productions.
page 193   From Shirmer/Hedrick Blessing.
page 194   From Shirmer/Hedrick Blessing.
page 195   Copyright Richard Barnes Photography.
page 196, *top*   From Doug Scott.
page 196, *bottom*   From Doug Scott.
page 198   Copyright 2000 Peter Bastianelli Kerze.
page 199   Copyright 2000 Peter Bastianelli Kerze.
page 202   Copyright Farr Associates Architecture, Planning, Preservation.
page 203   Copyright Farr Associates Architecture, Planning, Preservation.
page 204   From Pugh and Scarpa; photos by Marvin Rand.
page 206   From Barry Halkin.

page 207   From Barry Halkin.
page 209   From Herman Miller, Inc.
page 210   From Herman Miller, Inc.
page 211   Copyright Edward Caldwell.
page 212   Copyright Edward Caldwell.
page 214, *top*   Copyright Cesar Rubio Photography.
page 214, *bottom*   Copyright Cesar Rubio Photography.
page 216   Copyright 2000 Peter Hubbe.
page 217   Copyright J. D. Peterson.
page 218   Copyright J. D. Peterson.
page 220   From Doug Snower Photography.
page 221   From Doug Snower Photography.
page 222   Photo by Anton Grassl.
page 224   Photo by Kyle Johnson.
page 225   Photo by Mariusz Mizera.
page 226   Photo by Mariusz Mizera.
page 227, *top*   Copyright RMA Photography.
page 227, *bottom*   Copyright RMA Photography.
page 228   From Eckert and Eckert.
page 231   Photo by Murray Legge, AIA
page 232   Photo by Murray Legge, AIA
page 234   Copyright Nic Lehoux Photography
page 236   Copyright Edward Caldwell.
page 238   From Lara Swimmer.
page 240   Copyright Richard Barnes.
page 242   Copyright Mithun.
page 243   Copyright Mithun.
page 244   Copyright Mithun.
page 245   Copyright Mithun.
page 247   Copyright Croxton Collaborative Architects, P.C.
page 248   Copyright Croxton Collaborative Architects, P.C.
page 249   Copyright 2006 Tom Bonner.
page 251   Copyright Croxton Collaborative Architects, P.C.
page 253   Copyright Hester + Hardaway Photographers.

WILEY BOOKS ON
Sustainable Design

For these and other Wiley books on sustainable design, visit www.wiley.com/go/sustainabledesign

Alternative Construction: Contemporary Natural Building Methods
by Lynne Elizabeth and Cassandra Adams (eds.)

Cities People Planet: Liveable Cities for a Sustainable World
by Herbert Girardet

Design with Nature
by Ian L. McHarg

Ecodesign: A Manual for Ecological Design
by Ken Yeang

Green Building Materials: A Guide to Product Selection and Specification, Second Edition
by Ross Spiegel and Dru Meadows

Green Development: Integrating Ecology and Real Estate
by Rocky Mountain Institute

The HOK Guidebook to Sustainable Design, Second Edition
by Sandra Mendler, William O'Dell, and Mary Ann Lazarus

Land and Natural Development (LAND) Code
by Diana Balmori and Gaboury Benoit

Sustainable Commercial Interiors
by Penny Bonda and Katie Sosnowchik

Sustainable Construction: Green Building Design and Delivery
by Charles J. Kibert

Sustainable Residential Interiors
by Associates III

Environmental Benefits Statement

This book is printed with soy-based inks on presses with VOC levels that are lower than the standard for the printing industry. The paper, Rolland Enviro 100, is manufactured by Cascades Fine Paper Group and is made from 100 percent post-consumer, de-inked fiber, without chlorine. According to the manufacturer, the following resources were saved by using Rolland Enviro 100 for this book:

Mature trees	Waterborne waste not created	Water flow saved (in gallons)	Atmospheric emissions eliminated	Energy not consumed	Natural gas saved by using biogas
225	103,500 lbs	153,000	21,470 lbs	259 milion Btu	37,170 cubic feet